Silent Thunder

Breaking Through Cultural, Racial,
and Class Barriers in Motorsports

Leonard W. Miller

The Red Sea Press, Inc.
Publishers & Distributors of Third World Books

P.O. Box 1892
Trenton, NJ 08607

P.O. Box 48
Asmara, ERITREA

The Red Sea Press, Inc.

Publishers & Distributors of Third World Books

P.O. Box 1892

Trenton, NJ 08607

RSP

P.O. Box 48

Asmara, ERITREA

First printing, 2004
Second printing, 2005

Book and cover design: Roger Dormann

Library of Congress Cataloging-in-Publication Data

Miller, Leonard W.
  Silent thunder : breaking through cultural, racial, and class barriers in motorsports / by Leonard W.
Miller.
     p. cm.
  ISBN 1-56902-176-7 (hardback) -- ISBN 1-56902-177-5 (pbk.)
  1. Miller, Leonard W. 2. Automobile racing drivers--United States--Biography. 3. African American automobile racing drivers--Biography. I. Title.
  GV1032.M45 2003
  796.72'092--dc21

                                        2003013084

This book is dedicated to the 500 black race car owners and drivers that raced on America's speedways unnoticed before World War ll and to Benny Scott who could race in any car with grace, style and credibility.

Contents

Foreword vii
Acknowledgments ix

Chapter 1. "Yours Grow Up to Be Joe Louis":
    The Early Years, 1939-54 1
Chapter 2. The Learning Period, 1955-64 17
Chapter 3. Planting the Seeds, 1965-68 29
Chapter 4. Getting Serious, 1969-71 35
Chapter 5. Indy, SCCA, Expo and England, 1972-73 53
Chapter 6. Bringing Everyone Together, 1973-74 65
Chapter 7. Sponsored by Viceroy, 1974 71
Chapter 8. BAR's Greatest Moments, 1975 85
Chapter 9. Black Athletes Hall of Fame, 1976 115
Chapter 10. Miller Days, 1976-77 123
Chapter 11. Lowest of Lows, 1978 133
Chapter 12. Starting from the Bottom Again, 1979-81 145
Chapter 13. Bad Times, 1982-88 161
Chapter 14. Our Dirt Track Winner Reappears, 1989 171
Chapter 15. Changing of the Guard, 1990-93 177

Index..187

Foreword

From the moment I met Leonard Miller at the Harvard Club of New York City in 1995, I knew there was something special about him. His passion for and knowledge of motorsports was undeniable, as was his determination to involve African Americans in the sport he loved so deeply.

Silent Thunder is not simply an autobiography; it's an historical account covering four decades of the competitive nature and business of motorsports. From the cutthroat world of corporate sponsorship to team dynamics and car mechanics, the author had to learn every aspect of the sport and to overcome repeated and unnecessary hurdles because of his race.

Numerous articles have been published in sports journals and newspapers pondering the minuscule number of African Americans in auto racing. *Silent Thunder* provides fascinating insight into the struggles encountered by the few who have tried to break through the barriers and who have made a difference.

In stick-and-ball sports, breakthroughs have been forced by boycotts, white mentors, and super humans such as Jesse Owens, Jackie Robinson, and Alice Coachman. In auto racing, success is heavily dependent on large sums of money. African Americans have had difficulty tapping into corporate sponsorship dollars, thus crippling their participation in the sport.

There is also a cultural clash: Most African Americans are geared to socializing with family and friends on weekends, which is when most racing events take place. Such a time commitment often tears a family apart and deters interest in the sport, as Miller movingly describes.

In addition, many African American parents, having a negative image of auto racing as being a dangerous, blue-collar, red-neck sport, discourage their children from participating. What is not understood is that while most African American children dream of playing professional ball, the skills they acquire through this pursuit are not immediately transferable to another profession; whereas the mechanical skills one learns through motorsports can lead to lucrative careers.

Furthermore, African American attendance at racetracks is not high, thus the pool from which to interest participants is small. Leonard Miller describes various techniques he has used to diversify motorsports fans and to gain media attention for African Americans in the sport.

In 1999, at the Rainbow/PUSH Sports Conference in Washington, D.C., I heard about all the problems that would be facing African American race teams in the twenty-first century. These problems come to life and are dramatically illustrated throughout *Silent Thunder*.

Leonard Miller has managed to break into the inner circles of motorsports, as witnessed by his friendships with Dan Gurney, Carl Haas, Skip Barber, and African American NASCAR legend Wendell Scott. His years of experience and contacts provide not only examples of what to do and what not to do for those struggling to rise in the sport, they also provide inspiration.

This life story takes a behind-the-scenes look at several types of auto racing from a rare viewpoint and is a must-read for anyone interested in motorsports, sports management, sociology, or history. Although I had heard many of the stories through my eight years of knowing Leonard Miller and his son Lenny, the written text is transfixing, with every page introducing a new business or mechanical strategy, social issue, or personal drama.

This is far more than an auto racing book. The racing is just the setting. Leonard Miller shows through example how to overcome adversity to attain one's dreams.

Lisa Delpy Neirotti, Ph.D.
Director, Sports Management Programs
The George Washington University
Washington, D.C.

Acknowledgments

The experiences narrated in this book might never have been published if not for a humiliating experience at a meeting with an automobile manufacturer in the winter of 1995. As my son Lenny and I approached the parking garage across the street, he blurted out: "Dad, you have to write a book." He encouraged me on a weekly basis and, once I started, he would not let me stop until the manuscript was completed.

Thanks to Steve Lanier for introducing me to Ethan Casey, editor-in-chief of the global journalism community BlueEar.com. When Ethan flew over from London to meet with me for the first time, I knew instantly that he was the right person to edit the manuscript. As he received chapters I sent to him, Ethan became engrossed in the story and urged me to write a sequel. Ethan continued editing my manuscript even while on special assignment in Pakistan for the *Financial Times*.

Since I learned to write on yellow-ruled pads as a child, Jeanne Humphrey had to transpose my handwritten pages to a modern personal computer. My deepest thanks to her for diligently keeping my manuscript in order and for deciphering my hieroglyphics.

Thanks to Lisa Delpy Neirotti, Ph.D., for offering to write the Foreword. Lisa has kept in close contact with the team ever since we met at the Harvard Club of New York City in the summer of 1995, and she periodically assigns sports management graduate students at The George Washington University to study the barriers I have encountered at all levels of motor racing.

Finally, I want to thank Lillian Ridley for formatting the first chapter and encouraging me not to sugarcoat what I believe to be the truth.

Chapter 1
"Yours Grow Up to Be Joe Louis":
The Early Years, 1939-54

The Miller family's lifelong love of racing began in 1939, when I was five years old. At the time, I lived on the Hill miniestate in Wayne, Pennsylvania, with my parents, Julius and Ethel Miller. We lived in an apartment over the garage where I heard Mr. Hill, who was the deputy superintendent of the Valley Forge Military Academy, talk about boat-tail racing cars and the Indianapolis 500.

During the 1920s and 1930s Philadelphia's Mainline, named for the train line that began in Philadelphia and ended in Paoli, Pennsylvania, was home to many of America's wealthiest families. It was a prime area for employment in servant positions for first-generation Irish and Italian immigrants and a magnet for black people from Virginia, Maryland, and Delaware. My father and many of his relatives came to the area from Caroline County, Virginia. My mother migrated from Pennsylvania's "mushroom" country, Chester County.

Living in the heart of the Wayne community and attending the Radnor School District had other benefits, despite our race. The Depression began to ease during this period, and local parades became more in vogue. The local white bluebloods entered their restored cars in the Memorial Day and Fourth of July parades. Most of these were bright blue or yellow Model A and B Ford roadsters, Lincolns, Packards, Cadillacs, and Duesenbergs, with here or there a Cord or a Stutz Bearcat. Like many of the black servants' children on Philadelphia's Mainline, I was also exposed to fine horses, but I was drawn to cars because of their noise, bright paint, and extreme cleanliness.

An incident in the Hills' apple orchard in 1940 spurred me on to compete in the world of auto racing, as I've done ever since. My mother was walking my brother Dexter in the baby coach, with me by her side, when she came upon Mrs. Hill with one of her children. Mrs. Hill leaned over my brother's coach and commented on how cute he was. Then she said, "Your baby is cute, but our cute babies grow up to be George Washington. Yours grow up to be Joe Louis."

My mother, a very proud woman, stomped off in a fit of anger. When we were out of Mrs. Hill's hearing she said to me, "Leonard, you're going to be something in life and not have to be put down by white people." With that comment, she began to direct my path toward college and the white-collar world. Thus, the seeds were planted for a struggle between my mother's ambitions for me and my own.

Just before America entered World War II, my mother and father secretly built a house, and we moved to Rebel Hill, a community in nearby Upper Merion Township. Like most of our neighbors, everything at home was geared to growing food in our large Victory Garden, tending the chickens in the backyard, and feeding two hogs that would ultimately wind up being slaughtered every year. By late fall, all discussions concerning cars became nonexistent. The rest of our time was spent fighting discrimination on our bus route. The school bus drivers the Upper Merion School District employed passed the stops where the black students gathered and picked up the white students further down the road first. Then, the drivers would pick up the black students, who consequently had to stand in the aisles every day on the way to school. This was eventually put to an end in 1946, when my friend Arthur Scott, led all of us black students to riot on the bus, resulting in a reconfiguration of our bus route.

By 1947, youngsters like me turned their attention away from making World War II model airplanes to talking about cars. Then, in 1948, *Hot Rod* magazine began appearing at area drugstores and usually sold out within two days.

The only other black teenager within a 100-mile radius who was keenly interested in cars was Horace "Buddy" Sparrow, Jr. Our parents had been friends since 1929 and often exchanged visits on Sunday afternoons. They were also one of several black families that had enough acreage to drive cars around on their own property.

At this time, if you were a good boy, between the ages of twelve and fourteen, your father, brother, and friends would teach you how to drive. On farms in eastern Pennsylvania, boys learned to drive as young as seven. Both Buddy and I started driving at thirteen. By 1948, we were driving not only around Buddy's property but in the new Calvary Cemetery across from where we lived on Rebel Hill.

Like boys everywhere, boys where I grew up experimented mainly with three things: sex, cars, and alcohol. For Buddy and me it was cars only. Automatic transmissions were just beginning to emerge. Buddy's parents had a 1941 Chevy with a floor shift and we rode around his property and sometimes down the road. One day we began experimenting with shifting it without a clutch. After several weeks and talking to several mechanics, Buddy succeeded in shifting from first to second gear without the clutch. We learned that the transmission gear revolutions and motor revolutions had to be at a certain revolutions per minute for this anomaly to occur. Buddy, who had a keen ear, could listen to the revs of the motor and do this successfully ninety-nine times out of a hundred. After mastering this technique we taught it to all of our friends, beginning with my brother Dexter. This experiment set the stage for many street and racing application improvements in the years to come.

While Buddy and I continued to read every word of *Hot Rod* magazine as soon as it hit the newsstands, we found our black peers were interested only in stick-and-ball sports. By 1949, the Philadelphia area had only two bona fide black mechanics at car dealerships. Rice Innis was a mechanic at the Buick dealership in Wayne, where he had started washing cars in the early 1930s; and my cousin George worked for a Buick dealership in Philadelphia, beginning in 1929. Since most black parents, except in Detroit, saw no future in working around automobiles, they consciously steered us away from the industry.

By 1950, more car magazines had appeared. In addition to *Hot Rod* magazine and *Mechanics Digest*, *Custom Cars*, *HONK*, *Hop Up*, and several others came on the scene. I had car magazines all over the house. My mother admonished me almost daily to quit fooling around with cars, because she considered it a greasy, and dirty job. So I hid the magazines and read them at school or outside in the garage. *Hop Up* became my favorite, because it was pocket size and only forty-eight pages. I could conceal it in my trousers or in my notebook at Upper Merion High School without detection by my mom or the study hall teacher.

In 1950, the family had a 1937 flat-back Ford for transportation. We saw that street rodders took the motor compartment side panels off their cars to expose chrome water hosepipes, chrome acorn nuts on the cylinder heads, and a chrome carburetor air bonnet. I told Dexter and Buddy that we were going to do the same on Dad's '37 Ford. We found the correct diameter chrome plumbing pipe and installed it in place of the rubber water hoses on the motor. Then we took the P & W train on a Saturday to the Pep Boys store in Norristown to see how much money we would need for the other chrome parts.

Since Dad never looked under the hood anymore because Dexter and I took care of the car's maintenance, we rode around for a year before he realized what we had done. Until he caught me, I would drive the car beyond sight of the house and take the side panels off—especially at night, when I drove to street rod gathering places, or to church youth activities or to my friend Elias "Doodle Bug" Redmond's house in Mt. Pleasant.

When Dad finally caught on to what I had been doing, he told my mother. She fussed at me for days: How could I have deceived my father by playing hot rod with the family car? It took me a week to talk her out of removing the chrome from the motor. I promised her I wouldn't take the side panels off, then no one would see the chrome. After that I never took the side panels off, unless I was in the company of a lot of hot rodders. Until the car was sold, the chrome stayed in the motor compartment, which, in fact, enhanced the sale of the car.

At this time, my automotive education expanded tenfold. A

white neighbor had blown his brains out with a shotgun in front of his children, and their house stood empty for quite some time. Every potential buyer who learned about the suicide refused to buy the house, that is, until the Clappsaddle family finally purchased it.

William Butch Clappsaddle, a hot rodder with a duck-tail haircut and black leather jacket, appeared on the scene with the most beautiful green 1939 Ford coupe convertible I'd ever seen. His father, a dirt track racer, had bought the Gulf gas station on Lancaster Avenue in Bryn Mawr. Two days after the Clappsaddles moved in, I befriended Butch then looked over his car. Except for several upper-middle-class teenagers I knew in Wayne, this was the first time I'd seen a real car like the pictures of California hot rods in *Hot Rod* magazine. The car was nosed, decked, and dechromed. It sat low on the road with dual exhausts and chrome Cadillac hubcaps. It stood out in the crowd.

I couldn't wait to tell Buddy about Butch and his car. I was eager for him to meet me at Mr. Clappsaddle's gas station. Buddy turned me down flat. He wasn't going to hang around any white guys. I told him we had to learn about cars wherever we could. Finally, Buddy relented and visited the station with me on several occasions.

When I went to the Gulf station to watch Butch improve and maintain his coupe, and later began helping out, I learned to focus on the work at hand, to listen to technological concepts, and to develop habits of cleanliness. At seventeen, I began to learn about Gabriel shock absorbers and lowering the car's center of gravity and weight distribution. I also began to hear about debates on the merits of Smitty versus Belond mufflers, Amoco versus Sunoco premium gasoline.

After all the work we put into that coupe, Butch was racing another rodder down Lancaster Avenue one day, when the car turned over in front of Villanova University and was completely demolished. The car slid, upside down, almost a hundred feet before coming to rest. How Butch escaped severe injury or death, I'll never know! This serious mishap helped to raise my understanding of cars and racing to another level. If you as a competitor have any money at all, after a setback, you should begin a new project as quickly as possible before you lose your nerve.

Butch began his next car project with a vengeance. He bought a 1940 Ford Club Coupe convertible. Under his father's supervision and with the help of several of his regulars and Lump Delaney, a custom car builder of local fame, he customized far beyond what he had done with the coupe. Boxes labeled Offenhauser, Edelbrock, Moon, and Barris began to show up at the gas station. We hangers-on drooled as the parts were shown to us before assembly. By 1951, as Butch's convertible became ever more exotic, Dexter would accompany me to the gas station and anywhere else hot rods were being built. This only accelerated Mom's displeasure. Dexter had to follow my example; hide car magazines, and never read them in front of Mom.

I graduated from Upper Merion High School in 1952. By this time I had decided to buy a car and customize it, just as I had seen Butch do. Because I had been an honor roll student throughout my high school years I was accepted at West Chester State Teachers College with no problem. I had to save all my money for college and therefore didn't have one dollar to put towards a car. At the close of my freshman year, I got my chance to make enough money to buy a hot rod. My father found out that the Mainline Lumber & Millwork Company in Wayne was hiring summer help at union-level wages. Through his connections, I was hired. The black summer help was put in a segregated crew along with the regular black help emptying boxcars, stacking lumber, and loading trucks. Being part of this work gang became a blessing in disguise: Overtime was every day, six days a week.

Through my father I learned that Larry Desimone, a street rodder in Berwyn, had a '40 Ford Club Coupe convertible for sale for $250. After looking it over and determining that it was a basic hot rod that needed more work, I bought it on the spot.

But after I went out and bought the same model car as Butch, no one would help me, except Butch himself. A chasm developed between me and the white teenagers who hung around the gas station and worked on Butch's car. Butch himself would give me all the pointers and direction I asked for and would help me do minor chores, but he was the only white person who would go out of his way to help me.

My parents had always urged me not to let race hold me back in anything I wanted to do. So I got Buddy Sparrow and Dexter to help me. In other words, I had to use a black nucleus to move forward.

Keeping it very low key in my mother's presence, the three of us began transforming the '40 Ford into a street killer. First, we developed a budget. I had to have $600 for college tuition and room and board for the 1953-54 school year. Working six days a week with all the overtime I could get, I had $1000 left over for the car. The average salary for schoolteachers at the time was $2400 per year.

Since the white racers and rodders didn't bother with me because I had a car equal to theirs, I had to find a place to rebuild my car. Dad secretly loved cars, so he, Dexter, Buddy, and I built a crude garage with used lumber, second-hand doors, tar paper, and other materials that others in our tightly-knit black community had stolen from construction sites. After two weeks of putting every spare minute into building it, we completed the garage.

Listening to and watching other Ford enthusiasts, we decided to obtain a 1948 Mercury motor, locate a twenty-six tooth Lincoln transmission, add a three-quarter race cam, mill the heads, and construct a dual-point Lincoln ignition system. So out came the '40 Ford motor.

Then a stroke of luck presented itself. Dexter and I decided to go to Bill Jones's junkyard in Malvern for as many Mercury and Lincoln parts as we could afford. Mr. Jones, who was black, had served several years in Eastern State Penitentiary for racketeering during World War II. When he returned to Wayne, most members of the black community, especially the church people, ostracized him. But Dad always spoke to him on the street, and so did I.

Arriving at the junkyard, Dexter and I saw a group of fancy Cadillacs, Packards, and Lincolns parked out of sight in the back. As in most junkyards of the day, there were two very dirty and greasy attendants dismantling cars. They directed Dexter and me to go to the office, downstairs in the back.

I went down the steps to the basement and knocked. Mr. Jones came to the door. When he opened it, I saw cards and a pile of money on a table where four mobster types were playing poker. I told him what I was looking for and how much money I had: the paltry sum of fifteen dollars. He asked what we were hoping to do. I told him we were building a California-type hot rod. He remarked that my father was one of the few people who had treated him right since he had been paroled from Eastern State Penitentiary and invited me to take whatever parts we needed free of charge. Then he said, "You know about the three monkeys?"

"No," I said.

"Hear no evil, see no evil, speak no evil," he said. "Forget what you saw."

A few years later, I learned that the Mafia in eastern Pennsylvania moved its secret gambling rendezvous to remote black locations whenever possible. Providing venues for these secret games gave blacks more income in one day than running a legitimate business did in a month.

For the next two years, Dexter and I visited the junkyard whenever we needed parts. We bought everything there at huge discounts, except what we got at Hank's Speed Shop in Berwyn. We were able to get '41 Studebaker taillights, '49 Plymouth bumpers, seats, a Buick speedometer, springs, Cadillac hubcaps, wheels, starters, generators, brackets, and numerous other small items—all from Bill Jones. During the school year, I even slipped away from West Chester State Teachers College with my new girlfriend Rose to get parts to keep the car running and to customize it even further. Every time I visited the junkyard, I looked to see if the gangsters' cars were parked out of sight in the rear, which they often were.

It was also during this period that I became a charter member of the Barris Kustoms of America Club run by George Barris, one of the top custom car builders of the century. Barris designed custom cars for Hollywood, including the Batmobile for the 1960s TV series *Batman* and cars for *The Beverly Hillbillies* and *The Munsters*. Each membership card and decal came with a catalog. In the catalog, Dexter and I spied telescope Barris custom tips running through the lower fenders of a 1940 Ford. I saved up enough money to buy the exhaust tips and later had Lump Delaney install them in the lower part of my Ford's fenders, between the Studebaker taillights and the '49 Plymouth bumper. The setup was an attention-getter everywhere I went. Eventually, the Pennsylvania State Police made me disconnect the exhaust in the fenders because it didn't conform to state inspection regulations, which I moaned about for months.

In the fall of 1953, Butch Clappsaddle contacted me at the college, asking me to join his father's pit crew at Mason-Dixon Speedway, just over the Maryland state line. I had been to the track before and knew it was frequented by a bigoted, blue-collar bunch of locals from the West Chester and southern Pennsylvania region. I told Butch I would meet him at the track and help change tires.

This was the beginning of many years of going to the track alone. Teachers' colleges in the 1950s were very conservative and had rigid rules. One was that if you lived on campus, you were not allowed to have a car—and certainly not a customized California-type hot rod. To circumvent this rule, I rented a garage in an alley near the school.

West Chester in the 1950s was a very segregated town. Black folks were restricted to certain streets. The garage I rented was in a white working-class neighborhood. A white day-student friend told me about it and paved the way for me to rent it. I never started the car, with its deep, throaty Smitty mufflers, late at night; nor did I enter or exit the alley at the height of neighborhood activity such as picnics, outdoor birthday parties, or car washing. I avoided impressing the neighbors with my customized car. I learned early on that poor and lower-middle-class white girls loved both on-track racers and off-track hot rod cars, because of their mystique and innovation. Black girls loved to ride in big, fancy Cadillacs and Lincolns, especially in the northern cities on weekends, when everyone in the neighborhood could see them as they passed by.

One particular Saturday night, I eased my car out of the alley and down Route 202 to Mason-Dixon Speedway. Mr. Clappsaddle was running his '36 Ford coupe with a Ford V-8 in the Pennsylvania State Championship race. In those days stock car racers drove their cars to the track or had ratty-looking homemade trailers, which presented three problem areas that had to be addressed: brakes, tires, and tuning. Mr. Clappsaddle, Butch, Butch's brother, and I prepared the car for the heat race which, if I remember correctly, we won.

While getting the car ready for the feature, we noticed the cords showing through a tire. Since I was "showboat" fast with a four-way lug wrench, Mr. Clappsaddle told me to jump over the fence and take a tire off a friend's car that had the same size and bolt pattern. I climbed over the six-foot fence behind the pits to get the tire. Luckily, the car was in a well-lit area. As I proceeded to take the rim off the car I heard someone yell, "There's a nigger in the parking lot stealing a tire!" Two hillbilly types were having sex in the back seat of a nearby car. I noticed that they were half naked, and I hoped they would shut up. Keeping my head about me as they continued to yell and point, I got the rim off. Then I heard Butch yell, "Len, get that tire over here!"

The hillbillies were yelling, "The nigger done got the tire! Get him!" By this time, several policemen had arrived and were standing between me and the pit fence. They asked what I was doing at the Mason-Dixon Speedway. I said I was with the Clappsaddle pit crew. One cop said he hadn't ever seen any niggers on a pit crew at the Mason-Dixon Speedway.

"Sir, there's my crew over there yelling for me," I said.

The cops stepped sideways and turned around to see who was yelling. As they did, I bounced the tire over the fence to the crew. Mr. Clappsaddle finished fourth in the feature, one of his best finishes at Mason-Dixon Speedway that year. If the car had had new brakes and had not been driven on the street before the race, he could have won.

Riding back alone to West Chester that night, I came to the conclusion that my love for cars and racing would be a cultural nightmare. I was caught between black men who generally shied away from mechanical careers and white men with fearless John Wayne and Chuck Yeager attitudes who lived on the edge via motor racing.

In 1954, two events occurred that broadened my experience with cars and with people. The first took place in the spring of 1954, on a Saturday night during spring break. I was returning from Rose's house in the heart of the Shibe Park black community in North Philadelphia. My car was well known in the area; from 1952 to 1955, it was the only car of its type seen there. Everywhere I parked it, it drew a crowd. Rose never really liked the groups that formed around it or the questions people asked. On this particular night, I was returning home via Ridge Pike when a '48 Plymouth coupe with dual exhausts pulled up beside me at a light. The driver, who was black, turned down his window and said, "Blood, I've seen your car around my neighborhood, and it ain't shit!"

"Bro, you don't want to race me. I got too much for you to handle," I said.

"We'll see," he said.

We proceeded side by side up Ridge Avenue. I was not paying any real attention to him. He kept pulling up beside me. Finally I got tired of him, and I let him see the potential of my Lincoln transmission and dual Stromberg 97 carburetors with progressive throttle linkage.

Tromping the gas, I pulled ahead by twenty car lengths. He kept following me. As we neared Norristown on open road, his car was still in my rearview mirror. I got serious. I took the car up to 90-mph. He tried to hang tough, but lost control going downhill. The Plymouth hit the side of a small stone bridge, then turned up on its side, slid along the bridge, and landed on its roof. I stopped to see if it had caught fire. Seeing no fire, I called the fire department anyway and sped away. The next morning I saw in the newspapers that the driver of the Plymouth had broken his neck, and the police were looking for a Ford convertible that had left the scene. I put the car in the garage and kept it there for six months, until I felt everything had blown over. But I continued working to improve the car's overall performance. Every time I looked at the 50/50 heavy-duty Gabriel shock absorbers, I knew they had made the difference flying over the bumps in the road that night.

By early summer of 1954, I had improved the car even more—something every racer, vintage car owner, hot rodder, and drag racer must do to remain competitive. Horace "Buddy" Holmes, a man who lived with my Aunt Marion in Essex County, Virginia, said he wanted me to come down and help him at Uncle Jesse's gas station and show the white boys in the area that Negroes could build cars as well as they could. I took off for Virginia in early July, with Mom still yelling about me and my car.

I had been going to Caroline County since I was a baby, and on occasion I also visited Aunt Marion and Uncle Jesse for several weeks at a time in the town of Hustle in neighboring Essex County. Buddy and I pumped gas at their country store, and I helped him repair cars and farm equipment. Uncle Jesse had a thriving business in the black community.

On reaching Aunt Marion and Uncle Jesse's farm, I learned that Uncle Jesse had opened a City Service gas station on Route 301, halfway between Port Royal and the Route 17 and 301 highway intersection. The station was across the road from a genuine Southern, "gut bucket" black-owned blues roadhouse. Uncle Jesse wanted me to help Buddy pump gas on the weekends and on Saturday night, because the black community did a lot of home visiting, and roadhouse customers all filled up at the station.

The second night I was pumping gas, a car with South Carolina license plates pulled in. Not noticing me at first, they said, "Fill the car up." Then they noticed they were at a black-owned station. The driver yelled to the man sitting in the passenger seat, "We done pulled into a damn nigger station. Let's get the hell out of here. I ain't gonna give no goddamn niggers my money for nothin'—*ever*!" The area around the pumps was gravel. As the car sped off, gravel flew into the air, and a piece got in my eye. Buddy rushed out of the car pit and told me to stay calm. Then examining my injury he moaned, "I got you down here to embarrass these peckerwoods."

By the weekend, the patrons at the roadhouse had all seen the funny-looking '40 Ford Club Coupe convertible. They would stand on the dilapidated front porch and wait for me to come out of the gas station with the deep guttural sound of the Smitty mufflers growling so loud you could hear me shifting a mile away in the quiet Virginia countryside.

The next week, I took some time off to go over the car. Its weakest points were the shackles in the rear suspension area. In that era, you could lower the back end of a Ford as much as four inches by lowering the springs. Depending on the cars mileage and the bumpy roads encountered, they could loosen or break. This would cause the car to shift sideways, squirrel, or drop down on the rear fenders. Sure enough, looking at the shackles, I found one loose. I corrected the problem and told Buddy I was ready to meet the challenge.

Our opportunity came a few days later. We had run out of gas at the station, so we had to close down for the day. Oil companies in those days serviced black-owned gas stations last. As we got ready to go to the white-owned station on Route 17, Buddy started to sweat and stutter. He kept saying we were sticking our heads into the lion's mouth, and that we could end up being beaten half to death. I said, "Let's go!"

The Esso station was set on a hilly turn off Route 17, about halfway between the 17-and-301 intersection in Tappahannock. Being from Pennsylvania, I was not accustomed to pulling into a gas station meekly. I pulled right up beside a hot '49 Ford sitting in front of the garage doors. There also was a stock car sitting beside the station. I turned off the ignition.

There were about nine dyed-in-the-wool, pre-Martin Luther King white Southerners in and around the station—five young dirt-track-types hovering around three older men in bib overalls inside smoking corn cob pipes, and a customer having his car fixed. Inside the station hung a rebel flag.

A tough-looking dirt-track type came over and said, "What are you damn nigras doin' pullin' in here and blockin' my station up?"

"I hear you got the fastest car in the county," I said. "Do you want to race?"

Another hanger-on in bib overalls, looking like a character out of the movie *Deliverance*, said, "I be dog, we got a Yankee nigger here. Look at dem dere license plates—Peen-sul-vaya plates."

While the group stood around laughing at us, I was looking out the side of my eye at the '49 Ford. Buddy was about to bolt out of the car and run. I whispered, "Don't worry." With bravado, the owner of the Ford said, "I guess I got to teach a Yankee nigger a lesson," and everyone laughed.

I said, "Let's race from Route 301 and Route 17 crossroads to your Esso station." This was several miles. Laughing, the group agreed.

When the owner of the '49 Ford started it up, I knew he had a nonproduction cam. I knew he had headwork. I'd already noticed the dual exhausts, and the car sat low. I asked him what he had under the hood. He said he had a three-quarter race motor. I made a mental note that my twenty-six tooth Lincoln Zephyr transmission, '48 Mercury motor, dual Stromberg 97 carburetors, Weiand manifold, Moon fuel block, and progressive linkage would be his downfall.

Ever since junior high school, fifty-five years ago, right up to the present day, it has always been a source of amusement to me that most white men with U.S. roots have never asked me nor my son, Lenny, what we know about cars or airplanes. The group at the gas station, being no exception, automatically assumed that Buddy and I were inferior and dumb and therefore would be easily beaten.

The two cars went back to the 301-and-17 intersection, and we started side by side. The car in the lead would force the other car to come around on the wrong side of the road to pass. The first car to reach the Esso station would win. Beneath my dashboard I had a Buick 120-mph speedometer, courtesy of Mr. Jones's junkyard. Back then it was rare to see a tachometer in a street car. The Buick speedometer was vital because the car was capable of exceeding 100-mph without pushing the accelerator to the floor. Furthermore, it was large and round, so I could see my shift points better.

I jumped out into the lead and told Buddy the '49 Ford would have to outdo itself to beat me. Reared in the South, Buddy had never before witnessed a demonstration of sheer aggressiveness and fearlessness in a black person. The '49 Ford driver and his pal were stunned. That day the Lincoln transmission performed like a Concord, North Carolina Jerico transmission configuration does at a NASCAR short track today. The car propelled itself out in front two car lengths with no problem.

Halfway to the finish line, after our car bottomed out at the foot of a hill, the cable to the speedometer broke, shooting oil all over Buddy. Now I couldn't gauge my speed. Buddy, thinking fast, stopped the oil from spewing by sticking a wooden matchstick in the cable. As we neared the Esso station at about 105-mph, the Ford pulled alongside. Between my Smitty mufflers and his Belonds, in all likelihood the noise scared every animal within hearing range to death.

As Buddy and I passed the gas station in the lead, he said, "Let's get out of here. You've upset things around here." I told him we were turning around and going back. We pulled back into the station, with the '49 Ford following us. Everyone at the gas station was standing around in shock. The two young men in the Ford got out and walked over to us. I got out, but Buddy stayed in the car.

"What's your name?" asked the driver.

"Len Miller," I replied. "What's yours?"

He said his name was John, and that he had never seen a colored boy like me. "Len, you and your buddy are welcome here any time," he said. "You take care, you hear?"

Buddy and I pulled off. As we got further down the road, Buddy said he had to tell everyone about this. The white boys had wound up treating us with respect, and I pointed out that we had overcome racism, going from segregation to participation.

Two nights later, as we were returning to Uncle Jesse's farm, a highway trooper stopped us on Route 17. I didn't relish being pulled over by the police in a wooded area in the South in 1954. The trooper was civil and deliberate. "Where are you going, boy?" he asked.

"To my Uncle Jesse's farm," I said. "I'm his nephew."

"Is this the car that beat John's Ford the other day?"

"Yes."

"Get out of the car and stand over there. Have you ever run white lightning?"

"No."

Very methodically, the trooper checked the thickness of the car doors, inside the trunk, the back floor, and so forth. After completing his search, he said, "You tellin' me the truth? Get in this car and get goin'. I know Mr. Holmes, and he's pretty good for being colored. Now I want you and this car headin' back to Pennsylvania and out of this county in two days."

"Yes, sir," I replied.

With that ultimatum, I moved over to Caroline County to visit my grandmother and my cousin Charles Gray. After visiting Bowling Green and Milford, I headed back to Pennsylvania with a smile. I had made my point.

Chapter 2
The Learning Period, 1955-64

D uring my college years, I enjoyed taking relatives and friends out for a ride in my '40 Ford driving at over 100-mph. One such episode grew out of our Alpha Phi Alpha fraternity meeting in Philadelphia in the spring of 1955. The chapter president wanted me to scare several of the new pledgees, including Harry White, a friend I had known since I was fourteen.

The goal was to scare them enough so that they would seriously question the value of pledging to become an Alpha fraternity brother. I put Harry and two other pledgees in my car and proceeded up Broad Street from City Hall with the top down. By the time we approached Temple University, I was close to reaching 100. Harry was used to my daring antics, but the other two pledgees were petrified. As we passed Fisher's Restaurant, I finally hit the 100-mph mark, with the thundering Smitty mufflers so loud as to scatter the long line of would-be patrons standing outside the restaurant. I looked in the rearview mirror and saw one terrified pledgee, and the other about to faint. "Knew you wouldn't wreck," said Harry with bravado as we slowed down.

"Let's try it again," I suggested.

"Hell, no," he said. "Never!"

One Sunday, as we exited our family church, Second Baptist in Wayne, Pennsylvania my cousin Fret, now Reverend Daisey Thomas, said she would like to go 100-mph if it wasn't dangerous. I told her I knew where we could do it safely. One of the main topics of discussion that year was speed. In Pennsylvania every young person who even thought about cars wanted to brag about riding in a car that exceeded over 100-mph. This was probably true in most states, with the exception of California, where, because of the dry lakebeds, rodders and racers—including pre-World War II black drivers such as Mel Leighton and Rajo Jack's friend, Herman Giles—aimed at 200-mph plus.

We rode along the Pennsylvania Turnpike, near the Valley Forge exit, where I drove around to the front of the Howard Johnson's restaurant and then headed south toward Norristown. Since the turnpike was still under construction, there were only a few cars heading back to Norristown. Fret and I went over 100-mph without any trouble and broke the speedometer in the process. At church the following Sunday we recounted our experience. Of course, almost every young person there begged me to give him or her a 100-mph ride, but I wisely refused.

As one of only a handful of true black hot rodders in the greater Philadelphia area in the fifties, I rarely made the rounds of the root beer stands and drive-in theaters where whites hung out. I did race once at Hog Island, next to the Philadelphia Airport, but there were too many kids with Mafia-connected families and superkiller street-racing machines for me to have an even chance to win in a heads-up race. The worst thing about Hog Island was that you raced title for title a lot, that is, if you lose a heads-up race or races, you lose your car. I certainly wasn't dumb enough to risk losing my car, so I never returned.

While the white rodders and cyclists visited hangouts on the weekends, I drove my car with the hood off throughout the area's black communities. In Ardmore, I always stopped at Alice Tucker's house. Her mother and my mother had been friends for many years, and Alice attended West Chester State Teachers College along with me and Rose.

This particular Sunday afternoon, Mrs. Tucker admonished me for making too much noise with the car. "I could hear you coming from Spring Street," she said. "When the young people in the area hear you coming, they stop eating their Sunday dinner and run out on their porches to see you coming around the corner in that hot rod of yours. As a college student, you should stop running around in a car like that."

When Mrs. Tucker had finished scolding me, Alfred "Chief" Anderson, the famous black aviator and Tuskegee Airmen instructor, who visited the Tuckers frequently, told her to leave me alone. "It's rare in this area to see one of us take an interest in real mechanical things," he said. When Chief Anderson spoke, no one in the area questioned his opinions. He was revered as a kind of demigod because he was a pilot. Like most black families in the area that owned cars, in 1947, my mother and father took Dexter and me to Wings Field after dinner on Sunday afternoons just to see and stand on the very spot where Alfred Anderson took off on a flight.

On another occasion, as Chief Anderson walked past a crowd of boys and girls admiring the latest improvement I had made to the car, he whispered to me, "Son, keep the exhaust noise down as you come up on to this street. Drive easy; your car sounds like one of our red-tailed P-51 Mustangs taking off."

During my junior year at West Chester State I was required to take a speech class. The speech teacher was Dr. Bertha Tyson, a professor with a far-right political philosophy and a Victorian attitude. All of her students, from the 1930s on, gave their required speeches on topics that Dr. Tyson liked. In short, there were no speeches about Democrats, labor unions, minorities, motorcycles, or hot rods. I told Earl Miller and Karl Guttenburg, our class president, that I planned to speak on the need to develop drag strips for hot rodders as a way to reduce fatalities at illegal drag racing events on America's back roads. After I made my speech, Dr. Tyson berated me in front of the class and said schoolteachers should never dignify motorcyclists or hot rodders, whom she regarded as a despicable and disgraceful bunch. Sure enough I flunked the course, the only time in my entire life, including graduate school. When I took Dr. Tyson's class again the next semester, I spoke on the improvements needed in the state education system and received a B.

When you reach twenty-one and your interest in hot rods and race cars continues to accelerate, I believe you are destined to stay in love with cars for the rest of your life. When I began student teaching in the fall of 1955, I introduced the first automobile club at the high school. Initially the class met once every two weeks, then the club members wanted to meet every week. The club was made up entirely of white teenagers, primarily farm kids or kids who worked at local gas stations. Black kids didn't join because most of their parents didn't have cars, and because not many of the gas stations in the area hired black kids. Later I learned that their involvement in the automotive club had kept several kids from quitting school. I wondered what Dr. Bertha Tyson might have thought about that.

After the Dr. Tyson episode, my mother turned up the heat to get rid of the car. She didn't want me driving it to my student teacher assignment at West Chester High School. I put my car up for sale in the spring of 1956 and sold it just before graduation. A rich kid bought it and improved it over the next ten years. My mother was more elated about my selling the '40 Ford than about my graduating from college. She just knew there would be no more cars dominating my life. Never would she have dreamed what was to come.

After graduating, I married Rose and tried to obtain a secondary school teaching position outside the Philadelphia public school system. Black males had to teach in the northeastern urban school districts, because the white suburban districts didn't want black male teachers teaching white female teenagers. With my mother's help, I found a job teaching at the Bordentown State Reformatory in New Jersey. Although this was the last place a teacher would want to begin a teaching career, the experience turned out in many ways to be a blessing in disguise.

After my first year of employment, I was drafted into the army. After completing basic infantry and company clerk training at Fort Jackson in Columbia, South Carolina, I was assigned to Fort Bragg, North Carolina, one of the top U.S. Army posts in the world.

Fort Bragg comprised elite special forces units of all types, including airborne rangers, the 82nd Airborne, special on-ground forces units of all types, and an elite army manual development group made up of drafted soldiers with very high IQs from America's most prestigious universities. Sergeant Smith was my drill sergeant for eight weeks. Although Randall Robinson's book *Defending the Spirit*, refers to him in pejorative terms, my experience with

Sergeant Smith was very positive. He expected his black troops to be gung-ho, not pouters. I was in his platoon in 1957 when the National Guard was escorting Ernest Green and the rest of the Little Rock Nine to a newly integrated school every day. One morning in front of the company, Sergeant Smith became so indignant with another drill sergeant, who was white and from Arkansas, that he almost caused a riot.

While at Fort Jackson, I was given tests based on routine assessments and special interests. I scored 98 percent on the automotive test battery and 90 percent or better on all the other tests. Lieutenant Vega, my company officer, had induced me to take the Officers Candidate Test (OCT) because he thought I'd make a good officer. With two hours' notice, at 9 p.m., twelve of the unit's college graduates, myself included, were marched in lockstep for two miles to Fort Jackson's large mess hall to take the exam on wooden tables, with flies everywhere and in dingy lighting conditions. At midnight we were marched in lockstep back to our tents, mentally and physically exhausted. Eleven of us passed the test. Most of us declined going to Officers Candidate School because we were married and didn't want to serve an extra year in the army. In any event, I had taken the OCT under the worst conditions of any test I had ever taken, in or out of the army—and passed.

I was assigned to the U.S. Third Army's 45 Ordnance Battalion's Direct Automotive Field Support Unit at Fort Bragg. This was a one-of-a-kind unit, trained to back up the 82nd Airborne on the ground by repairing jeeps, trucks, and other vehicles under extreme battlefield conditions. This company of over two hundred men was mainly composed of enlisted and drafted soldiers from the Deep South and included only four blacks: Henry Hazelton, who dispensed parts, two mechanics, and me. I was the company's shop clerk. The men in the company included dirt track racers, drag racers, sports car racers, auto body specialists, welders, assembly line operators from United Auto Workers, several recruits from bootlegger families, and NASCAR enthusiasts.

Although off base the racial segregation was ironclad, the unit melded because the army had been desegregated for nine years and the young Southern white soldiers accepted being integrated with blacks – at least on the surface. The company comprised young men with the same interests, which enabled everyone to communicate easily, and everyone was proud to wear the patch of the Third Army, historically one of the finest U.S. fighting units ever to take the battlefield.

The special unit next to us was the munitions handling company, which had a heavy black complement. Black soldiers in that company would always ask us, "How do you get along with those KKK rebels?" I told them I had no problem during the day, although at night several of the South Carolina dirt track racers would hand out printed cards saying, "Help integration! Take a nigger to lunch!" Otherwise, there were no real racial problems.

Until this time, I had paid no attention to stock car racing in the South. As I was from Pennsylvania, and black, my background and experience were centered around local, independent asphalt tracks, Langhorne Speedway for Indy cars, and the Indianapolis 500. Conversation in the company always centered around Grand National racing (NASCAR). The two tracks mentioned most were Darlington and Daytona. On Labor Day weekend, when the Darlington race was held, the Southern soldiers in the company would gather around the radios outside the barracks or sit in cars to hear the whole race. Great cheers would go up when Fire Ball Roberts would take the lead. Other names would be bandied about, like Lee Petty, and their favorite, the flamboyant Curtis Turner. The dirt track racers lived and breathed cars and trucks twenty-four hours a day. Most of these soldiers with Southern racing roots had no interest in seeing the base movies—except when it was *Thunder Road*, the 1958 film starring Robert Mitchum. The bootleggers and NASCAR types went to see this later-to-be-cult movie almost every night during the week it was shown. Going to see the movie for myself gave me more insight into how they thought. Years later I mentioned to my son Lenny that Dale Earnhardt would have fit in with this group better than any driver in NASCAR today, because he was self-educated, superaggressive, and capable of impossible driving feats.

I soon noticed that the Southern-born soldiers exhibited a pride in serving the United States as a group, whereas most of us non-Southerners felt pride only as individuals. Still today throughout the South, at Concord Motorsport Park and many other short tracks, I see evidence of what I experienced at Fort Bragg: devotion of almost one's entire life to getting a race car to the track every Saturday night, with the hope of reaching NASCAR's Winston Cup level. I equate it to a black youth from a public housing project putting all his efforts into basketball with the hope of reaching the NBA. The difference is that NASCAR's Winston Cup hopefuls garner a lot of useful automotive technical knowledge that might lead to other opportunities. In contrast, basketball hopefuls do not build solid, in-depth skills that might lead to everyday business success when they retire.

Because of a shortage of specialists in the fields of writing, teaching, and accounting at the post, I was transferred to headquarters company to finish out my army active duty. The civilian principal welcomed me with open arms. At the time, West Chester was recognized as the best teachers college on the East Coast. I wound up teaching sergeants, men who had fought in both World War II and Korea but had not finished high school. I taught English and American history as part of their high school equivalency diploma program. While at headquarters company under base commander General Robert F. Sink, I met and associated with a number of bright soldiers such as (Marty Wasserman, Brock Brower, Michael Kenneth Absher, and Shirley Wooster), all of whom went on to become outstanding professionals in civilian life.

After receiving an honorable discharge from the army, I returned to my old job as social adjustment teacher at Bordentown Reformatory. In just the twenty months I'd been away, the racial composition of the inmates had changed. When I was first hired in 1956, the inmate population was primarily Irish, Sicilian, and Polish. When I returned in 1959, I noticed that the racial makeup had begun to shift towards a black and Puerto Rican majority, who were mostly from Newark, Jersey City, Camden, and New York. These two groups brought a completely different culture to the reformatory. White inmates became afraid of being beaten up or raped. This climate provoked an increase in escape attempts, although this was never officially documented.

The superintendent, Albert C. Wagner, was very protective of his institution. The New Jersey State Police and the Department of

Corrections vied with each other in capturing escaped felons from the state's penal institutions. Because I like adventure, I volunteered to be deputized to apprehend escaped prisoners. At first, Mr. Wagner paired a teacher with an experienced corrections officer. My partner was Richard Smith, who remains a friend to this day. Teachers in the group were William Fauver, who later became commissioner of corrections for the state of New Jersey; Richard Seidel, who later became assistant commissioner; Joe Call, Jesse Milby, and me. Superintendent Wagner knew that Richard Seidel and I were the best "wheel" men at the reformatory, because he had caught us playing recklessly with our vehicles as we traveled to and from work. In fact, we almost got suspended once for scaring our colleagues with our antics.

By 1961, Superintendent Wagner allowed Jesse Milby and me to team up, without having a corrections officer present, to help apprehend a white inmate who had escaped. Sergeant Bernie Inman was in charge of the group delegated to capture him. As usual, Mr. Wagner emphasized that we were to apprehend the escapee before the state police did. One of the reformatory's "rats" told officials where his friend was headed. The Superintendent radioed the state police, gave them my license number, and let them know I was deputized. This allowed me to drive over the speed limit without being stopped.

Sergeant Inman had devised a very savvy inmate escape philosophy, based on time of day, season of the year, and psychological profile. With the rat's information, he developed a dragnet from the back of the reformatory's farm west to Route 130 and struck a line from the old school house about three miles up Route 130 and across to the New Jersey Turnpike, halfway between Exit 7 and Exit 7A. Since the sergeant had the two-way radio in his car, Jesse and I rode behind him awaiting instructions. About an hour later, one of the spotters saw the escaped inmate running like a deer for the turnpike, over open ground.

Now, this was the era of straight police cruisers. The Bradley, British Land Rover, and other four-wheel vehicles weren't in production or used at the Department of Corrections. Since my souped-up Volvo P-1800 with Dana posi-traction was the best vehicle available to get across the open cornfields, I got the call.

Jesse and I were two out-of-character sights. We wore dress clothes and had a twelve-gauge shotgun sandwiched between us and our heads were hitting the roof of the Volvo as we bounced over the corn rows.

This inmate was indefatigable. As so many police officers often say, the strength, speed, and stamina human beings can muster when they're trying to avoid apprehension is truly remarkable. He zigged and zagged without losing stride. Finally, we caught up to him, and I deliberately brushed him with the Volvo, causing him to flip in the air and land on his back. Jesse got out of the car with the shotgun and told him to stay down. As if on cue, a rousing cheer from the large group of corrections officers echoed across the countryside. I felt like a victorious Christian gladiator in the Roman arena. After the felon was handcuffed and taken away, Jesse and I returned to the reformatory with the corrections officer. As we walked back towards the front entrance, several white inmates yelled out, "You yellow nigger, we're gonna kick your fucking ass!" It was a source of amazement to me that inmates in a penal system know about every major event, even a secret meeting, within minutes of its occurrence.

This and a subsequent episode were brought to the attention of the Central Intelligence Agency's secret regional office in Philadelphia in 1961. Like NASCAR driver Steve Park hanging up on Dale Earnhardt when he first called, I hung up on Mr. Z of the CIA several times when he called me at home in the evening. Finally, in 1962, I agreed to meet him at the CIA's secret office at Fifteenth and Market Streets, where the Municipal Services building now stands.

I soon discovered that the CIA had developed a prescreening system for 2500 young, aggressive Americans who had a base IQ of 136 as well as certain secret "007" specialties. Without my knowledge, my name appeared on the list. After the most extensive testing in every conceivable aspect of human behavior I have ever encountered, I was named one of the final eight candidates. If I remember correctly, in 1963 the CIA had 10,000 employees, three of them were black. Two were black women. One could duplicate any document in the world as authentic as any original; the other was a world-class call girl, able to make a foreign diplomat ejaculate nine times in ten minutes and tell on his mother, not just his country's secrets. The black male agent was assigned undercover to the U.S. Air Force in France.

What I learned about myself from the CIA experience propelled me beyond typically black, naïve thinking and made me very cognizant of the dark side of human nature.

At that time, according to Mr. Z, the CIA had become an Ivy League club, above the fray. The secret "007" side was dependent on immigrants from countries like Hungary, double agents, and turncoats from Russia. These groups and others did the hit man work and apparently were assigned to carry out orders without question. I have never seen, before or since, such a complete dossier on my life. The CIA was interested in me because of my knowledge and experience with cars, my ability to blend in on the cocktail circuit, and my having the right complexion, which could be lightened or darkened to look Hispanic or Arabic.

During this period, the CIA became concerned about American diplomats who were being ambushed in moving vehicles. In countries like the Philippines, communist insurgents were making noises about assassinating U.S. government officials. Since neither government nor police agencies had firmly established defensive driving schools in the United States, the CIA recruited people like me who could spirit American diplomats out of harm's way to safe airports and other destinations.

I had no problem taking on this type of duty. This was before insurgents, terrorists, and opposing spies had the ability to stand at a distance and send a stinger missile up the exhaust pipe of your car. I was told quite bluntly that no one would expect a black man to be "smart" enough to do dangerous assignments or even be in the CIA.

After successfully completing the first battery of tests, I was told that I was being considered for a backup desk position that would eventually lead me to an embassy appointment, with the secret assignment of being a "roadblock breaker." Moreover, I was to keep the cars clear of explosive materials. But that's a chapter for another book.

My most memorable experience in the bowels of the CIA's Langley, Virginia, headquarters was a series of meetings with a psychiatrist on the topic of why I refused to be given a Peace Corps cover to spy on black leaders in Africa. From this experience, I learned that those professionals who operate above the law are no different, whether they are from America or any other country. If the CIA crest had been removed from the wall behind him and replaced by the Nazi banner, one would not have noticed the difference. He viciously attacked my race, my self-esteem, and my loyalty to my country. I countered that I was not going to befriend black leaders in Africa only to "rat" on them. Now that the CIA had tested me with every conceivable IQ and performance test known in the U.S., I realized more about my overall capabilities and was more self-assured than ever before. I told the doctor that I had been more loyal to the United States than its institutions and opportunities had been to me.

By the end of the week, he became totally fed up with me. He threatened to plant a story in *The Washington Post* branding me a homosexual and pedophile, going so far as to say the story would center on the restroom at the Hotel Harrington, where a lot of Washington's closeted gay professionals rendezvoused. I told him I didn't care whether he ruined my life or not; to reiterate I refused to be assigned to the Peace Corps in Africa for the purpose of spying on black government officials there.

On the eve of my last day at the CIA headquarters, I knew the psychiatrist had only two options left: He could make me disappear forever, or he could release me. Fearing the worst, instead of taking the secret bus to Langley, I drove. If I were to disappear, they would have to make my car disappear too. I gave everything important in my pockets to Rose before I left the International Inn, not knowing what was going to happen to me that day. After much deliberation in an office in the bowels of the CIA that morning, the psychiatrist and others decided they would release me if I signed certain documents promising not to reveal anything about the CIA to anyone for two years. For fifteen years, I told no one about my experience with the CIA, even when I knew members of the University of Pennsylvania's psychology department were secretly conducting tests for the agency in the 1960s. Rose was glad the job went south, because she wasn't looking forward to my disappearing into the unknown all the time.

After the short-lived CIA experience, I settled in as director of education at Rahway Prison in Rahway, New Jersey. In the 1960s, this was the fourth toughest prison in the United States.

All these experiences—in the army, at Bordentown Reformatory, and Rahway Prison, with the CIA—served to enable first me and later Lenny to withstand long periods of auto racing competition under a degree of strain that most blacks, with the exception of Wendell Scott, have not been able to sustain over long periods. As an example, Wendell had to swap motors between his race car and truck to make it to the racetrack, then take the race car motor out of the truck and put it back in the race car and race. Then at the end of the racing event he had to go through the whole routine again to return home.

Chapter 3
Planting the Seeds, 1965-68

I n 1965, when he was four years old, my son Lenny began to ride with me on Saturdays to Wilson Haines Volvo in Mt. Holly, New Jersey, where Norman Pine was the service manager. Norman and I hit it off immediately, because both of us strove to buck the norm. He had prepared a Volvo PV-544 to run in H/gas class at the Atco Dragway. Given his aggressive nature, Norman had made inroads into the Volvo factory in Sweden. As most auto enthusiasts of that period remember, Volvo's PV-544 was one of the most detuned, well-built economy cars manufactured after World War II. A woman I knew in Pennsylvania parked her PV-544 under a large snow bank in near-zero temperatures from November of one year to April of the next, where with just a few turns of the motor, she started the car up and drove away.

Norman enjoyed great success racing heads up against H/gas competitors. He was less successful when handicapped against other classes. Since Lenny was too young to go into the pits, my friend Kenneth Tyler would accompany me to Atco to follow Norman's progress. It was during this period that I realized how difficult it would be to get more than one black friend to go to the track with me. My friends' roots were in the black middle class; they attended church faithfully every Sunday morning and just as faithfully watched football on TV every Sunday afternoon.

After much deliberation, I decided to start drag racing my Volvo

P-1800. I discussed my decision at length with Wilson Haines, explaining that I'd like to have the car prepared at his dealership. But after Wilson had made the decision to allow Norman to prepare my car at the shop, he committed suicide and left the task of managing the shop to Norman, who also performed all the mechanical duties until the dealership went out of business. This left me out in the cold. Rose was happy that I was forced to stop because our second child, Stephanie, was on the way.

During spring of 1966 a friend introduced me to Tony Hill, a talented English mechanic who agreed to help me prepare the Volvo P-1800 motor for the drag strip. With a growing family and rapidly increasing professional responsibilities, I had to budget my finances very carefully while making preparations to enter the 1966 National Hot Rod Association (NHRA) M/S automatic class. To this day, I have no hesitation in developing a motor program. Because of my unsolicited exposure to the CIA and my personal experiences, I never developed a local-gas-station attitude towards motor preparation. In this case, it was necessary to search the world for a Volvo racing exhaust system. The two best exhaust systems manufactured for the Volvo were the Kirk & Potter systems. Volvo supplied its new "B" camshaft. Norman made the valve assembly modifications to direct the gas in and the fumes out faster.

Again, not wanting to go to the track alone, I paired up with John Griswold, another pioneering black street-class drag racer who owned an H/S automatic Plymouth Barracuda. He ran his car mostly at the now defunct Vargo Dragway in Cross Keys, Bucks County, Pennsylvania. John was a personal friend, even before we began drag racing together. Since most of our friends showed little interest in any type of auto racing, John kept his drag racing activities to himself. At the same time, other things just as intense as racing were going on in my life. I was now employed as a Senior Social Research Scientist at New York University's Graduate School of Social Work, where my research tasks included participation on a national manpower project funded by the U.S. Department of Labor.

I was assigned to the riot-torn areas of South Central Los Angeles (Watts), Chicago, San Francisco, and New York. The New York surveys and analyses were headed up by my colleague and friend

Jack Tannenbaum. These were heady times. Each team member's assignment was to interview street gang leaders, high school students, community activists, civil rights activists, looters, and local government officials.

Making the mental transfer from interviewing black folks and gang leaders in the riot-torn black areas of Harlem, Chicago, Watts, and San Francisco to discussing drag racing technology on the weekends was extreme, to say the least. But having had my mental capacity tested by the CIA enabled me to handle it without undue stress. Jack and I both traveled so much that we were approved for United Airlines' exclusive 100,000-Mile Club for traveling that distance in one year. Being a member of that club was the best perk a frequent air traveler could get, and it was free. Alas, it was short-lived, because Ralph Nader challenged it as discriminatory against the average traveler.

I was alarmed about this depressing state of urban black communities and even more so about good, mostly single mothers who had to contend with the loss of their children to gangs, drugs and truancy. In Watts I was most impressed with Randy Thomas, a very bright, street-wise student at Barringer High School, and Ted Watkins, an adult community leader who tried to lift the area economically after the riots. Thomas and his best friend Elliott Smith became truly committed to the quest for fair treatment of blacks in motorsports into the twenty-first century.

Interviewing gang leaders was an eye opener. In different circumstances, most of them could have been innovative small company presidents. All were smart and charismatic. The most organized gang I interviewed was the white gang called the Mission Rebels in San Francisco. This gang reached out and helped the down-and-out in the Mission district, but could fight or instigate a riot against the police if necessary.

The most intelligent and violent gang leader I interviewed during those two years was Chino Garcia, leader of the Real Great Society. His gang operated out of New York City's lower east side. Chino was tall and tough looking; he towered over the rest of the gang members. He was reputed to have killed five people, so his authority was never questioned. At the height of his gang power,

Chino could assemble up to five hundred Puerto Rican teenagers to fight their adversaries to the death if necessary. Chino was a visionary; he and his lieutenants diversified from pure gang activity into small businesses and night clubs.

I was unimpressed with the black gang leaders. In Chicago, Los Angeles, and Harlem, they relied on naked intimidation and raw physical power to control their members and the neighborhood. They seemed committed to destroying themselves and the good members of the black community who just wanted to be left alone. Most of the black gang members I met could hardly read. The only national black leader who tried to turn the black gangs into productive thinkers was Ben Chavis, during his tenure as president of the National Association for the Advancement of Colored People in the early 1990s.

After seeing so much despair in America's major cities, I looked forward to retreating to the drag racing world on weekends. Vargo Dragway was my favorite strip to visit. Bucks County, Pennsylvania, was one of America's most serene and beautiful counties, and the competitors at the track were of different races, colors and creeds added to that. The days were crystal clear, and the timberline near the track was an artist's dream.

It was at Vargo that I first met Alex Baynard, who later became an integral part of the Miller Brothers drag racing effort. Both John Griswold and I went out of our way to talk to Billy Young, the first black Pennsylvanian to own a slingshot dragster. We marveled that his black driver, Little Huk, looked so young. Everyone got along like one big family. The track was a Shangri-La for me and an ideal oasis in the midst of a nation filled with strife. My best afternoon at the track in the M/S trophy class was knocking off eleven competitors.

Like most independent drag racers, my money was tight at the beginning of the 1967 racing season. Plus, the competitive drag racers were habitually improving their cars. I had to make the tough decision between staying home until I could be truly competitive or racing every week for the sake of being at the track as an also-ran.

Tony Hill and I decided to go back to the drawing board and improved the motor again. We changed the front shock geometry to enable the front of the car to shift weight to the back for better traction, installing a 50,000-volt ignition system and replacing the 4:11 rear end gears with 4:88 ones. This change influenced my decisions to develop the next drag racer solely as a racing car. At high speeds on the street, the high winding noise kept Rose irritable, though Lenny said it was neat. I continued having better-than- average success at Vargo Dragway and less success at Atco Dragway in New Jersey, but I won my class at both tracks.

In 1968, I continued to improve the Volvo by experimenting with the valve train, rear end gear ratios, different size racing slicks, and suspension geometry. These changes made me more competitive in the M/S Stock class, so I ran at both Englishtown, New Jersey, and at Atco. That year's most memorable moment was at Atco Dragway, within a few weeks of Dr. Martin Luther King's assassination. Like most Americans, I was thoroughly upset about what had happened in Memphis. In fact, a moment of black rage overcame me that night. With my youngest brother Bruce helping me out in the pits, I cut the Christmas tree lights (starting line) with a vengeance. In addition to beating all my competitors that evening, I broke my seat. I was so full of rage that when I pulled the gear shift lever from first down to second, I kept hitting the side of the seat. As anyone with Volvo P-1800 driving experience would agree, it had the slowest-shifting transmission in the world, so I had to get the best shifts out of it at all times, or I would be certain to lose the round. My rage about Dr. King's death energized me that night as I shifted gears like a madman.

It was also in 1968 that I met Wendell Scott and his friend William Jackson at the NASCAR Grand National race at Trenton Speedway in New Jersey, as well as Malcolm Durham, one of the top touring drag racers in the United States. Malcolm was also the best black drag racer in the country, idolized by all the black drag racers wherever he appeared with his Strip Blazer Chevrolets. Malcolm's advice during that year led me to sell the Volvo and roll over into the semiprofessional trophy ranks with a team approach. Malcolm said racers must decide whether they are going to race for fun or to win. He thought too many black racers ran for fun and were more interested in betting on or against each other's cars than in understanding the art and science of racing.

Chapter 4
Getting Serious, 1969-71

In the winter of 1969 I asked Kenny Wright, a family friend, and my brother Dexter to discuss mounting a drag racing effort, beyond the interest of black racers at the time. Most black racers were stuck in the secondary level of racing, striving only to beat other black racers and betting large amounts of money on individual runs rather than mounting serious development efforts in the National Hot Rod Association's trophy or money divisions.

Dexter had become interested in an automotive career as a result of my hot rod activities in the early 1950s. He had graduated with an associate of arts degree from Virginia State College in 1958 and, thanks to my participation in a panel discussion at the United Nations in 1966, was by '69 working as the new automotive service manager at the Sears 69th Street store in Philadelphia.

Jack Tannenbaum, an NYU colleague who conducted social research in the same group that I was assigned to, was a friend who participated in the panel discussion with me that year. Gen. Robert E. Wood, chairman of the board of Sears & Roebuck, was the guest speaker. Because of Martin Luther King's impact at the time, Wood mentioned in his speech that there was a need to promote Negroes at Sears in every department. Like many corporate leaders, then as now, he was having a hard time finding qualified blacks, and wanted the audience to make recommendations. I rushed up to the stage and, after much difficulty, got a chance to talk with him about the racial discrimination Dexter was exposed to at Sears's. Wood said he would look into the matter. True to his word, he had Dexter's qualifications checked out, and Dexter was promoted.

Kenny Wright was an auto body man, one of two trained black auto body men on Philadelphia's Mainline in the '60s. Jackie King, another friend, was the other one. Kenny worked at the Philadelphia School District's JFK Automotive Center, which trained inner-city black and Hispanic youth for apprenticeships in the automotive industry. Among the center's specialties were bodywork and painting.

An individual or team operation must have motor and suspension/body specialists, plus a team manager, to have even a remote chance of winning any type of auto race. At the meeting, we had these bases covered. The first thing we did was to incorporate, not only for tax purposes but to minimize disrupting attitudes e.g., *I'll take my parts* whenever there might be a disagreement. Once at Atco Dragway, I saw a car almost completely dismantled when the handshake partners became angry with each other.

I adhered strictly to the objective business approach that Joel Kirshner, my business mentor taught me: race at the level of a realistic budget. In further discussions with local professional drag racers and auto specialists, we selected V/S as a class that we could run within budget the entire year. I learned early on that most racers start with what they own, whether the car and equipment are competitive or not, or by the seat of their pants. This approach is practically a guarantee that a racer will run poorly every week or run out of money halfway through the season.

Next, we had to determine the best power-to-weight ratio car eligible to run in the class. Again, too many racers are loyal to a manufacturer for the wrong reasons. We selected a 1955 station wagon because, from a power-to-weight ratio point of view, it was at the top of the class.

We turned to K & G Speed Shop in Havertown, Pennsylvania to put the motor together. In the winter of 1968, Chris, the technician specialist at K & G Speed Shop was on the cutting edge of drag racing component technology. He turned us on to Sissell Automotive in California, the most prominent company developing killer six-cylinder motors. His logo was 6=8 (six cylinders having the power of an eight cylinder car).

Dexter found a loophole in the NHRA rules that permitted a six-cylinder Corvette motor with three one-barrel carburetors in the V/S class. We canvassed the U.S. and found a Corvette linkage setup at a Chevrolet dealership in Atlanta. After installing the linkage to the carburetor, Dexter didn't like the setup because it was flimsy and didn't open the three carburetors evenly. He concluded that a customized throttle linkage setup had to be made for the carburetors.

During the period while the motor was being built and Kenny was preparing the car after school at the JFK Automotive Center, Dexter told me to look around for someone who could make a linkage that would open the carburetors evenly. I remembered what a CIA agent and a safe cracker at Rahway Prison both had told me a few years earlier: "Whatever you can imagine that can be made, is being made in the world somewhere." With that in mind, I began to inquire after the name of a company or person who could produce a one-of-a-kind custom carburetor linkage for our specific application.

After making numerous phone calls, I found the people who made the best custom carburetor linkages in the most unlikely place—on 201st Street in New York City, just above Harlem. The name of the shop was Accurate Carburetors. After I told them what I was looking for, they said they could take care of the problem.

I took Lenny and Stephanie along with the mounted carburetors traveling by Amtrak from Trenton to New York City. We then transferred and took the A-train—the same A-train in the title of one of the most famous jazz renditions of all time—through the heart of the million-resident black community. The children and I arrived looking very suburban, carrying a Corvette carburetor setup through miles of subway train, and a community that had just been involved in riots. We got off the subway at the north end of Harlem and walked a block and a half to Accurate Carburetors. The shop was a throwback to the 1930s. The two partners looked like members of a 1939 European Alfa Romeo or Bugatti racing team, with aprons and dress caps. Although the shop appeared disorganized, both men knew exactly where every part was, on the workbench or in the bins behind them. After looking over the setup for a few minutes, they said they could adapt a Jaguar carburetor linkage to the setup with no problem.

Three weeks later I returned to Harlem alone, again by public transportation, and finally picked up the setup. By March 1969, the car, now named Mr. Diplomat, was finished and ready for the first drag race at Englishtown. Dexter had to finish putting it together by himself because, as a result of the *Pueblo* incident, Kenny was called up to active duty as a member of the navy reserves.

The Sunday we were to go to Englishtown, Dexter got the flu. Like many drag racers of that era, we flat-towed our car to the track. It was kept at my Aunt Lonia's garage, up the street from Dexter's house. She helped me hook up. Then I towed the station wagon from West Conshohocken, Pennsylvania, to Englishtown, New Jersey. At the track, the towing tires had to be changed to slicks, the air pressures had to be checked, and all the other routine procedures necessary for preparing the car for competition had to be completed. By then everything connected with the competition preparations had to be done by me alone.

In an attempt to save money, we had not had the motor dynoed before installing it. As a result, a serious problem surfaced after the first practice run. The station wagon barreled off the line and died at 4300 revolutions per minute in second gear. It should have wound out at 5200-5400 revolutions per minute in third gear. After it performed the same way the second time down the quarter mile, I decided to shut it off and ponder what to do next. Because I didn't have time to research the problem, I decided to bluff my first competitor rather than loading the wagon up and go home.

Because V/S was an unglamorous competition class at the bottom of the drag racing ranks, casual racers with street cars tried to steal wins to impress girlfriends, relatives, and colleagues who knew nothing about the sport. On this day, four such racers had entered V/S. When they saw our intimidating and professional-looking station wagon, three of them decided not to race that day. The fourth appeared on the line as my sole competitor.

When we staged our vehicles at the starting line, I messed with his mind by entering the staging box late, revving the motor and making short, aggressive braking stops. When the staging lights came on for the run, he became so eager to beat me off the line that he redlighted. All I had to do was putter down the track and get the trophy.

Later, after having the Holley carburetor representative research the fuel problem with the motor, we learned that the carburetor needle steps were for a racing hydroplane application, not an automotive application. This was why the motor peaked at 4300 revolutions per minute. The lessons learned that day have stayed with me ever since. Gas station bay-type racing preparation gets you 75 percent of the way to where you want to be without testing the motor on a shop dynamometer first. Dynoing and performing other prerace research and checks makes the difference in having a competitive race car at any level of racing. I also vowed that day never to go to the track again and do the work of an entire pit crew.

The three-carburetor side draft setup continued to pose major problems throughout the 1969 racing season. To alleviate some of the hassle, we started racing at the McGuire Air Force Base drag strip south of Trenton, which was one-eighth of a mile long. The shorter track allowed the station wagon to go through the lights at peak power at the end of each run.

During the season we returned to Englishtown Raceway Park several times. The first time we returned, the number two carburetor malfunctioned in practice. A group of us, along with Jerry Martini, owner of a Mobil station in Pennington, New Jersey, who helped Dexter and me out from time to time, were wondering what to do, when a former inmate whom I had taught at the Bordentown Reformatory wandered by and poked his head in. His nickname was Whitey, and he looked like a smaller, less muscular version of the Russian boxer who fought Sylvester Stallone in *Rocky IV*. Whitey had been incarcerated at Bordentown in the '50s because he had been part of one of the biggest illegal "chop shop" car rings that had ever operated in Newark.

He asked me what the specific problem was, then looked at the carburetor setup and disappeared. About fifteen minutes later he returned with a nearly new Corvette side draft one-barrel carburetor and handed it to me. He said, "Mr. Mil, this should solve your problem," and disappeared in the crowd. Thrashing at breakneck speed, we switched carburetors and won the V/S class that day.

As we were packing up to go home, an announcement came over the public address system. A 1936 Cord Replicar owner from New

York was stranded and couldn't get home, because someone had removed one of his carburetors from his motor. The announcer requested that the carburetor be returned, and no questions would be asked. On hearing the announcement, we stopped in our tracks. In the heat of the battle that afternoon, it had never occurred to me that Whitey might have stolen the carburetor.

As I looked over the parking lot, I saw an immaculate Cord Replicar with a well-dressed man and woman standing beside it. They looked as if they should have been at Lime Rock, Connecticut, viewing a road race, instead of spending the afternoon at a blue-collar dragway. We quickly dismantled the carburetor. I went over and diverted the couple's attention by asking them what the problem was, while a member of the crew set the carburetor on their hood. After hearing their story, I directed their attention to it. "It appears that someone returned it while we were talking," I said. They were so relieved, they looked as though they had seen the Holy Grail.

Before the 1970 racing season began, the NHRA made our 1969 setup illegal because 1955 Chevrolet six-cylinder station wagons were never produced with three one-barrel side draft carburetors. As a result, I had to revert to the standard Chevrolet one-carburetor setup that appeared on six-cylinder passenger cars. This change made me return to the drawing board, using Sissell Automotive's 6=8 motor configuration (six cylinders having the power of an eight cylinder car).

It was also in 1969 that we met Joe Gerber, president of the Race of Champions, the biggest annual Modified car race in the Northeast. It was at the 1969 Grand National race that Joe sowed the seeds that led us to move over from drag racing to stock car racing. At the same time Jim Cook, who promoted the Indy car races at the Trenton Speedway in those years, advised me that road racing and Indy car racing were the way to go. Two years later I took Cook's advice, much to Gerber's disgust.

Meanwhile, we decided to enter the 1970 drag racing season to get name recognition. We wanted to run every week at the Atco Dragway in New Jersey, because it was closer than Englishtown or Cecil County, Maryland. By this time the Vargo Dragway had closed. Next we needed to figure out if we were going to run in the trophy class or the money class. To ensure that we would be competitive all season we entered the trophy division, because it was less expensive. If we had gotten one of the local beer company drag racing sponsorships for that year, we would have competed in the money class. We, then, identified our technical resources. In addition to K & G Speed Shop, Dexter had identified Alex Baynard, Tony Pizzi, Ollie Volpe, and drag racing legend Bill "Grumpy" Jenkins as excellent resources. They were all drag racing specialists in different areas. Alex we met while racing at Vargo Dragway. Dexter knew Jenkins through his position at Sears. Jenkins took a liking to Dexter because Dexter never wasted time buttering him up like other local drag racers.

With the best resources, Miller Brothers and Kenny Wright improved the V/S Chevy station wagon another 50 percent over the previous season. The first improvement was changing the intake manifold and going back to using the sidedraft carburetor. Lenny, now eight, was given weight-stripping tasks such as removing sound-deadening materials and getting in tight spaces with wrenches. Because of church youth activities on Sundays, Lenny couldn't attend races. When he did go to the track we usually won, and he developed a winning attitude.

Formulating an incorporated team with assigned responsibilities allowed us to grow both on and off the track. When United States Auto Club (USAC) and NASCAR's Grand National cars were at the Trenton Speedway, I would go into the pits and meet new contacts there instead of going to Atco Dragway with Dexter and Kenny. When black stock car pioneer Wendell Scott came to the Trenton Speedway, I made certain Lenny and I attended the race. By 1969, I had come to know Wendell quite well. It was during this period that he informed me that Elmo Langley was the most racist Grand National driver he had encountered over the years, and that Richard Petty and his family treated him better than anyone else in NASCAR.

On opening day we flat towed Mr. Diplomat to the Atco Dragway. While Dexter was finding a place to park in the pits, I scouted out the competition. Looking around, I spied two very poorly constructed V/S cars and one pretty decent 1960 Plymouth Slant Six. I noticed that one of the two young men uncoupling the Slant Six was black. I walked over to introduce myself and to take a closer look at their car. The white partner greeted me, but the black partner shunned me. After some small talk, I informed the white partner that we would be competing in the same class. The black partner stood by the car looking at me with disdain. I realized then I had met my first "Oreo" racer—black on the outside, white on the inside. My mother always said that Oreos, in general, are far more dangerous than Uncle Toms, because Oreos have no allegiance to anyone, especially not to blacks.

With Kenny Wright's driving, Dexter's mechanical expertise, and technical advice from other sources, Mr. Diplomat began to win. Week after week, we knocked off the Oreo's Plymouth Slant Six—though when we were racing at Englishtown or at McGuire Air Force Base, the Oreo's car won. Kenny was even featured as Driver-of-the-Week in the 8 August 1970 edition of the *East Coast Drag News*.

As the season progressed, the Oreo refused to speak to us. He could not figure out how a black team continually beat him and his partner. The final blow to his racing ego came when we won the 4th Annual New Jersey State Championship V/S class on 19 August. He turned his back on us when we passed by his pit and cut his eyes at us in the staging lanes.

Things came to a head on the last weekend of the Atco season— a day Dexter, Kenny, and I will never forget. Morale was very high at the start of the day. We were announced as ninth in the points standing in the trophy classes out of at least 350 competitors. This was the first time a black team had achieved top ten status in either division since the track's inception.

On hearing that we were in the top ten, the Oreo asked the technical inspectors to look at our motor, paying the necessary tear-down fee to have the procedure done. The tech inspectors had Dexter remove the cylinder head from the motor. While they were in the midst of CC-ing the heads and checking the camshaft lift, Dexter's name was heard over the loudspeaker; he was wanted on the phone. Since he was busy removing the head from the motor, he sent me to the telephone. His wife Phyllis was on the other end, in the middle of an emotional crisis. She was going to commit suicide if Dexter didn't come home, she said. I tried to calm her down, telling her that we would be home in several hours. But she wouldn't hear it. She said she was sick of being alone on weekends, unable to attend social events because we were drag racing. From the end of World War II through the late 1980s, in the corridor between Washington, D.C., and Harlem, the black middle class partied on weekends like it was always New Year's Eve. Phyllis wanted to be a part of that scene and felt she had been denied the opportunity.

After hanging up I called my parents, who lived next door, and asked them to check on Phyllis. My mother gave me a tongue-lashing. "Leonard, racing is tearing this family apart," she said. "I don't know why two college graduates are fooling around every week with uneducated poor white trash. You need to be home in church on Sunday and Dexter needs to be able to take his wife out to social affairs."

My mother then knocked on Dexter and Phyllis's door. Getting no answer, she went into the house, found Phyllis on the kitchen floor with her wrists slashed and a bloody butcher knife nearby, and called the rescue squad. At the track, I told Dexter what Phyllis had said. He didn't believe she would follow through with her threat. He thought she was just frustrated and venting.

The tech inspector finished with the wagon and declared it legal to run. But in trying to get the wagon back together we couldn't finish the job, because we needed another head gasket. As the team manager, I made a decision not to run. We had played into the Oreo's hand. His Slant Six won that day. We went over to the tower and received our awards for finishing in the top ten points standing, while the Oreo looked on in disgust.

When Dexter got home, there was a message on his front door telling him to go to the Norristown hospital. When he got there he found our parents in the waiting room. Phyllis had to be admitted for psychological testing for a few days. Later that evening, my mother said she wanted to talk to us. Mother really hated racing. She wanted us to be white-collar workers—that was her definition of success. She believed Dexter would be better off making five thousand dollars a year as a banker in a suit and tie, than making ten thousand as a mechanic. She also thought drag racing was a sport for poor white trash.

Throughout the winter of 1970, Mother continued to talk to us about drag racing. She just did not understand what we were trying to do. My father never said anything, so long as we were winning. Rose never said much either. I always made time for her and our children; they were always my priority. I also made a point of attending professional and social functions that Rose and I agreed were important.

At the end of the 1970 season, Dexter and I decided to continue racing and to move up to a faster class. We quietly met with Alex Baynard and Ollie Volpe, who was white and a key team ally. After a number of bench racing sessions, Dexter and I decided to sell the V/S Chevy station wagon.

In 1971, we changed our name from the Miller Brothers Team to Miller Brothers, Volpe & Baynard. The change allowed us to expand our vision. We now had Volpe's motor knowledge and Baynard's expertise in suspension and exhausts. We bought and entered a 1969 427-cubic-inch big-block Camaro in the NHRA B/S money division. Baynard was the designated driver, because we wanted to draw in sponsorship dollars for a black driver.

Tony Pizzi, a specialist in big-block drag racing motors, built the power plant. The car could almost run on the national speed record for that class when Ollie spent quality time prepping it before each race. Grumpy Jenkins supplied us with one of his special ignition systems.

At local drag strips in Pennsylvania and New Jersey, the car became known as a runner in the B/S money class. The car won so much that at one special event at Atco betting fans, mostly black, wagered a total of $25,000 on it. They would walk through the stands yelling, "betting B/S black."

When Alex eliminated all competition except for the last car at this special event, the black betting fans were ecstatic. They continued to chant, "betting B/S black." But at the last round, Alex barreled off the line even with his opponent, losing the race at the end of the quarter mile by half a car length. Everyone lost their money. Now the fans were chanting, "Betting white the rest of the night, betting white the rest of the night." Since we knew many of the black fans who had lost their money, we packed up and left the track early. The last thing we needed was a fight.

We ran into a similar incident at Englishtown Raceway Park later in the season, with better results. This time Brooklyn Heavy's people bet on us. Heavy was alleged to be the biggest member of the black Mafia in Brooklyn, and among the top black Mafia leaders in the United States. He bought three Pro-Stock Dodges from Ronnie Sox, the legendary Chrysler drag racer, which allowed him to run even with the white competitors. Another black drag racer named Rapid Ronnie Lyles, who also had a large black following from Brooklyn, was running a car that day too.

Brooklyn Heavy's Bedford-Stuyvesant entourage coming into the Englishtown track was a sight to see. At least fifty cars, each with at least four people inside, followed Heavy's rig to the track that day. Some of the women in the caravan looked like characters in movies such as *Fort Apache, The Bronx* and *New Jack City*. Others were so daring and comely that both racers and spectators gawked as they passed by. The men in the group were a mixture of black Mafia types, pimps, gang bangers, petty crooks, and honest people getting out of the city on a hot Sunday afternoon. Including Ronnie Lyle's group, the caravan was at least three hundred strong. Heavy's gang did not bet foolishly or lightly. In fact, they bet on very few black drag racers. Occasionally, they would bet on Heavy's Pro-Stockers, our Miller Brothers car, and Rapid Ronnie Lyles. The rest of the time they bet on white drivers.

Some of the serious bettors would fan out through the pits, watching and listening to the cars run. They would write notes and the precise times of the runs. Usually these bettors had number-writing or gambling backgrounds. One of the serious Brooklyn bettors asked us how we were doing. From the way he was dressed, he looked like a high roller or a pimp. He struck up a conversation.

"Hi Mil, what's it like?"

"Good," I said.

"How good?"

"Real good."

"Good all day long?"

"Can't go that far."

"How far?"

"Can't say all the way," I said, ending the conversation.

"Thanks, Mil. I'm dropping duckets on you, bro. Don't let me down."

"Oh, here we go again," said Dexter, who had overheard the conversation. But we won that day, and Heavy's gang went home with smiles.

After the Englishtown race, Ollie wanted to drive. He thought he deserved a chance, because he did more work on the car than Alex. Because of Ollie's continuous complaining, Alex began to hold back and withdraw. He didn't want to fight over who would drive. Ollie took over both the mechanical duties and the driving. By this time Kenny Wright had stopped participating because of personal problems.

Later in 1971, we were running at the national record level almost every week. So we decided to enter the car at a Northeast Division 1 race in Montreal. The division drew all the best drag racing cars in the Northeast and throughout most of the United States. The team set out for Canada.

At Montreal Ollie broke the national record, clocked at over 130-mph. At the end of the run the distributor broke. The Jenkins distributor was unique, so we could not go to a trackside vendor to get the part we needed. We had to borrow or buy a distributor, so Ollie could back up our record for the NHRA record book, as required by the rules. Searching through the pits, Dexter and Ollie found another Pennsylvanian whose distributor was the same as ours. But, although he had been beaten in the first round of competition, out of meanness he refused to lend it to us. The team was through for the day. To make matters worse, when we returned to the hotel a crew member named Mousy walked through a clear plate glass door in the lobby, completely destroying it. It was a long ride home.

During this period I was spending more time with Wendell Scott, who had also introduced me to Mel Leighton, a black sprint car owner and driver who had attempted to enter a car in the Indy 500 in 1949. In line with more than sixty cars, Leighton had been told to withdraw his entry because blacks were not allowed to enter the race. I explained to Mel and to Wendell the reason I was disenchanted with drag racing from a marketing and sponsorship perspective. I saw drag racing as the least feasible racing environment for blacks over the next twenty years.

Wendell and Joe Gerber pushed stock car racing as the way to go. Mel, on the other hand, pushed USAC and Sports Car Club of America (SCCA) open-wheel racing for sponsorship opportunities. Mel persuaded me to switch my efforts to open-wheel racing, and suggested I fly out to his house in Los Angeles to meet Benny Scott, a second-generation black race car driver. His father, Bill "Bullet" Scott, had raced in the California black auto circuit in the 1930s. Leighton had been one of his good friends.

My family and I flew out to L.A., and Lenny and I went to Mel's house to meet Benny Scott. Mel gave us a lesson in black racing history. He explained the obstacles we would have to overcome to be successful as black racers. He said Benny and I had the best chance of any black combination to succeed at the higher levels of racing. By the end of the meeting, Benny and I had become fast friends. We still visit today.

When we met, Benny had never owned a brand new race car. Every car he owned had been second hand. The first was a go-kart, a miniracer powered by a lawnmower engine, which he built with a friend at his father's gas station when he was thirteen years old. When his father died suddenly, his wife and three children had to get out to work, so Benny had to build and race his cars on a very limited budget. This made him an excellent welder, chassis builder, and motor builder.

Mel stressed that it would be easier to set our sights on the Indianapolis 500 than on other types of racing efforts, because of the sponsorship money that was available. He felt there was no way a black drag racing effort could be sold to corporate America. He said that we had the proper educational backgrounds and experiences to fit in with either the "sporty car" or the "Indy" racing crowd. When we told Wendell Scott about the meeting, he was very unhappy that we were not going to mount a black stock car effort in NASCAR.

To make matters worse, I let Wendell down on the most important business opportunity of his life. He brought me a film script on his life to review, with an opportunity for 25 percent equity. Wendell trusted my business judgment and decided he needed an ally when negotiating his film rights. He made this decision just before the screenwriter Ken Voss, a Formula Vee driver I was acquainted with, began shopping it around Hollywood. One autumn night, Wendell drove the five hundred miles from Danville, Virginia to Trenton in a downpour to show me the script.

Wendell arrived at my office around 9 p.m. and let me read the script. It was a straightforward folk hero story. Wendell said that for $3000, I could own 25 percent of the script. I had only $800 available; all my spare cash was tied up in my own racing expenses. Because I was so focused on my own affairs, I did not take the time to call family and friends to help out. I didn't even think about giving Wendell a postdated check. I simply told him I didn't have the money. Wendell returned to Danville empty-handed and highly disappointed.

A few months later Greg Simms, a local Afrocentric educator, called. He was outraged that the story about Wendell Scott had become a black exploitation movie. He had learned about it through a friend at Third World Film Productions. Apparently, because the plot had been changed to a comedy, the supporting actors and actresses had tried to engineer a sit-down strike on the set. According to Simms, they had been rebuffed by Richard Pryor, the leading actor. Allegedly Pryor had said, "You niggers can get fired if you want, but this nigger is going to do what this white man wants as long as I get paid."

When the movie, *Greased Lightning*, came to the Ewing Drive-In Theater outside Trenton several years later, Lenny and I went to see it with our friend Ron Hines. Pryor's portrayal of Wendell Scott was a disgrace, and the film made a mockery of Wendell's contributions as a black pioneer in NASCAR's top racing division. I called Wendell and told him so. In his easy, nonthreatening manner, he replied, "Miller, that is why I drove seven hours in the pouring rain from Danville to Trenton to get you involved."

At the Black American Racers Association event honoring him several years later in Washington, I asked Wendell how he had done financially on the movie. He told me he had received only $25,000 for signing over his movie rights. He was supposed to have gotten a small percentage of the U.S. gross profits, not the European. Greg Simms's sources said the movie never made a real profit here, but did well overseas. Although years have passed, I still get angry at myself for letting a friend down when he needed me most. I could have helped or at least advised him, instead of being selfishly wrapped up in finding sponsorship for Miller Racing, Inc.

After meeting Benny Scott in L.A., I returned to the East Coast and contacted black tennis great Arthur Ashe's law firm, Dell, Graighill and Fentress, for the purpose of seeking Ashe's assistance. Contact with the firm opened doors for us. Lee Fentress suggested a racing team could be developed using an integrated approach. The firm represented an Indy car driver named John Mahler, who might be interested in being part of such an effort. In record time, Fentress assembled a group to mount the effort for Mahler to enter the Indy 500 and other select races in 1972. With Mahler's help, we were able to get three investors: Brig Owens, safety for the Washington Redskins; Richard Duetsch, a friend of the Kennedy family; and Paul Jackson, at the time the largest black contractor in the United States.

Jumping from a regional drag racing effort to an Indy 500 and SCCA Formula A effort was not as impossible as it seemed. Having been raised in the backdoor of Philadelphia's Mainline society in the '40s and '50s, I had routinely overheard million-dollar deals in the making and had absorbed the skills for making them through osmosis. I learned what went into such deals: expertise, money, and trust. While Ollie Volpe and Dexter finished the drag racing season, I met several times with Mahler and Fentress. From our meetings we formed Vanguard Racing, Inc. Benny agreed to be the black driver trainee for the Indy 500. With the new racing company established, Miller Racing, Inc. was put on the shelf. Dexter eventually concentrated on successful show car efforts, and Ollie moved up through the racing community, eventually working as Moroso's NASCAR representative in the mid-1990s.

In November, we finalized our racing plans for 1972. Mahler would enter Indy car races and counsel Benny on his driving techniques. Fentress was to represent Richard Duetsch. I was to go with Mahler and look for associate sponsorships for both drivers. Fentress through one of Duetsch's business interests had already lined up Harbor Fuel Oil as primary sponsor for Mahler's car.

Originally from Bettendorf, Iowa, Mahler was considered a ladies' man. He had fighter-pilot dash and good looks. He was a professional tennis instructor and a college graduate, and he always had an unlit cigar in his mouth, like the legendary open-wheel car owner Carl Haas. And he was always pulling mischievous pranks with passenger cars and trucks. On a trip to Goodyear Tire & Rubber Company to meet Mike Babbich and Leo Mehl, director of the motorsports division, during the winter of 1971, we encountered an Ohio snowstorm before we arrived at our hotel. As we entered the driveway of the Holiday Inn, Mahler who was driving my new Buick Electra 225, asked if I would mind if he scared the people standing in front of the hotel. In the driveway under the overhang of the lobby was a solid sheet of ice. He said he was reasonably certain we would not crash through the plate glass window. I was up for it, so I said, "Let's do it."

Mahler engaged the Buick into a beautiful power slide on ice. Using the accelerator, not the brakes, as his control, Mahler went down the driveway at a 45-degree angle. The people standing out front started screaming and running everywhere. Several slipped on the ice.

As Mahler came under the canopy, he did a 360-degree turn with the Buick, slid almost perfectly up to the curb in front of the lobby door, and stopped. People were peering through the plate glass window in shock.

Before we could get out of the car, the hotel manager stormed out the door in a rage.

"What are you trying to do, kill somebody?" he demanded. "Who do you think you are, an Indy car driver?"

"Yes, I am," Mahler replied.

"Don't ever pull a stunt like that again," was all the manager could say in reply.

But the crowd was impressed. The women thought Mahler was cute. A number of them asked for his autograph, and by the time we reached the front desk, two had given him their telephone number. The next day we had a very successful meeting with Mehl and Babbich at Goodyear's headquarters in Akron. Associate sponsorships were coming together for the 1972 racing season.

Chapter 5
Indy, SCCA, Expo, and England, 1972-73

B y February 1972, John Mahler, Lee Fentress, Richard, and
I, were ready for the racing season. We were to use Mahler's
McLaren chassis to qualify for Indy with an Offenhauser
motor prepared by Louie Unser. Vanguard then bought a McLaren
M10-A for Benny to campaign in the Sports Car Club of America
(SCCA) Formula A Southern Pacific Region under Mahler's tutelage. Goodyear and the Champion Spark Plug Company were associate sponsors. Mahler was a driver who could qualify despite
mediocre equipment and long odds. (Wendell Scott had the same
knack in NASCAR's Grand National Series.) We had to practice,
qualify, and race with the same Offenhauser motor. The heavily
sponsored teams had one motor each for practice, qualifying, and
the race, plus a number of spares.

With a shortage of crew, Benny had to assist Mahler. With over
sixty cars attempting to qualify for the thirty-three-car field, Mahler
qualified twenty-ninth. He got every ounce of horsepower out of the
Offenhauser and fought the wheel around the speedway without
kissing God's hand. I was ecstatic.

In the 500, Mahler finished twenty-second. He made the mis-
take of trying to race the front runners instead of saving his equipment. He redlined the Offenhauser one time too many, and about
halfway through the race it finally blew. Considering the circumstances, all of us at Vanguard were more than satisfied. This experi-

ence and others with Mahler that year hooked both Lenny and me on big-time racing for good. When Mahler stayed at our house, Lenny would eagerly sit near him and take in all his experiences and racing stories.

While the team's eyes were on Mahler, Benny entered select SCCA Formula A races in the Southern Pacific Division. He won four races and earned first-place honors in the class by the end of the season. When one of his many first-place trophies was presented to him in Denver, several of the sporty-car types who had tried for years to win a coveted first-place trophy for bragging rights were in shock. One blurted out, "Can you imagine a baboon has won the first-place Formula A trophy?"

Benny could not believe what he was hearing. When he told me what had happened, he said it was the first time he had encountered such a racist remark. I told him that any time a black, especially a black man, achieves honors in a new venue, he's always going to be taunted by some of the whites whom you've surpassed. Jackie Robinson got so tired of the taunts that in later life he stopped saluting the U.S. flag.

The goals we set for 1972 were achieved. With Mahler having qualified, Richard caught the Indy bug. This was the first time I was close enough to see how America's rich can pole vault into the top rung of a sport without having to learn the business of that sport from the ground up.

Through Fentress, Duetsch informed the rest of us that he was going to field a race car for John Mahler in the 1973 Indianapolis 500, with the hope of a higher finish or, as a long shot, winning the race. He added that he would match dollar for dollar any black investment in, or donations to, Benny's 1973 racing season other than from Brig Owens, Paul Jackson, and me, up to a limit of $250,000.

Brig, Paul, Benny, and I set out to talk to black potential investors or donors who were wealthy or had disposable income of $10,000 or more. Benny talked to Muhammad Ali, who told him he was crazy and a fool trying to kill himself driving a car without wings at over 200 miles per hour. Brig met with black professional athletes who loved cars. They told him a black could never qualify for the Indy

500, and that they weren't going to waste any of their money trying to do the impossible. Paul talked to several well-heeled black contractors, who rather than with putting a black driver in the race, were mainly concerned with getting free VIP tickets to the races for their families. One physician I contacted even laid a stack of hundred-dollar bills out on a table and said, "Len, this money is for taking my white sweetie to the French Riviera. Look at the stack and weep."

Since we could not obtain one dollar from well-heeled blacks, we voted to disband Vanguard Racing in the winter of 1973. But Benny and I vowed to keep racing. We met in Chicago at the Airport Hilton with Rowland Jefferson, M.D., a wealthy black surgeon and race car owner who later wrote and produced the black film *Disco 9000*. Marvin MacAfee, his chief mechanic, also attended the meeting.

As at most black meetings I've attended involving setting up a new organization, Dr. Jefferson raised the question of who was going to be president and who was going to speak to the media and appear on TV. I was taken aback by this initial emphasis on leadership fluff. Benny and I had not yet broached the proposed team's PR aspects; all of our premeeting discussion had been about the practical aspects of getting Benny to the Indy 500.

After several hours of discussion, we decided to buy Benny a used Formula Super Vee to participate in SCCA events across the country. We tried to talk Marvin MacAfee into becoming Benny's chief mechanic on a part-time basis. Marvin declined because he had to get paid for any mechanical work. He did say that if sponsors could be found, he would quit his job for a $25,000-a-year salary. We couldn't do either, so he declined giving Benny any assistance at all.

Returning to Los Angeles after the meeting and thinking over our 1973 racing plans, Dr. Jefferson decided to throw his money in with ours and get Benny back on track towards Indianapolis. A white investor from California who had been following Benny's career and wanted him to go further also contributed some money.

Benny located a used Formula Super Vee, including all the spares and an open trailer, and found a young mechanic named Denny who worked at a Porsche dealership. Benny's wife, Schill, performed most of the gopher duties. My tasks were to obtain a sponsor and to keep his name in front of the public.

In the midst of getting ready for the 1973 racing season, I received a flyer from Operation PUSH advertising its Chicago Expo, stating that 500,000 visitors would attend, and that VIPs from America's top corporations would be present. Since we now needed sponsorships for several black race teams and exposure for the newly formed Black American Racers (BAR), I looked further into appearing at the PUSH Expo. I convened a meeting with Ron Hines and several other members of the association, and everyone thought it was a good idea.

Expecting that 500,000 visitors would pass through the exhibit, we decided to take both an Indy car and a NASCAR Grand National car. Leonard Manley supplied Valvoline's Indy show car, and George Wiltshire supplied his own NASCAR Grand National car.

Since the race cars took up a lot of booth space, I had to buy six booths. Since we had more than enough display room, and decided to sell BAR T-shirts, patches, and decals. And, since no one had any money, I underwrote all the expenses through my company, Dynamic Programs, Inc.

In all, we had twenty in our group, including Ron Hines; former civil rights worker Leo Lilliard; an avid racing fan Eugene Gadson, Ph.D.; drivers Coyle Peek, Benny Scott, and George Wiltshire. Also part of the group were Mel Scott and Percy Jones, who owned a well-stocked African artifacts store in Trenton.

The Operation PUSH Expo personnel directed us to stay in a black-owned hotel, if at all possible. The group thought it was a good opportunity to spend money in Chicago's black community. When we went to check into the black hotel we had chosen, no one stayed in his room more than a few minutes. All the rooms assigned to the group reeked of marijuana and worse. The stench was so strong that you could almost get high just from breathing. The group nominated me to get our money back immediately. I told the manager our group wasn't used to this type of accommodation. Worse yet, I said, we might be injured or killed. We were very worried about the possibility of a stray bullet fired by a drug pusher whistling through our rooms if a drug transaction went sour. The manager let us check out without any problem. While we were loading up, a bellman told us someone had been shot through the walls the night before. We headed to the Hyatt without looking back.

The racing exhibit was placed on the back curtain wall in the minority business section of the Expo. Before the exhibit closed, the Indy car had almost been stolen. Several marginal businesses were in financial trouble on the first day, unable to pay the union for setting up their exhibits. They didn't have enough money to adhere to the six-foot rule. The union contract with the convention center stipulated that one of their workers would set up and dismantle the booths under six feet in height. Helpers would be assigned if the structure were complex and if heavy boxes had to be moved around by hand. If the booth measured more than six feet in height, a helper was required at all times, and the costs doubled. Three marginal vendors went bankrupt before the Expo was over.

A union official in New Jersey had prepared me for this situation ahead of time. He said, "Take a thousand dollars in cash for booth erection. When you pay cash on the spot, you'll go to the head of the line. Tip the workers five dollars, and most will lower the time recorded to do the work. Don't worry where the cash goes." During our five days at the Expo, BAR received exemplary treatment from the union. We never had to wait for service, and I could go to the front of the line at the service request desk while the marginal small-business owners were disputing over the union charges.

Most of the black and other minority businesses were located in one area, and the Fortune 500 companies and Johnson Publishing Company, one of the leading black-owned businesses, were located in the main exhibit area. The minority-owned businesses represented a cross section of products. Some were counting on the proceeds earned at the Expo to make their yearly profits.

Like many vendors, anticipating 500,000 visitors passing through our exhibit area, we signed up for the daily Brink's Armored Car Service. For the first two days of the Expo most of us had to cancel the service because of extremely low sales.

When the Expo opened, we were swamped with black schoolchildren. The convention center parking lot was a sea of yellow school buses. The teachers, both black and white, were proud to expose their classes to black businesses and products. Many of the black kids who passed through were hungry, more interested in food than in being exposed to black culture. Many begged for coins persistently. Leo, Ron, and others in our group gave out coins to the really hungry kids until they ran out of change. Since Benny, Coyle, and George had their driver's uniforms on, they couldn't give the kids change even if they wanted to.

The ice cream man, the only white vendor on the floor, made a lot of money during the Expo. He was located between entry and exit doors of the minority business area, near our exhibit. About 100,000 kids bought ice cream cones at about 30 cents each. There would be at least a hundred kids in the ice cream line in the morning and fifty in the afternoon. While the black vendors were standing around going broke, the Brink's armored car started making two stops at the ice cream stand each day. The vendor was moving ice cream so fast he had to park a large refrigerated truck just outside the convention center so he wouldn't run out. The white ice cream vendor made a killing, while the black vendors were killed.

Although Reverend Jesse Jackson's staff advertised PUSH Expo heavily across the United States to entice the black middle class, only the true believers showed up during the day. The black middle class mainly showed up at the special musical events to be entertained by the Jackson Five and other famous black acts. Most couldn't have cared less about what Reverend Jackson was trying to do.

The highlight of the Expo was an impromptu ceremony by a black third grade teacher and her class in front of our booth. They presented Benny, Coyle, and George with $2.57. The presenter, a bright black girl, said on behalf of her class that they had collected the money among themselves to help us go racing. At the conclusion of her remarks the entire class clapped with approval. All of us were deeply touched; tears came into the eyes of several of us. The $2.57 was never spent. It's still in our racing files somewhere.

Percy Jones and Mel Scott, along with six other black vendors we knew from the New York/New Jersey area, took a financial beating by going to the Expo. Four of the vendors went bankrupt within six months. Percy and Mel never really recovered financially. The products they had bought plus their other expenses amounted to over $25,000. The expenditures wiped out their cash reserves and eventually forced them out of business. Like all the vendors, they had counted on the black middle class to buy from them.

Except for the $2.57 from the kids, the Expo was a bust for all of us black racers. The corporate representatives stayed as far away from us as possible. The black auto dealers present for the most part wanted to be patted on the back for their achievements at the receptions and luncheons. They looked on the black racers as stealing their spotlight. As a result of this experience, we vowed never again to appear at any event without being sponsored.

Benny entered most of the SCCA Formula Super Vee races in 1973. Because we were unsponsored, we regularly finished in the middle of the field. To race on the East Coast I had to build a one-and-a-half-car garage, so Benny could set up the car and make repairs. For a month during peak season, Benny and Denny the mechanic were guests at our home in Lawrenceville, New Jersey.

It was during this period that Lenny became addicted to everything about race cars. It began when Benny stayed with us and worked on the car ten hours a day. Lenny and his friend Eddie Greatti would come home from school and head straight for the garage to perform gopher duties. They became so obsessed with racing that they put together a go-kart.

The go-kart almost caused a quarrel between me and Rose in the midst of a car crowded household. One day at my office in Trenton, I got a call from Chief Seabridge of the Lawrence Township Police Department, telling me that Lenny had been pursued down Allwood Drive in a go-kart with the throttle cable tied around his thumb, clocked at 35-mph. "Please talk to him and call me back," said Chief Seabridge. Because I was a vice president of the Lawrence Township Democratic Club and a supporter of the police department, I scolded Lenny and Eddie, and considered the matter closed.

Our best finish of 1973 was at Pocono. Benny finished second, in spite of several German Formula 3 drivers working together and boxing him in on the last lap. This was the first time Benny and I had experienced slip streaming, now called drafting, by two or more drivers working together.

At the Pocono race Ed Henry, marketing director for Carling Black Label Beer, took notice of Benny's outstanding driving ability and came over afterwards to say he was bringing over the company's president and his wife to meet Benny as a formality, because he had decided to become an associate sponsor of the team for $25,000. (Ed and I had been talking for several months about the possibility that Carling might sponsor our team.) I asked Schill, Benny's white wife, to stay in the background for a few minutes while Benny talked with the president and his wife. Alas, while the president was congratulating Benny on his performance and relaying all the good things Ed had told him, Schill walked up to the group and butted in.

Picture the group: Ed Henry was dressed like any motorsports manager in the summer, in a banlon shirt and khakis. The president was in a sports coat, shirt and tie, and khakis. His wife was dressed like a wealthy South African white woman just returning from a croquet game at an exclusive country club—white hat, long white dress, white shoes. Benny was dressed in his driving suit, I in a Champion Spark Plug banlon shirt. Schill was dressed like Daisy in the "Li'l Abner" comic strip, in denim shorts and a short-sleeved blouse.

When Schill said she was Benny's wife, I saw the $25,000 sponsorship disappear before my eyes. Without pausing in what he was saying, the president of the company formed a plastic smile on his face. His wife turned red with shock, then a pale white that blended in with her clothing, and frowned. Ed did an excellent job of trying to continue our conversation, all for naught. The president and his wife quickly excused themselves and left the rest of us standing there. Later I heard that the company almost fired Ed for considering Benny for sponsorship.

In the twelve years that I knew Schill, this was the only time we had a big difference of opinion on the role of a driver's white wife. After Carling retreated, Schill pressed the point with me: A wife should not be hidden in the background because of her race. I countered that, in 1972, white male captains of industry and their wives didn't accept sponsoring black men who were married to white women. Black male entertainers and athletes who were married to white women were less likely to sponsor a black race car driver too, because they tried to be accepted by the white community by sponsoring white causes and organizations.

"I don't look at race," rejoined Schill. "We're all human beings and should be respected equally."

"White corporate America in general is not the least bit interested in sponsoring a black man with a black wife, let alone one with a white wife," I replied. "That is the sad fact of the matter." I did agree, though, that in an ideal world, Schill was right.

At the end of the 1973 racing season, Dr. Jefferson dropped out for the classic racing reason: he was on the West Coast and felt he could not meet with me regularly or attend any of the races. He also wanted to develop his own race team on the West Coast, where he could show his friends the car on occasion at his convenience.

Before I explain how Ron Hines, Malcolm Durham, and I got Black American Racers Association (BARA) off the ground, I must tell the story of Coyle Peek, who came to be Benny's backup driver in training during the 1973 season. On occasion, as we marketed BAR and Benny Scott to potential sponsors, the "what if?" factor came up. If Benny quit or got hurt or was killed, what would happen to the program? To overcome this problem, BAR sought out a backup driver. While we were doing this, Coyle Peek called from Long Island and we went over his experience on the telephone. He had read about our Indy project in various newspapers and magazines.

Coyle had been introduced to auto racing through the Sports Car Club of America (SCCA) in 1970. His racing idol was Bobby Unser. When asked what else he was interested in, his answers were modeling and becoming a movie actor. At that point I should have terminated any further discussions with him, but I didn't. Coyle had some limited Formula Ford experience, but he liked to pass himself off as a Formula Atlantic driver (the series above Formula Ford). He could spend an hour talking about the Formula Atlantic Brian Hart motor, without coming up for air.

Since BAR was continuously trying to find drivers capable of moving up the ladder in the shortest time possible, I decided to send Coyle over to England and enter him in five Formula Ford races. In the 1970s England had the most competitive Formula Ford Series in the world. Drivers would leave the United States and compete in the British Formula Ford Series to see if they had the right stuff. Coyle and I contacted several Formula Ford driving coaches in England, settling on Peter Semus of S.H.A.R.P. Racing Limited as his tutor.

As the day neared for Coyle to board the plane to London, he began to procrastinate wondering whether he should go. He postponed his flight twice, using flimsy excuses. When I mentioned the situation to Ron Hines, he said, "Can't you see? Coyle is scared. He's never been more than a thousand miles away from home in the United States."

When I confronted Coyle, he admitted he was scared to go to another country by himself. I told him Peter Semus would be looking after him on and off the track during his stay in England. Peter reassured him too. The next week, Coyle finally got on the plane.

In England, Coyle proved he could drive a race car, competing at Silverstone and Mallory Park. Of the five races Coyle entered, his best finish was second at Mallory Park. All the races he entered had large fields of thirty or more cars and were very competitive. Peter was satisfied with Coyle's driving ability, saying he was aggressive and charged through the field in the sprint races and made clean passes while moving through his field of competitors. But Peter cautioned me that Coyle had a need to impress people off the track beyond his station in life. He also remarked that Coyle projected an image more like a movie star than a race car driver.

When Coyle returned to the United States in the summer of 1973, he was buoyant. We thought it was because of his racing success in England, but it turned out he was appearing on the upcoming *Ebony* magazine eligible bachelor list. When the *Ebony* issue with the bachelor list appeared on newsstands shortly thereafter, Coyle received seventy-nine letters from young women around the country. At first I was amused. But soon it became very clear that Coyle was more interested in replying to the seventy-nine letters than in even discussing racing. He got so wrapped up in impressing young women, that he canceled any meetings having to do with racing. Apparently, he thought he had done enough racing for the year.

Coyle asked for expense money to go to the track to see Benny race at Watkins Glen, then showed up with three starlets on his arm. He went to the team registration building in town and talked the registrant into giving him the remaining team pit passes. Anyone in racing who's been involved in a situation like this knows what problems this can cause when the legitimate crew members can't obtain their credentials. Coyle had created my first problem of the day.

Since Lenny was too young to be allowed in the pits, I asked Coyle to let him tag along with him for the day. Before Coyle, Lenny, and the three women left me, Coyle asked me for fifty dollars to buy sandwiches and drinks during the day, because he was broke. As I gave him the money I said, "Make certain Lenny eats." At the end of the day, as Benny, Ron Hines, Lenny, and I were returning to our motel, Lenny mentioned that he was real hungry, because he hadn't eaten anything all day. That night was the beginning of the end of Coyle Peek's affiliation with Black American Racers, Inc.

But it took several other incidents in 1973 before his affiliation was finally terminated in late December. The first was his compelling need to call a number of the young women who had written letters to him following his appearance in *Ebony*. It got so bad that when he visited my office in Trenton, he would make individual calls costing seventy-five dollars each. Anne Stumpo, my personal secretary, put locks on certain telephones and almost denied him entrance to the building. Finally, Coyle was banned from using the phones at all.

Another incident caused a commotion at the Dover Speedway in Delaware. Earlier in the year, Coyle had met George Wiltshire at Reverend Jackson's Expo in Chicago and had told him that he wanted to be a NASCAR driver. On the Dover weekend Coyle, carrying his driver's suit to the speedway wanted to have pictures taken by George's race car and towing rig. As he was doing this, a curious crowd gathered. Coyle was directing the photographer and posing for pictures at the same time, as if he were on a Hollywood movie set. Bill Gazaway, NASCAR's operations chief, spied Coyle with the small crowd around him. Gazaway, who ran NASCAR's field operations with an iron fist, and who had never seen nor heard of Coyle Peek before, was livid.

He sent an official down to Wiltshire's rig to bring Coyle back to report on what he was doing in the pits in a driver's uniform. Gazaway, an old-school operations man, reminded black folk of a movie version of a Confederate colonel or a blood-and-guts World War II marine sergeant. He asked Coyle a number of blunt questions—though none Coyle couldn't answer. Coyle didn't even have the proper pit credentials. When Gazaway learned this, he immediately had an official escort Coyle out the pit gate.

On Monday, when Coyle told me what had happened, I chewed him out again. I said, "You're more interested in pretending to be a model or a celebrity than in driving race cars. You're on the verge of not being a part of the team any more."

The final straw came at Christmas time. Coyle promised several women that he was going to give them the most cherished gift they'd ever receive. The women waited anxiously for Coyle's gift. A week before Christmas, they received an elegantly wrapped gift containing a gold-plated frame filled with a personally autographed picture of Coyle in his driver's suit.

When one woman in New York City received Coyle's picture, she smashed it into small pieces. When another in Mount Holly, New Jersey received hers, she told Coyle to come to her house and pick it up. Shameless, he picked up the picture because he wanted to save the frame. To make matters worse for Coyle, I told him he was also through with the team because he was not focused on race car driving but on being a celebrity. Coyle disappeared from the scene and never drove a race car again.

Chapter 6
Bringing Everyone Together, 1973-74

During the winter of 1973, in addition to the racing team, the Black American Racers Association (BARA) was incorporated. I had formulated the idea along with Ron Hines, whom I had met at a black racers' brainstorming session at Eugene Gadson's home in Lawrenceville, New Jersey, several years earlier. Ron arrived at this suggestion because of the Vanguard Racing experience that had brought the black racing community together across the country in 1972. We discussed the idea with Wendell Scott, Malcolm Durham, Sumner "Red" Oliver, and Benny Scott. Red said an association of black racers was long overdue. There had not been a racing group of any type since the two known associations organized in the 1920s and 1930s in Indiana and in California.

The task of organizing the association was left to Malcolm, Ron, and me. I was elected chairman because of the varied secretarial, accounting, and legal resources at my disposal through Dynamic Programs, Inc., my manpower-consulting firm, that would facilitate getting the group off the ground fast. Malcolm was named president because of his national success and track record as the most noted black drag racer of the 1960s. He had a following of at least 50,000 fans nationwide, many of them black. It was Malcolm who contacted Margaret Ricks, Yvonne Savoy, Harry "Pinky" Pinkard, Billye Jean Armstrong, Sylvia Proctor, and others and all of them were extremely dedicated to performing the necessary organizational tasks, several of them later became officers.

Ron was the linchpin of the group. He had all the positive attributes of a superior athlete, a skilled academician, and an engineer. He also had the good looks and excellent manners that made him attractive to most people he encountered. He was one of the first black students to graduate from the prestigious Phillips Academy in Andover, Massachusetts, in 1959. He also graduated from the University of Pennsylvania with a degree in mechanical engineering and belonged to the Kappa Alpha Psi fraternity. While at Penn, he became the first black captain of the track team. He later became an integral part of the separate organization Black American Racers, Inc. (BAR) along with Benny Scott, Tommy Thompson, and Bruce Driver.

The goals of BAR, Inc. were to publish a yearbook, to create a Black American Racers Day at a drag racing facility, and to raise the visibility of black contributions to motorsports. We also decided to recognize those corporations that contributed to the development of black racing and racers.

Eugene Wells, a childhood friend to several of us and a motorsports hustler of the first order, came up with the idea of sponsoring a Black American Racers Day at Englishtown Raceway Park in 1974. He said that Englishtown would draw black fans in large numbers from Philadelphia and New York City and from all points in between. The Englishtown officials agreed to the Black American Racers Day, but Hines, Wells, and I were made responsible for organizing and running the special program. We decided to run an eight-car, Pro-Stock Eliminator race among the East Coast's best black Pro-Stockers. Malcolm, as president of BARA, would participate automatically. We concentrated on getting seven more cars to take part.

Hines and I decided we first needed to contact Brooklyn Heavy. He owned three Pro-Stockers, and Willie "Camrod" Campbell had one. Brooklyn Heavy also attracted a huge black following at Englishtown Raceway Park whenever he appeared. After many attempts during the winter of 1973, I reached Heavy by phone at his place of business in the Bedford-Stuyvesant section of Brooklyn, and we set a date to meet. I contacted Hines, and together we journeyed to "Bed-Sty" to see Heavy. This was one trip we would never forget.

Hines and I drove from Trenton to Brooklyn in the middle of the week, early in the spring of 1974. We arrived after dark, around 8 p.m. As we drove toward Bed-Sty, Hines grew more uncomfortable. It looked liked Beirut, Berlin after World War II, and parts of Chicago's public housing neighborhoods combined. There were no pedestrians, no police cruisers. But we knew we were being watched.

As we neared Heavy's street, a guy who looked like an NBA power forward stepped in front of the car. We braked. This guy was the neighborhood's unofficial traffic cop; to see Heavy, we had to get through him. He stood about six-feet, nine inches tall, and his name was Tree. We identified ourselves. He said Heavy was expecting us. We followed him around the corner to a small row of well-lit buildings.

Tree showed us where to park. When we got out of the car, we were surrounded by some of the toughest-looking characters we'd ever seen in our lives outside of the movies. At this point Hines was ready to return to Trenton; this was not our type of crowd. Tree told everyone to stand back, and that we had business to discuss with Heavy. One street gang tough pointed to me and said, "He look like FBI."

Inside Heavy's auto repair shop, we had to wait until he finished talking to two white men who looked like characters out of a *Godfather* movie. While we were waiting, Camrod Campbell came out to greet us and ushered us through the door to an adjoining building. We were surprised to see a full-blown cam-grinding shop in the heart of one of America's most blighted ghettos.

When we returned to Heavy's office, the two white men were leaving. As soon as we started talking to Heavy about the Black American Racers Day race, we heard a commotion in the shop. A middle-aged man who looked like a numbers runner or a dope peddler pulled his new Oldsmobile 98 into one of Heavy's garage bays. A crowd began to gather, gawking at the car. When Heavy went to see what was going on, he became angry and turned to the crowd and said, "*Who* is the king?"

"*You* the king, Heavy," they replied.

"Since *I'm* the king, you get that piece of shit the hell outta my garage," he said. "Cause I'm gonna show you what the king can buy."

Heavy proceeded to the sidewalk, to a friend's car. He called back over his shoulder to Camrod to look out for the two of us until he returned. Then he jumped into the car with the two unsavory types and sped down the street, heading for the local Cadillac dealer.

About an hour later, Heavy drove into the shop in a brand new white Cadillac with every available option. Once out of the car, he told one of the young toughs in the crowd to go out in the street to check the sticker price on the Olds. The young man returned, and Heavy had him announce the price to the crowd. Heavy then had a very attractive young black woman announce the sticker price on his car. The Cadillac clearly was more expensive. The crowd cheered. "Don't *ever* park your piece of shit in my garage again," Heavy told his would-be usurper. When he was done, someone yelled out, "Heavy, you the king!"

After all the drama had subsided, we started the meeting all over again. Hines went over all the details, including the payout. Heavy agreed to bring his cars to the track when we agreed on a date.

On a clear, hot summer day in 1974, the top black Pro-Stockers on the East Coast showed up at Englishtown Raceway Park. At least five thousand black fans from Brooklyn, other parts of New York City, New Jersey, Philadelphia and Baltimore filled the stands. The total attendance was more than 25,000. Hollywood Sam, who had a speed shop in Detroit and was the leader of the black drag racing community there, had one of the Detroit Pro-Stockers appear. This gave us enough cars. One of Heavy's cars won top eliminator honors—but when we paid out in the tower after the race, Eugene Wells refused to pay Heavy. Wells was always scheming. Once, he sold a hundred cases of oil that Pennzoil had contributed for distribution to the black racing community. Eventually one of his schemes landed him in the Burlington County Jail in New Jersey. On this occasion, Wells figured Heavy didn't need the money, so he decided to keep it. Somewhat petulantly, Heavy said that was not the deal he'd made. So we made Wells pay Heavy. Several years later the FBI published a Black Mafia List, and Heavy was on it. Later he was busted for drug distribution and got seven to fifteen years in prison. With that, black attendance at Englishtown Raceway Park dropped dramatically.

In the midst of organizing Black American Racers Day however,

Hines and I were determined to publish a yearbook, because very little had been written about black racers since the early twentieth century. What turned out to be the only issue of the *Black American Racers Yearbook* was published in 1974. Ron and I wrote all the articles, and Malcolm Durham solicited almost all the advertising to underwrite the costs. The yearbook was the first published chronology highlighting our achievements since blacks had begun racing in 1910. It included a short article on the Gold & Glory Sweepstakes that had taken place on the Fourth of July in Roby, Indiana, from 1924 to 1936. After all the work Hines and I had done to publish the yearbooks, some black racing fans still refused to buy it because it was thin compared with other auto magazines. In the collectors' markets, copies of the yearbook now go for at least ten dollars. When it was originally published, the price was one dollar.

Another association highlight in 1974 was the banquet and workshops held at the Holiday Inn in Trenton, New Jersey. The Reverend S. Howard Woodson of the Shiloh Baptist Church gave an inspired, racing-related speech, and approximately 150 racers from around the Northeast attended. Special guests included Bill Singer, the track announcer at the Trenton Speedway; James P. Young of Champion Spark Plug Company; and Ray Heppenstall, designer of the Howmet turbine race car. Racing legend Red Oliver was honored for his contributions and pioneering efforts in black racing. In 1929, Oliver was the first black person to receive a AAA mechanic's license, which allowed him to become a mechanic in the Indianapolis 500. He was also honored for having provided lost historical material on black racers before and after World War II. On his many visits to our home, when he accompanied George Bignotti's team as a crew member to the Trenton Speedway, he spent hours educating Lenny on how blacks survived repression by corporate sponsors and others in the field of motor racing since 1910. Red Oliver passed away in 1997, at the age of 98.

Chapter 7
Sponsored by Viceroy, 1974

To prepare for the 1974 racing season, I told Benny we had to raise our visibility before submitting our proposals to major corporations. Corporations, I added, basically did not want to deal with drivers on a face-to-face business basis, and the racing entity should be incorporated for a number of reasons. We decided to incorporate the race team under Black American Racers, Inc. (BAR) in 1973. This would ensure that our proposals would be reviewed at the large corporations, if nothing else for the sake of curiosity. Mo Campbell, whom I had known for several years, was brought in as a stockholder and vice president to contact major corporations for sponsorship.

In addition to contacting the Ted Bates Advertising Agency about sponsoring a black driver, Mo approached Vel Miletich/ Parnelli Jones team, which included pros such as Al Unser and Mario Andretti. Mo really tried to position BAR for Kool cigarettes sponsorship but he was told that Kool's marketing program was geared toward Diana Ross concerts and other black musical events, and that he should meet with the Viceroy brand manager concerning sponsorship. After pitching the value of the team to Viceroy's marketing division, Art Heller and others at the Bates agency which had agreed to take us on, presented the BAR package in Louisville, Kentucky where the Viceroy division was located in the Brown &

Williamson complex. The marketing program was accepted with the assistance of Lenny Lyles, a key black executive and a former NFL player.

Mo and I attended Madison Avenue meetings during the winter of 1973-74. The biggest issue was always having enough money to race a full season in the Formula Super Vees, later called the Mini-Indy cars. At a meeting in January, the gloves came off. Executives from the Ted Bates Advertising Agency, Brown & Williamson Tobacco Company, and their public relations representatives were splitting hairs over the team's motor budget and other equipment costs. I tried not to fly into a black rage, but I had seen this kind of racism up close and personal before. For the most part it was subtle here, maybe even unconscious. Still, I was angry; at one point Mo had to physically restrain me. After Mo settled me down, I posed a question. "If a race motor costs $24,000 on average for a white-sponsored team," I asked, "how can a black team build the same motor for $12,000?"

Silence. They sat back and thought a while, and then they agreed. After that, everything seemed to run more smoothly. They did however question me about the racial identity of Benny's wife. I said she was white.

A week later, I was summoned back to New York City for an off-the-record meeting, without indicating the meeting's purpose. Mo was there too, and neither of us had asked whether Heller had invited the vice president of the Bates agency to attend the meeting. The VP said that BAR should select another driver for the team. We demanded to know why. He started talking in riddles, posing questions but avoiding answering mine.

I knew exactly what he was implying, what he was not saying, and I knew why. Benny Scott was black, his wife was white, and in that VP's world an interracial couple should not be promoted through an advertising campaign about to be launched for a black racing team. I tried to tell him that her race had nothing to do with our racing or our corporate sponsorship. He continued to dodge my questions concerning anything related to Benny's interracial marriage. Eventually the VP asked me to step into the hall, where I was told the following story:

The Champion Spark Plug Company had wanted to include real car-related ads in *Ebony* magazine and in other black publications. An executive at the J. Walter Thompson Agency, which represented Champion, found a black car enthusiast on Long Island who owned several vintage cars that by Pebble Beach standards were real winners.

The plan was to visit the man's home and take pictures of him and his cars. On the designated day, a film crew showed up to shoot the ad. The car enthusiast and his children met the crew in front of the house. The crew requested that the man's wife also be included in some of the pictures with the cars. The man went into the house, and a short time later the wife came out, well dressed but with a bright blonde bouffant hairdo.

The ad crew started whispering among themselves; they didn't know what to do. The crew leader told them to start shooting, but first to take all the film out of their cameras. They took the shots as planned, then returned to New York City. Although the man was paid, the ad campaign was quietly canceled.

I got the message. After the meeting, Mo and I were forced to find another black driver to replace Benny. When I told Benny what transpired, he simply said he understood I had to play the game or the team's potential sponsorship may be canceled before it ever got off the ground. It was in the best interest of the team. Wendell Scott said there was a black NASCAR Sportsman driver in Tennessee who could be a substitute. His name was Randy Bethea, and he had qualified on the pole (first) in the NASCAR Sportsman race at Nashville in 1973.

Mo found Randy in Daytona, preparing to run in the Permatex Sportsman race during the 1974 Speed Weeks. Randy was mostly known as a stock car driver, was good-looking and in good physical condition, and Campbell thought he would be acceptable to corporate sponsors. We just wanted to know if he could make the car turn right. Many stock car drivers start out learning to turn left on circular tracks and later have a hard time learning to turn right for road courses, and we hoped Randy would be the exception.

Campbell explained our goals to Randy: We wanted to enter a black driver in the Indy 500 and other major races. Randy indicated that if we were serious about hiring him to drive the Viceroy Formula Super Vee, he would move to Pennsylvania immediately. We returned to New York to present his racing credentials and experience to Brown & Williamson. Randy had won the 1970 Tennessee State Hobby Division Championship. He also raced in the NASCAR Sportsman division in 1972 and 1973. Although he did not win any races in those classes, he won numerous heats and pole positions and usually ran in the top ten. After the presentation, we all agreed to have him flown to New York City so he could meet the group personally.

I was unable to meet Randy at Penn Station in midtown Manhattan, but I tried to give him the basics of moving through the big city without incident. I told him not to buy diamonds or watches from the vendors in Penn Station. I told him not to look up at tall buildings, because it would make him an easy mark for street hustlers and con artists. I told him not to talk to anyone.

"Don't worry, I'll be fine," he told me.

When he arrived at Penn Station, someone talked him into buying a fake diamond ring for much more than it was worth. Someone else approached him again outside the station and talked him into buying a watch. When he finally arrived at the meeting, he asked me for a loan because he had spent all his money. When he got to the Bates office, he stood around staring like he had just made his first trip to the big city.

But everyone at the meeting liked Randy. He had a great sense of humor, and his signing enabled us to get our program off the ground. There was so little time before the March press conference, and we had to outfit Randy, build a car, and move him to Pennsylvania.

We hired Ray Heppenstall to build a new English Royale Formula Super Vee for the 1974 Volkswagen Gold Cup Series of twelve races. Heppenstall worked unceasingly, continuously trying to get the car ready in time for the national press conference at the New York Hilton.

When we got there, we had the car photographed in front of the hotel. It had only just rolled into position, when a fire inspector appeared to check whether there was any fuel in it. From our previous experiences at the Chicago Operation PUSH Expo, we already knew not to have fuel in the tank of a race car at a hotel or convention center. The fire inspector then measured the distance from the lobby entrance to the car's position on the sidewalk. He found everything was okay. He then measured the distance from the taxi stand to the car and concluded that the car was too close to the stand area and had to be moved several inches forward. Once that had been done, everything went smoothly.

Everyone affiliated with Black American Racers, Inc. knew this was a historic event. All the major sports reporters from the New York City papers appeared, plus the national black press, two New York City TV stations, members of the Eastern Motor Press Association, and Chris Economaki, publisher, *National Speed Sport News*, who stayed with us for both the press conference and the luncheon. A small number of motorsports writers also appeared from the foreign press.

Abe Procrasa, a very able PR man, put on a flawless production. He announced the purpose of the press conference, then turned it over to Robert A. Pittman, vice president for marketing at Brown & Williamson. Pittman made the most balanced presentation to explain why Brown & Williamson was sponsoring a black racing team and marketing Brown & Williamson's Viceroy cigarettes. Of all the black and motor racing press conferences I've attended over the past thirty years, this one was the best.

The black press was ecstatic. It would be the first time they could interview and showcase a black race car driver as well as an entire black family. The black photographers took a group picture of my mother and father, my wife and our children and me.

The next day we had to determine how we were going to get Randy enough practice time within the next week for him to familiarize himself with upshifting, downshifting, double clutching, heel and toeing, and trail line braking. Ray Heppenstall came to the rescue. He was planning to go to Summit Point, West Virginia, with his other customers, who included Bill Alsup and Walter Wilkins. Under most circumstances, it would have been easy to get to Summit Point. But 1974 was the height of the oil crisis.

To get to a racetrack, real racing enthusiasts can come up with all types of imaginative schemes. Heppenstall had a friend who owned a gas station in West Chester, Pennsylvania. The friend said he would have enough gas for the Heppenstall team to get to West Virginia and for the five race cars as well—if he went along for free. Heppenstall rendezvoused at the gas station after midnight and loaded six fifty-five-gallon drums of gasoline in his van and in Bill Alsup's pickup truck. Then he returned to his shop in Glenside, Pennsylvania, where he met up with the rest of the group. Lenny and I rode to West Virginia in the back of the van. Lenny sat in the back in a lawn chair between four fifty-five gallon drums of fuel.

At the track, Randy had a hard time getting used to the Royale Formula Super Vee. He did a lap in the car and returned to the pits, saying he felt like he was driving around in a coffin. One of the West Virginians standing around interrupted saying, "That's why the Grand National drivers nicknamed you Snowball"—a reference to a black man's skin turning white when he's scared. I let the remark pass. We had a serious problem developing, and I didn't want to get sidetracked dealing with crude racial remarks.

After two days, Randy had made little progress on his lap times. Heppenstall secretly expressed his displeasure to me behind the truck on the last day of practice. By the time we loaded up the race cars and gassed each vehicle, Heppenstall wasn't saying much to Randy. We then headed back to Pennsylvania, in all sorts of vehicles looking like the A Team. In Pennsylvania we siphoned off gas from the barrels to give Bill Alsup enough to make it back to Vermont.

After that practice weekend, both Mo Campbell and I were worried that Randy wasn't going to make it. After Viceroy had rejected Benny Scott for reasons beyond my control, I kept in contact with him every week. By the time of the press conference, I had agreed to help Benny secretly in building a Formula Super Vee for the Robert Bosch Volkswagen Gold Cup Series. Because we didn't have cutting-edge horsepower, Benny decided to develop a new aerodynamically sleek body for his Tui racer. Since he had to do most of the work himself, the car couldn't be ready for the upcoming Lime Rock, Connecticut race.

At Lime Rock Randy and the team met with a string of bad luck. The Viceroy Special Super Vee qualified twenty-first in a field of thirty-nine cars. A first-lap mishap involving six cars put Randy out of the race, with only minor suspension damage. At the Laguna Seca race in Monterey, California, another first-lap multicar crash sidelined the car and caused extensive damage that could not be repaired in time for the race in Ontario, California, the following weekend.

Randy's third race took place at Road Atlanta on 21 April 1974. His practice times were so slow that Bobby Allison, who was appearing in a match race with a NASCAR Grand National car, took Randy around the track a few times to show him how to negotiate the course. Randy rode squeezed between the right side of the roll cage, with Allison flogging the car around the racetrack. Allison's tutelage helped somewhat.

Randy, however, crashed the car in the first lap of practice, because the throttle stuck open, damaging the Formula Super Vee beyond trackside repair. Since we were sponsored, I had to race around the pits to see if someone would rent us a car. In those days the top Formula Super Vee teams carried one car to the track, so I had to concentrate my efforts on renting a backmarker's car and then have Heppenstall work all night with the crew to improve its suspension geometry. A backmarker team agreed to rent their unsponsored car to BAR for $1000 and have their driver sit out the race.

The next day Randy started in the rear of the field, based on promoters' choice. There were forty-two cars to start the race, but the promoters added our car, to make it forty-three. Randy ran a lackluster race all day without crashing the car, moving his position from forty-third to thirty-first place. In fact, he drove the car all day as if he were driving the first lap of a warm-up session. The crew's morale was very low on the return trip to Pennsylvania. The crew member par excellence that weekend was Bob Sprull, who later became a crew chief for Roger Penske in Championship Auto Racing Teams (CART). In addition to his exceptional mechanical skills, Bob had Formula 1 standards and double-checked his work without close supervision.

After the Laguna Seca race, I contacted Benny Scott to see if he could get his car ready for the 30 June race in Mid-Ohio. A week before Mid-Ohio, he called and said he and Schill would tow from California and enter the race, if I had access to spare parts in case they were needed. I said, "Try to make the race at all costs."

The luck with the Viceroy Formula Super Vee changed on 29

and 30 June at the Mid-Ohio race course in Lexington, Ohio. The International Motor Sports Association (IMSA) sanctioned Robert Bosch Volkswagen Gold Cup race drew fifty-two entries, the largest Super Vee field ever. Bethea was thirty-third fastest, ran a good clean race, and finished twenty-fourth overall.

In addition to BAR's entry, Benny Scott and I made an unsponsored entry under the name of Benny Scott Racing. Unhappy with our current situation, I spent more time assisting Benny than working with Randy. In fact, Benny pitted on the grass near our official entry. Although he was faster in practice than Randy, he was driving with lesser equipment. In the race, Benny had moved up to eighteenth place when his car got entangled with two other cars and couldn't continue, resulting in a long, lonely tow back to southern California. After the race, Ray Heppenstall and I again had a long talk about Randy's lackluster performance. I then had to tell Randy privately that he was on the verge of being replaced.

With my family, including Lenny, in tow, we drove to Road Atlanta for the 7 July race. Mo Campbell went ahead to drum up some PR. Because the race was taking place near Atlanta, we knew there would be interest from black fans. Al Anderson, president of Regal Racing and Anderson Communications, was instrumental in getting fifty black fans to the track.

Disaster struck Randy Bethea on 6 July, while he was practicing at Road Atlanta. He ran off course between turns nine and ten, flipped, spun wildly, and came to rest with a totally demolished race car. Hearing the bad news, Rose and I made a beeline to the track's medical facility. When Randy was taken out of the ambulance, Rose, unable to see him in such bad condition, collapsed in my arms. After the doctor and his staff evaluated the extent of Randy's injuries, I immediately had him transferred to the county hospital. The urgency of Randy's condition had to take precedence over my family, which caused Rose some consternation.

Leaving my family in the care of friends at the track, I headed off to the hospital with Mo Campbell. We sat in the waiting room for an hour, until the doctor came out and said Randy had a severely broken foot and two sprained knees. My family and I stayed an extra day to make certain he was being taken care of properly. He was on crutches for several months afterwards, but IMSA's on-track driver insurance coverage was just enough to get us through the ordeal without undue financial stress on him or on the team.

Immediately after returning to Trenton, Mo and I called the Ted Bates Advertising Agency for an emergency meeting. We proposed that Benny Scott be the Viceroy Super Vee Gold Cup driver for the rest of the season. The driver change was sanctioned, and that evening we called Benny and told him the good news. He was elated. I asked Schill to try to be as low-key as possible, though she needn't be invisible or stay away from the track. Coming from a liberal southern California background, she couldn't fathom people in the East objecting to a black man being married to a white woman. She said she'd do the best she could, but countered that she was Benny's wife, and that the conversation offended her.

After the emergency meeting, a press release was immediately sent out announcing that Black American Racers, Inc. was naming Benny Scott of Hollywood, California, as driver of the Viceroy Formula Super Vee for the remainder of the season. Now we had to pull all our resources together overnight and get Benny to the East Coast within a few days. After arriving, Benny was immediately scheduled for a press conference and lunch in midtown Manhattan to announce him as the new driver.

Benny started his first race as the Viceroy Formula Super Vee driver on 14 July at Watkins Glen, with a thrown-together race car. He started from the twenty-fourth qualifying position and charged up to twelfth place on the first two laps. Although his assault was blunted because of a faltering motor, he finished a creditable eleventh overall. In a press interview after the race, Benny said, "With motor, suspension, and brake modifications to my car, I plan to be much more competitive from now on." He added, "Finally, I will have some real backing with the help of Viceroy and Black American Racers. I am very excited and will be working one step at a time to compile the strongest record I can. I want to get to the Indianapolis 500 as soon as possible, and that's just what Len Miller and Mo Campbell want. We are well on our way."

After Watkins Glen, the team traveled to the Charlotte Motor Speedway in North Carolina. Benny was tired; he started fifteenth and finished fifteenth. It was the kind of day that race car drivers like to forget. Rose, Lenny, and Stephanie attended the races at Charlotte with me. Viceroy had come up with sponsorship to pair NASCAR superstar Cale Yarborough and Freddie Phillips, a fellow hard charger in the Formula Super Vee Series, in a companion race, to race as a team with Benny. Cale, being the superstar, took the wheel of the AMC Gremlin first. He drove the wheels off the car. The brakes failed quickly when Cale went up front. Then the motor went sour, sidelining the Gremlin for the day. Benny was highly disappointed that he hadn't gotten a chance to drive.

The next day, Ron Hines and I were late leaving the hotel with my family. As they still do today, the North Carolina State Police patrolled every highway and driveway within five miles of the track, and Ron got a ticket for driving 80-mph. Because we were far above the speed limit and from out of state, Ron had to pay at the police station immediately. Without any hesitation, Ron asked the trooper if he could ride with him to the station, so the rest of us could get to the speedway on time. The trooper had a hard time believing I was a car owner, but he finally consented.

As we came out of the tunnel to the infield a short time later, we saw Ron standing along the pit road, waving at us with a big smile. The troopers at the police station were NASCAR fans and had taken him directly to the track, where Ron had run into Cale Yarborough at the pit pass checkpoint. Cale, at the height of his racing career, wasn't questioned by any workers at the pit gate about anything. He told Ron to jump in the car with him, proceeded through the tunnel, and let him out—without Ron having to show any credentials. Being recognized by the right people can eliminate a lot of unnecessary hassle.

Elkhart Lake, Wisconsin, 20-21 August, 1974. The Elkhart Lake race weekend was a watershed for BAR. The team became self-contained and increased its suspension geometry knowledge, and Ron Hines, Mo Campbell, Benny Scott, and I jelled as a unit. But Ray Heppenstall, who maintained BAR's race car, entered his own car with Al Holbert, Jr. against ours. This is always a kiss of death in racing—when a rent-a-racer shop enters its own car against its best-paying customers and then pays more attention to the shop car than to the others. When I confronted him, Heppenstall said he wanted a winner in his shop that would bring in new business, because none of his customers had won any races thus far that season. I disagreed with his approach. Within the next ten minutes, we parted ways in a friendly manner, without throwing wrenches in the air, kicking oil cans, or cursing each other in public. In the back of my mind as I walked away, though, I did wish we could have taken his best mechanic, Bob Sprull, with us.

I hated putting Benny under undue stress. It's enough for a driver to learn the lines of a long road course, without being burdened with pit road problems. But the separation from Heppenstall was done, and it was up to me to solve the problem.

After a ten-minute standup meeting in the middle of the field behind the pits, we decided to make a motor change and to enlist the services of the Bear Brake & Alignment trackside demonstration equipment to get our toe-in, toe-out, and alignment baseline. The Bear people agreed. As always, if you're a sponsored race car you can get more professional support under adverse circumstances than if you're a lone, private unsponsored racing team. I then approached Carl Haas, a legendary race car owner and parts importer for Lola in Great Britain, hoping to work a deal for spare parts, because we had none.

While Ron, Benny, and I were scrounging around, the news spread like wildfire around the track that BAR had separated from Ray Heppenstall. The gossip crossed over the track to members of the Black Volkswagen Club from Milwaukee. The president of the club cornered me and demanded to know whether we were going to race, because he had more than sixty members who had come just to see Benny. After I had reassured him and crossed the track to speak to the group, everyone settled down.

Returning to the pits, I noticed Benny surrounded by a camera crew and reporter. Because of all the prerace publicity *Players*, the black equivalent of *Playboy* magazine, had sent a crew out to interview Benny and the team for a feature article. When a team is thrashing around, trying to prepare a race car for qualifying, a camera crew sticking mikes in your face is somewhat overwhelming. But we all got through the situation without harsh words. It was worth being accommodating to the *Players* crew because the feature article had been excellent publicity for Viceroy, Benny, and the team.

Benny qualified the Viceroy Black American Racers Tui in the middle of the large field. Ron Hines and I then took time out to sample some of the tantalizing food for sale at the track, prepared by a volunteer church, the Rotary Club, and other groups. We always looked forward to the friendliness and the wonderful spread at Elkhart Lake, especially the corn on the cob. Before the race began John Zeitler, one of Ray Heppenstall's competitors, offered his help and queried Benny about how the car was handling. Benny explained that he needed to compensate for two corners on the track. Zeitler, then, made a chassis change that made a positive difference.

Our race strategy was for Benny to drive aggressively but calculatingly. We had no spares, and without discussing it with Benny, I had decided to buy a new Lola T-324 from Carl Haas. Benny wanted to charge, but he had to make sure to make no mistakes. He drove the Black American Racers Viceroy Formula Super Vee up one place at a time until the checkered flag dropped, finishing tenth and earning the team its first Volkswagen Gold Cup Championship point of the season. Mo Campbell remarked that we actually had done better under stress than we had ever expected.

Lime Rock, Connecticut, Labor Day Weekend 1974. As in the preceding two years, the entire family looked forward to going to Lime Rock, Connecticut. Lime Rock was like Mid-Ohio and Elkhart Lake: set in serene surroundings and attended by the nicest Americans you ever wanted to meet. The fans rarely used profanity, you never heard racial slurs, and everyone, even children, used the trash barrels for depositing their refuse.

Anne Stumpo, my administrative assistant, my youngest brother Bruce, and his wife Evelyn accompanied us to the track. My family stayed at the Black Berry River Inn, where a number of the Formula Super Vee owners and teams stayed every year. The setting at the Black Berry River Inn was more like being on the Formula 1 scene. The food was gourmet quality, and the tenor of the racing conversations was at an extremely high level.

Back-to-back racing for weeks at a time allowed for little mid-week preparation. Beginning the twenty-first century as a spon-sored team, would have allowed BAR to have a backup car to enter the race at Lime Rock. In the 1970s, it was rare for a Formula Super Vee team to have a backup car sitting in their trailer. As a result, each team had to prepare its car as best it could under severe time con-straints, in addition to traveling from Wisconsin to Connecticut.

The 1974 Labor Day weekend at Lime Rock was upbeat, the weather was superb, and there was a large crowd. All through the weekend, Rose and Anne Stumpo kept asking if Paul Newman, another racing enthusiast, was at the track, because they wanted to get a glimpse of the most popular movie star. He was, but, since they did-n't have pit passes, they didn't see him.

As at Charlotte, Benny started fifteenth on the grid. At the drop of the flag, Benny established himself as a force to be reckoned with, charging up through the field. Like several other drivers in the series, including Bob Lazier, Bill Alsup, and Howdy Holmes, Benny would always charge downhill on road courses without letting off the accelerator pedal. Mark Donohue and Mario Andretti were among the best at this. Benny used this part of the track, coming down the hill under the bridge, to gain on the slower drivers coming on to the front straightaway. Benny exhibited some of the most aggressive driving of the five-race weekends in the car that year, put-ting the Black American Racers Formula Super Vee in eighth place at the finish, earning three more championship points, and estab-lishing himself solidly as one of the top ten drivers among more than sixty racers.

Watkins Glen, New York, October 1974. Between Lime Rock and the Watkins Glen race, the new Lola T-324 ordered from Carl Haas at Elkhart Lake was delivered as promised and made race ready by John Zeitler. We wanted to be well prepared, because it was the most important race of the season. This was the year the Formula 1 World Drivers Championship was decided at the Glen, with over 100,000 race fans in attendance. To increase our odds of making the starting grid, we brought our other car along for backup. This was the first time in our racing careers that we had the luxury of a backup car.

Benny flew in early from California to shake down the new car. He was impressed, because it was fast out of the box and felt solid and the power was up. After the first official practice session, only the brakes needed adjusting. Benny felt confident the new car was a contender. But as he was increasing his speeds during the qualifying sessions, the motor blew. Despite this, he placed in the twelfth starting position. Zeitler and crew had to work most of the night installing a new motor and checking over the entire car for the race the next day.

It turned out to be a beautiful fall day with warm sunshine. The Formula Super Vee race was set to start at 2 p.m., but tensions had begun to rise at dawn. As Benny's car was pushed to the grid, everything looked good. The car was fully prepared, and Benny was relaxed. When the green flag fell, Benny held his twelfth-place position down the main straightaway and into the first turn. The next time he came around in front of the pits, he was in eleventh place. In the following lap the forerunners came around—but Benny and several other cars were missing. Interviewed later by the press, Benny said, "I had just settled into the pace and was making my move up through the pack. We were all pretty close, about a foot or two apart, and entered the loop as a group at 100-mph. Right in the middle of the turn, one of the guys in front spun his car. I had nowhere to go and T-boned him. We were through for the day. We've had a tough weekend."

Chapter 8
BAR's Greatest Moments, 1975

T he 1975 racing season started out on a high note, with Black
American Racers Association, Inc., sponsoring an elaborate
banquet in honor of Wendell Scott on 25 January at the
Hospitality House Motor Inn in Arlington, Virginia. Because all the
black racers in the Washington area and beyond idolized Wendell,
the 300 tickets available for the affair sold out quickly. Wendell was
the main speaker, because the association wanted the attendees to
hear about his experiences. His episode of having the "colored"
ambulance reassigned to take white drivers to the hospital at the
Atlanta Speedway one year and struggling-to-get-to-the-track stories brought tears to the eyes of many. A local group, Armageddon
Soul Band, provided upbeat music throughout the evening.

As the association's secretary and chairman respectively, Ron
Hines and I worked to obtain honorariums and gifts for Wendell. As
usual, this proved to be an almost impossible task on behalf of a
black driver. After numerous letters and phone calls however, we
succeeded receiving contributions from only three corporations,
though all three gave willingly. Bill Dredge and the STP Corporation gave an honorarium. Viceroy gave an honorarium that Leo G.
Bell, manager of minority affairs presented to Wendell. Bill Broderick of Union 76 provided the nicest gift, a twenty-piece Wilton
Armetale special edition dinnerware set. Later Broderick would be
nicknamed "the hat man" in NASCAR circles, because he was

expert at changing sponsor hats on the winning Winston Cup driver's head in the winner's circle after every major race.

NASCAR sent a high-level official to the banquet. Tom Binford, board member of the United States Auto Club and chief steward of the Indianapolis 500, gave a personal donation to the affair and to everyone's surprise and delight attended. Binford, one of racing's most influential leaders in the 1970s, unreservedly wanted black drivers and black teams to participate in the sport. Many of us blacks who have been involved in racing since the 1950s were saddened when he passed away. Racing today needs another Tom Binford, someone who looks at all those participating in racing as racers first and not as an ethnic entity.

The biggest disappointment of the affair was the snub from the Ford Motor Company. I tried in every way possible to get Ford to participate. Wendell drove Fords throughout his career, and this would have been the ideal time for the company to recognize him for his achievements and his loyalty. Several BAR members had been intending to buy Fords who before the banquet bought Chevys instead. A group of us estimated Ford lost at least three million dollars in sales by failing to give a measly $500 honorarium to one of its greatest drivers. Years later, a Ford rep told Bobby Norfleet, a black NASCAR participant, that Ford didn't need to advertise its products on a black Craftsman Truck team, because their factories were operating at full capacity in 1999, thus blacks would add nothing to Ford's bottom line.

In all types of racing, being properly sponsored allows a team to get a big jump on unsponsored cars. Sponsorship allows the team to tow anywhere in the United States without having to worry about having enough gas or having to sleep under the truck, as A.J. Foyt did when he towed unsponsored from Texas to enter a race at Pennsylvania's Reading Fairgrounds.

Our team made the long tow to Sebring, Florida, to open the season on 22 March 1975. In those days, the race at Sebring was run on a rough concrete airstrip. Benny qualified sixth and jumped into the lead at the start, but a punctured tire forced him out of the race on the fourth lap. It was a long tow back home. Most of it we spent keeping each other's morale up by talking about how super competitive the car had been.

On 29 March, BAR made its first trip to the Daytona International Speedway. Daytona was a tough closed course to negotiate for all Formula Super Vee drivers because of wind gusts that appeared there without warning. Just before the Formula Super Vees entered the road course portion of the track, several drivers went airborne and wrecked their cars. At one point I thought a gust of wind was going to lift Benny over the wall, but he managed to set the car down safely on the track and he finished tenth.

It was at that race that Benny and I first met NASCAR's Bill France, Sr. and Bill France, Jr. John Cooper, whom I'd known since the early 1970s, brought them over to meet us and look at our team. Bill Jr., did all the talking and specifically asked how we had gotten Viceroy as a sponsor. He also asked why we raced open-wheel cars instead of stock cars. I don't remember what our answer was at the time, but as the years have gone by, I've come to believe that we should have expressed an interest in stock cars to him. They both wished us good luck and proceeded down pit road to greet other teams. We returned home still in the top ten in points.

From 18-20 April the team journeyed to Road Atlanta in Braselton, Georgia. It was very important that BAR maintain its momentum there. The team entered the new Lola T-324 Super Vee that Carl Haas sold us. It proved competitive right out of the box. The Ted Bates Advertising Agency again hired Anderson Communications, a black public relations firm in Atlanta, to develop the off-track events.

It is extremely difficult for any sponsored race team to fit in large public appearances in conjunction with practice and qualifying sessions. Since this is where corporations get a return on their sponsorship dollars, it's necessary to stretch the crew's, driver's, and owner's physical and mental capabilities to their limits. This is what occurred on this jam-packed weekend.

Late Friday afternoon, 18 April, Ron Hines, Benny, and I met with Mayor Maynard Jackson in his office for a photo session for the mayor's proclamation designating Sunday, 20 April as Black American Racers Day in Atlanta. We were to take a picture in front of our Viceroy truck, with the mayor reading the proclamation. While

Benny was talking about racing in general, an aide rushed into the room and said that Hosea Williams, the civil rights leader, was picketing the Viceroy truck. Al Anderson quickly changed the itinerary and had the TV camera crew take a picture of Ron, Benny, and me standing beside the mayor in his office. Benny then gave the mayor a Viceroy helmet for his desk. (When I spoke to Mayor Jackson in 1997, he told me he still displays the Viceroy helmet in his study.)

After the photo op, I rushed outside to confront Hosea Williams. He had fifteen or twenty demonstrators marching around the truck, protesting some of the mayor's policies that according to him, were adversely affecting black people. The demonstrators were hard-core believers, militants, idealists, and renegades. I asked Williams why he was demonstrating against a black racing team, of all things. He said, "Brother, I can get my views on TV news by using you." With TV and radio crews surrounding us, I said nothing. But I had the truck removed immediately.

That night on the news there was a short blurb on the Black American Racers Day ceremony, and a bigger one of Hosea Williams and his demonstrators marching around our truck, the Viceroy logo in plain view. When some of the backmarker and unsponsored race teams saw us on TV, the next day at practice they demonstrated their envy with derisive remarks masked as humor.

Saturday, 19 April was a full day, from 5:30 a.m. to midnight. The first order of business was to get ready for both practices, then to qualify the car in the afternoon. After qualifying, the car immediately had to be cleaned up and transported to downtown Atlanta for display at the Viceroy buffet dinner and dance. During this period it was rare for any team to have a show car specifically for off-track events. When there were time constraints, the team manager always had to hope the car would not be demolished on the track before a scheduled event.

In any type of racing, most teams attempt to enter the first race of the season to test itself against the competition. Some enter because, prepared or not they're obsessed with racing, while others, like hand-to-mouth racers, enter because they've saved enough money over the winter to get to the first race of the season. This time, fifty-two racers were present to qualify for a forty-car field. Only about fifteen of these cars had full sponsorship. Benny qualified sixth on the grid. Because we had to get the car to the big Viceroy event downtown, the team left before the rest of the qualifying was completed.

That night's festivities, organized by Anderson Communications, were among the most memorable off-track events we had ever attended as a team. The only comparable event that year was Bobby and Al Unser's mother's chili party on the *Queen Mary* at the inaugural Long Beach Grand Prix. Three hundred-fifty people showed up for the Viceroy festivities. All the major black politicians, community leaders, and car club members were in attendance. Friends flew in for the event, including Leon and Mary Bass, Dick and Gloria Brown, and Oscar Porter, one of the wealthiest blacks in the Bahamas. Leon Bass became famous in the American Jewish community in the 1980s for his total dedication to speaking out against the Holocaust. He was a black World War II U.S. Army veteran, who had been relegated to cleaning up Jewish corpses in Nazi concentration camps at the end of the war.

At most major inaugural racing dinners, when there is no racial diversity, the menu is not an issue. With heavy black participation at this one, veggie and cheese trays had to be minimized because blacks prefer hot hors d'oeuvres at receptions. The hotel chef was informed that the roast beef had to be medium, not rare, and the string beans had to be seasoned and not half raw. If these considerations had not been met, the festivities would have failed on the food choices alone. The Viceroy Formula Super Vee was placed in the corner of the ballroom, with spotlights beaming down on it. Rose and Mo Campbell greeted everyone at the door. The band's upbeat rock-n-roll, soul and country music kept the dance floor filled to the max all night. One Goodyear executive commented that it was the best racing party he had attended in years.

The highlight of the evening came when Mayor Jackson presided over the drawing for the Viceroy high-dollar helmet. A pretty young black woman came forward to claim the helmet and a kiss from Benny. At the moment Benny went to kiss her a young black man yelled out, "Don't you dare kiss my girlfriend!" Startled, Benny and the girl changed their posture and shook hands instead. I remarked to Oscar Porter: "America is really messed up. A black man won't let a relatively famous black driver kiss his girlfriend for fear she may run off with him, and a white beauty queen is maybe afraid to kiss a winning black driver because she might be labeled a "nigger lover!" I was referring to an incident in 1972 when Benny Scott won a SCCA race. The rest of the night went off without incident.

The Friday night affair drew about eighty blacks to the track the next day, because the black community had seen both the car and the driver on TV at the banquet with Benny receiving a proclamation from the city of Atlanta. Reverend Andrew Young even tried to figure out how he could cancel his church service to attend the race.

Benny put on a show for the fans. The Lola came from the sixth starting spot into second place going into the first corner. Benny battled among the top four cars throughout the race. Slipping to fourth, seven car lengths behind the leader, he made a brilliant move that I had seen Bobby Allison do with a stock car, i.e., slingshotting past Richard Melville on the next-to-last turn and tucking into the approaching sharp right turn in front of the hard-driving Jamaican. As he was closing in on the leader, time ran out, and he finished third.

When Benny took his place in the winner's circle with the first- and second-place finishers, the fans broke out into a loud cheer. Those who had shown up for the first time were particularly ecstatic when Benny's official interview brought out another resounding cheer. "It was one of the hardest races I've ever driven, and I'm pleased to bring the Viceroy Black American Racers Lola in third," he said.

The most blatant incidence of racial prejudice Benny or I have ever encountered at a track on a race weekend, then or since, was at Laguna Seca in Monterey, California, on 4 May 1975. We never expected that it would happen in northern California, of all places.

The weekend began out with John Zeitler towing the car from Connecticut to Monterey. Benny and Schill drove up from Los Angeles in their van. I flew to San Francisco to meet Ernest Howard—one of my best friends and president of Social Dynamics, Inc., one of the two top black consulting firms in the U.S., co-founded by Ron Dellums—who later became a congressman—and his wife Freddie.

The Howards and I drove down from San Francisco in their

almost new Jensen, an exotic British sports sedan. On the outskirts of Monterey, down by the sea, a number of Viceroy banners were being swept into the surf by the wind. It was an odd scene. Camel Cigarettes was sponsoring the race. I later found out that our Viceroy Cinderella team's publicity had completely overshadowed all the Camel prerace activities, and that the local Viceroy cigarettes marketing representative was an eager beaver and had put up 200 banners. He later told me that his Camel counterpart had paid a college student $100 to cut them all down.

When we signed in for my pit passes and two VIP passes for the Howards, I noticed the track manager, Mr. Hugill, looking at me. I made a mental note of it and proceeded out the door. When we arrived at the pit gate, the official wouldn't let us in, and proceeded to give us directions to the grandstands.

"I own the Viceroy car," I said.

By now, several other officials had gathered around. They all laughed.

"There's no way a colored person could be the owner of the Viceroy car," said the official who was doing all the talking.

I jumped out of the Jensen and showed him all my credentials. He just looked at them and said, "You could have stolen them." Then the track PR director happened by and told him to let us in. Here I am with one of the wealthiest black men in the United States accompanied by his wife, trying to get to our team's race car and being abused worse than I would be in the state of Mississippi. It ruined the rest of the day for all three of us. If I had had a run-in with another racist that same day, I'd have gone to jail—after putting that racist in the morgue.

The next day, Benny qualified the car on the pole (first). The press was elated because they had a chance to write a unique story line for a change. But this wasn't to be. The track management held a secret meeting with the Camel representative present to determine how to stop Viceroy from overshadowing Camel, the track sponsor. They decided to change the venue for the pole sitter press conference, and then invited several of the other drivers to appear at another hotel to talk about their experiences in Formula Super Vee racing. The drivers had no idea the pole sitter interview had been canceled.

Benny and I arrived at the hotel, where the press conference was to have been held, only to find the pressroom empty. Only by inquiring at the press registration desk, did we discover that the pole sitter press conference had been canceled and another was being held instead a few blocks away.

About fifty reporters attended the substitute press conference looking to interview Benny Scott. Not seeing him up front, most of them left. Leon Mandel, one of the leading motorsports magazine editors in the country, Fat Sam the black San Francisco disc jockey and talk show host; and a small group of others caught up with Benny and me in the parking lot of the first hotel.

They had reached the same conclusion I had—that the track management had two fears: Viceroy overshadowing Camel and Benny's being black. Fat Sam wanted to head back to the inner city and round up a few hundred demonstrators; Mandel discussed the possibility of developing an article about the situation. I didn't want to do anything prematurely, because we knew Benny was capable of winning the race. I did say I'd call Robert Pittman, Viceroy's vice president of marketing, and fill him in.

By this time, especially with the added stress, Benny was bushed. We headed back to the Blue Lantern Hotel, where we each had a box full of messages from reporters. I went to my room and called Pittman to bring him up to date. He agreed to come out to Laguna Seca in Brown & Williamson's corporate jet.

Benny and I had both decided to turn off the phones in our rooms. That didn't work, because the reporters tracked us down at the hotel. I told Benny to refer all questions to the team manager, then went across town and got another room in another hotel under an assumed name, so I could think.

Watching the evening sports news, I noticed that Benny's pole (first) position was being downplayed, and nonnewsworthy track information was being highlighted. Now I was totally upset. After figuring out what to do, I created a secret message system. I would relay messages through the Howards' room. They would deliver them to Benny, who in turn would relay necessary information to John Zeitler. We decided to pull the car out of the track compound and secretly prepare it over at the Tomato Factory shopping center after 9 p.m., in the parking lot under the lights. The reporters wouldn't be looking for us there, and very few fans hung out there.

We had one big advantage over all the other teams in the race: the first gear in the Hewland transmission. Over the winter Zeitler had found out that there was a Formula Ford first gear that would allow Benny to go through turn nine a tick quicker than his competitors. There were only five of these gears, available only in Europe. Since BAR had entered Coyle Peek just a few years earlier in Formula Ford races in England, I tried locating the gear. Because it was useful only at Laguna Seca, American Formula Super Vee teams didn't bother spending time looking for this rare piece of equipment. After several months of looking for it in England, the Formula Ford racing group we had done business with several years before found the gear we wanted and shipped it to us. Having the gear made us confident, especially sitting on the pole.

The crew went over every nut-and-bolt in the car and checked the clutch, special fittings, and suspension, while Schill looked on. As every racer knows, a sponsored car draws a lot of attention; even nonracing fans become curious because of the sponsor's name on the car. Before too long, two beautiful women came over to look at the race car and told us they were Las Vegas showgirls. One had a see-through net top with her nipples showing. When the crew saw these women hanging around, their ratchet-wrenches began singing in the night and all fatigue left them. When Schill spotted them, she marched over and pointed out that the driver was her husband. Eventually they left. We later found out that one of them was on the lam from her Mafia don boyfriend and had nowhere to stay that night. But the ladies had given us the extra lift we needed and by midnight, having checked and double-checked every inch of the car, the crew turned in. I went back to my secluded hotel room.

I couldn't sleep though. At 5 a.m. I called Benny to see if his mother and sister had arrived at the Blue Lantern Hotel. "Yes, they arrived Saturday evening," he said.

"Anything could happen today," I said. "We may have to put our lives on the line." Benny said he was ready, but he wanted his mother and sister to stay at the hotel. "You have to come over here and tell her," he said.

I went over and told Mrs. Scott in general terms about the problems we were having at Laguna Seca, and that Benny and I thought she should listen to the race on the radio instead of going out to the track. Mrs. Scott said his daddy had to go through the same thing as a race car driver in the 1930s, and that she was aware of what Benny had to do. Then she said she would hold me responsible if he came home to her in a box.

Around 7 a.m. Benny, Schill, and I set out for the track. John Zeitler had the car ready. Everything went well during practice. At the end of practice, a member of the track staff whispered to me that the track manager had instructed the track announcer to refrain from mentioning Viceroy or Black American Racers, and not to highlight anything concerning Benny Scott. According to this informant, the track announcer protested but said he would comply. I didn't mention this to Benny, because I didn't want to upset him and distract him from driving.

As the cars lined up on the grid, Benny was surrounded by at least fifty reporters and media commentators, including Fat Sam. Out of the side of my eye, I could see the track manager seething. The black Viceroy driver had pushed any mention of Camel out of everyone's mind.

The Brown & Williamson local marketing representative and two ranking vice presidents were enjoying every minute of the coverage. Then the track manager turned the harassment up another notch. To everyone's amazement, he ordered the pace car off the track. He allegedly said to one of his staff members, "Let's see how these black boys can handle the start on their own." At this point, my sublimated black rage surfaced. I quickly told the Brown & Williamson executives, Jim Young of the Champion Spark Plug Company, our associate sponsors, Ernie and Freddie Howard, and John Zeitler that I was throwing down the gauntlet. By this time, the reporters knew something was amiss and started crowding around again to find out why the pace car had been moved off the track. "Ask the track manager," I said. If BAR's sponsors had not been staunchly supportive, I would have expressed some very hostile feelings that would have caused a lot of controversy in the press the next day.

The beginning. My 1940 Ford, semi-custom Club Coupe convertible with a
1948 Mercury ¾ race motor. Photo taken in 1954.

Morning instructions (I'm on the left), U.S. Third Army, Direct Automotive Field Support Company, Fort Bragg, Fayetteville, NC, 1957.

My 1965 Volvo P-1800 with a drag strip motor.

I'm flanked by Grant King and my wife Rose, at the Pocono International Speedway, Pocono, PA in 1972.

Top 10 awards winner at Atco Dragway, Atco, NJ, in 1970, (9th place) Trophy Class out of 365 race cars (from left), assistant track manager, me, Kenny Wright-Miller Brothers driver. *Source: Unknown*

Kenny Wright in 1970, "Driver-of-the-Week," *East Coast Drag News*
Source: Images Unlimited

John Mahler, Vanguard Racing's 1972 Indianapolis 500 driver. Race car: McLaren, Offenhauser 4 cylinder turbo-charged motor prepared by Louie Unser, brother of the famous Indy drivers Bobby and Al Unser. *Source: John Mahler*

John Mahler contemplating his driving strategy while sitting on pit wall at the 1971 Indianapolis 500.
Source: Unknown

Ready for the crowd at Rev. Jesse Jackson's Operation/PUSH
Expo, Chicago, 1972 (from left), me, George Wiltshire-NASCAR
driver, Benny Scott-Black American Racers Formula 5000 driver
(seated in Valvoline Indy car) and Coyle Peek Black American
Racers entrant in the Professional Formula Ford Series in the
United Kingdom. *Source: Unknown*

Dexter Miller, original crew chief, Miller Brothers 1969 B/S Camaro at
Englishtown Raceway Park, Englishtown, NJ in 1971. "Mousy" a crew member standing in background.

Alex Baynard winning a round in the Miller Brothers, Volpe & Baynard B/S, 1969, 427 cubic inch Chevrolet Camaro at Atco Dragway, Atco, NJ in 1971. *Source: Bruce Miller*

Miller Brothers (Miller Racing, Inc.), Volpe & Baynard, 1969 S/S, 427 cubic inch Chevrolet Camaro at Englishtown Raceway Park, Englishtown, NJ in 1971. Alex Baynard (left) talking to crew under the hood.

With driver Benny Scott in Champion Spark
Plug's "Fast Track to Indianapolis" commercial
advertisement at Laguna Seca Raceway,
Monterey, CA, spring 1972. *Source: Champion
Spark Plug Company*

My two children, Stephanie R. Miller (left) and
Leonard T. Miller (right) sitting on pit wall at
Watkins Glen in 1972. Benny Scott's SCCA Vanguard
Racing McLaren M10-A, Formula A in background.

Talking last minute strategy prior to a Watkins Glen SCCA Formula A race in 1972. Benny's wife, Schill Scott (foreground), my son Lenny, standing behind pit wall looking at me and Benny Scott. *Source: Rose H. Miller*

Reading *Stock Car Racing* magazine on a family Christmas vacation at the Caracas Hilton, Caracas, Venezuela in 1972. *Source: Rose H. Miller*

In England, Coyle Peek contemplating his driving strategy prior to the September 1973 Mallory Park, Professional Formula Ford Series race. The race car is a Royale RP16 powered by a Ford Scloler 1600cc motor. Our Black American Racers truck in background. *Source: Peter Semus*

Randy Bethea (driver) sits on a Formula Super Vee at the New York Hilton hotel press conference in 1974. Pictured (from left): Ron Hines, mechanic, Alfred "Mo" Campbell, vice president and me, president. *Source: Associated Press*

The Black American Racers Association organizational meeting at Malcolm Durham's Supercar Engineering race shop in Hyattsville, MD, summer 1973. Pictured (from left): Malcolm Durham, legendary drag racer, me, Wendell Scott, NASCAR's most famous black driver, Ron Hines, automotive engineer.

Top: Viceroy Lola T-324 Formula Super Vee in action with Benny Scott at the wheel.

Bottom: Atlanta Mayor Maynard Jackson signs proclamation for Black American Racers Day. Pictured (from left): mechanic Ron Hines, driver Benny Scott and myself as president look on. *Source: Anderson Communications*

Top: Benny Scott's excellent 1975 season in the Black American Racers/ Viceroy Lola T-324 Formula Super Vee earned BAR a chance to crack international auto racing's big league Formula 5000 Series.

Bottom: Benny Scott behind the wheel of the new Black American Racers/Viceroy Lola T- 332 Formula 5000 car. Scott and the BAR team (from left): vice president, Mo Campbell, myself as president, and chief mechanic, Grant King on the verge of competing against auto racing's greatest teams and drivers including Indianapolis 500 winners Mario Andretti, Al Unser and Gordon Johncock. *Source: Brown & Williamson Tobacco Company*

Benny Scott at speed in the Viceroy/Black American Racers Lola T-332 in the inaugural Long Beach Grand Prix—1975. *Source: Roar in the City—John E. McCollister*

Benny Scott driving the Black American Racers/Viceroy Lola T-332 in the inaugural Long Beach Grand Prix. Benny finished 11th out of 52 entries in his first Formula 5000 race of 1975. *Source: Brown & Williamson Tobacco Company*

Pictured (from left): Arthur Fletcher, a friend, representing the Richard F. Nixon White House as speaker at the Black Athletes Hall of Fame in 1976 with me and Benny Scott. *Source: Douglas Hayes*

1976 Black Athletes Hall of Fame inductees, New York Hilton hotel, (from left):Benny Scott, Don King, John Henry Johnson, formally a Pittsburgh Steeler and me. Notice the fancy tuxedoes. *Source: Douglas Hayes*

I'm being inducted into the Black Athletes Hall of Fame by actor Bill Cosby and founder Charles Mays. *Source: Black Athletes Hall of Fame*

My usual two minutes with ABC television's Howard Cosell at the Black Athletes Hall of Fame private reception with Benny Scott looking on. New York Hilton – 1976.
Source: Douglas Hayes

My wife and I sitting with D. Parke Gibson (left) at the1975 Black Athletes Hall of Fame dinner in Las Vegas. He was the first person to calculate the immense buying power of the black community in America. *Source: Brown & Williamson Tobacco Company*

Tommy Thompson receiving the 1977 SCCA Northeastern first place trophy for the Formula Super Vee class. (from left): Kenny Wright, crewman, Tommy, trophy queen and me, team manager. *Source: Unknown*

Tommy Thompson with Mario Andretti, Trenton Speedway, Trenton, NJ—1977. *Source: David Innes*

The Milwaukee Mile, Milwaukee, WI, 1978. Tommy Thompson noticing something amiss up the track while I make a last minute adjustment as the track official looks on. *Source: Bob Merritt*

Tommy Thompson at The Milwaukee Mile, Milwaukee, WI two weeks before his fatal tragedy in 1978. (from left): Tommy, me, Ron Hines, crew chief. *Source: Bob Merrill*

Albie Robinson in action at the Flemington Speedway, Flemington, NJ in1979. Car maintained by Les and Gloria Katona, Lawrence Engineering, Trenton, NJ. *Source: Ace Lane, Jr.*

Another exciting feature win at the Flemington Speedway, Flemington, NJ in 1981. *Source: Unknown*

Bruce Driver and Darryl Carmen sharing checkered flag at the Flemington Speedway, Flemington, NJ in 1980. Darryl Carmen was the rookie champion and Bruce was the winner of the race that weekend. Foreground (from left): Al Tasnady, track official, Darryl Carmen, Bruce Driver, Bruce's girl friend and me. Background (from left): Carmen's crew, Paul Kuhl, track owner and Ron Hines, Black American Racers mechanic. *Source: Ace Lane, Jr.*

Bruce Driver feature winner, Sportsman class, Flemington Speedway, Flemington, NJ in 1981. Pictured (from left): Bruce's girlfriend, Flemington starter, Mark Blackwell, co-owner and crew chief, Bruce Driver, Ron Hines, Al Tasnady, track official and me. *Source: Ace Lane, Jr.*

Explaining the inner workings of the motor racing business at a private reception in Washington Crossing, PA in 1989. Foreground (from left): Dr. Walter P. Lomax, Jr. and me. Background: Mr. and Mrs. Frank Hague (center) and Wilhelmina White (far right). *Source: Leonard T. Miller*

Bruce Driver and me after being awarded "Rookie-of-the-Year" in 1989 at Shangri-La Speedway in Owego, NY. *Source: David Henderson*

Bruce Driver revving motor for private reception guests, (from right of race car): Bruce Miller, my brother, Lenny, my son, me, Herb Jones, co-owner and Gail Huggins. Background: Vernon Hammond, Claude Houston (partially obscured) *Source: Rose H. Miller*

Chris Woods getting his start as a crew member with Bobby Fuller and family. NASCAR Modified driver Rick Fuller (on far left) in his early years, Bobby Fuller holding checkered flag and Chris Woods (on far right). Year unknown. *Source: Unknown*

Chris Woods and the "Brady Bunch" celebrating one of his multiple Street Stock wins at Riverside Park, Agawam, MA in 1991, prior to moving south to Concord, NC. Chris's mother (kneeling bottom left with trophy) Chris's father (standing back row, far left) wearing white cap. Kevin Manion, nicknamed "Bono" (standing to Chris's right) was crew chief for Dale Earnhardt, Jr.'s NASCAR Busch Series car in 2003. *Source: Unknown*

Joe Gerber and me at the 1993 Rainbow/PUSH Conference in Chicago. The affair was hosted by Charles Farrell. *Source: Leonard T. Miller*

I'm strapping in at the Skip Barber Racing School, Lime Rock, CT—1980. *Source: Unknown*

Tuskegee Airman, Alfred "Chief" Anderson in a biplane at Buhl Field, Langhorne, PA. He encouraged my motor racing interest in my hot rod days. Photo taken October 1973. *Source: Leslie Hayling, D.D.S.*

Dr Pepper Coastal Plains Speedway win, July 7, 2001, in Jacksonville, NC—
First corporate win for Dr Pepper Company—Pictured (from left): Chris
Courtney, Tanna Townsend, Jefferson Hodges, Morty Buckles (Miller Racing
Group, driver), Al Anderson, Morty's brother, Shane Buckles, Morty's wife,
Maria Buckles. *Source: Leonard T. Miller*

Miller Racing Group/Dr Pepper partnership. Unveiling the race car in New York City at the 2001 Rainbow/PUSH Conference (First genuine sponsorship since Brown & Williamson Tobacco Company in the 1970s). Pictured (from left): Jack Kilduff, president, Dr Pepper, Leonard T. Miller, co-owner, me, co-owner and Miller Racing Group driver, Morty Buckles. *Source: Photo by Beverly Swanagan, Swanay Production*

I now had to do everything: push the car into place, strap Benny in—which I very rarely did in the eight years we raced together—and adjust the carburetors. At this point, I remembered Kipling's poem "If," which had been drummed into me when pledging Alpha Phi Alpha as an undergrad. My mother's long ago comment flashed into my mind about black men having to endure twice the stress of white men in anything they try to accomplish. I also thought of Jackie Robinson, my number one sports idol.

While I was pondering these thoughts, Benny looked up and said, "What do we do, Len?"

"Bring the field around at a snail's pace and let their carburetors load up, since you're in total control of the field," I said. "Clean out your carbs first coming out of turn nine and accelerate hard as you approach turn one."

"Why is the pace car being removed from the track?" asked Benny.

"Don't worry about it; take control of the pace lap," I said. It was not the time or place to tell him.

When you race with the same drivers and teams for over four years, their moves and strategies become fairly predictable. Bill Neuhoff, on the outside of the front row, was the only question mark, because we knew very little about him. We knew the drivers in the next three rows would hold their lines and not create hair-raising problems on the start. All of these drivers—Howdy Holmes, Eddie Miller, Herman Johnson, and Bob Lazier—went on to Indy cars. The other driver in the group was Richard Melville from Jamaica who was the other black competing in the series on a regular basis.

As the twenty-nine Formula Super Vees came around to the start/finish line, Benny's carburetors loaded up with fuel. This wasn't in the script. Bill Neuhoff jumped ahead of Benny and took the lead for the first two laps. On lap three Eddie Miller blew by Benny and dropped him to third. Benny looped the car on lap four in turn six. No one could believe how the car righted itself without any damage or tire problems. Benny had now dropped to ninth place.

With twenty laps to go and with the Black American Racers Formula Super Vee performing flawlessly, Benny put on a driving clinic. He broke Mario Andretti's track record of 100.822-mph. "Benny Scott is closing the gap on the leaders, breaking the track record," said the announcer. A few laps later the announcer said: "Benny Scott in the Black American Racers Lola has set another miles per hour record today." Then on lap twenty, he said: "Benny Scott in the Viceroy Black American Racers Lola has broken his own miles per hour record. The new course record is now 101.179 miles per hour."

Two laps from the finish, the race boiled down to a two-car battle between Benny and Freddie Phillips. As they came around turn nine for the white flag, a wisp of blue smoke came from Phillips's tailpipe. Benny had the nose of the Black American Racers Lola almost up Phillips's exhaust pipe. Benny tried both inside and outside moves all around the track on the last lap. Fred, who had had a life-threatening crash at Laguna Seca in 1974, blocked the track as best he could as they came out of turn nine heading for the checkered flag. With 30,000 fans on their feet, Freddie beat Benny by a tire tread.

The track manager and the Camel cigarette folks were sick. Viceroy and Black American Racers had almost completely over-whelmed their well-planned weekend promotional programs. "What a great job," I excitedly told Benny when he pitted. "We showed the track manager that he couldn't treat us like runaway slaves."

"That's all well and good, Len, but we didn't win the race," he replied, in true driver's fashion.

Thinking our racial problems were finally over for the weekend, we began to relax. Relaxing lasted five minutes at best. While Schill, Viceroy VIPs, the Howards, Jim Young, and Assemblyman Willie Brown (who later became mayor of San Francisco) and his wife were congratulating Benny, the disgruntled tech inspector told us to get the car over to the impound area immediately. Several minutes later the track's public relations representative, who had given us the heads-up earlier, came by and whispered that the track management had instructed the tech inspectors to tear down the Viceroy Black American Racers Lola to the last bolt to see if something illegal could be found on it, which would at least guarantee a hard time putting it back together for the race the following week at Riverside.

My sublimated black rage began to erupt again. Not wanting to upset the group standing around, especially Benny, I headed to the track office. By the time I climbed the hill, I was ready to burn down the office and go to jail. I found the track manager in his office and confronted him. The Camel rep was also present. After a very heated exchange along racial lines, the track manager said he was delaying the winner's circle press conference for a while and sneered at me. "You're not going to make a eunuch out of me," I said and stormed out the door in a rage.

After leaving the track office I immediately found John Bishop, the president of IMSA, the sanctioning body, and told him what had transpired. He told me to call him during the week. Then I went back to the Howards and the Browns and told them what had happened. Assemblyman Brown promised he would have his staff in Sacramento research which civil rights laws had been violated.

While we were huddled, John Zeitler informed me there would be a longer delay for the victory ceremony, because the Black American Racers car had to be torn down further. Tearing it down almost to a bucket of bolts, the tech inspectors could find nothing wrong with the car.

By the time the inspection was finally done, most of the fans had drifted away from the winner's stand. This was what the track manager had wanted. Some of the press left also, because they had to catch planes out of town. When the trophies were handed out, Benny refused to go to the platform. Benny just wanted to get some breathing room away from everyone and be alone, like a gunfighter after a battle. Schill couldn't believe the stress we had endured that day. She towed the race car and we rode in silence back to the Blue Lantern Hotel to say good-bye to Benny's mother and sister.

They had checked out and were sitting in the restaurant. When we approached their table Mrs. Scott said, "You brought my boy back in one piece, but Benny, you didn't win the race!"

"I tried, Mom, I tried," said Benny.

"If your daddy were living, he would have been proud of you," said his mother.

The racial stress, on top of the normal race-weekend stress, took its toll on Benny and me both mentally and physically. No white

American would ever be able to comprehend what we endured that weekend, but facing it together bonded us for life.

Several months later, the Laguna Seca saga finally ended. Willie Brown discovered that a small portion of the rear of the track was on Fort Ord Military Base property. This stroke of luck brought the track under the jurisdiction of federal civil rights laws. With unyielding support from the International Motor Sports Association, the Fédération Internationale de L'Automobile, and Assemblyman Brown, the track manager was eventually removed from his position.

While Schill drove, Benny and I slept all the way down the Pacific Coast. On Tuesday we reviewed our situation. We had to reassemble the car, and Viceroy wanted it painted in their new color scheme. In 1974, there were no race shops like the NASCAR shops found nowadays around Charlotte, North Carolina, where a team can paint and dry a body panel in thirty-eight minutes. Benny contacted a friend who had a race shop north of Los Angeles. He told us to bring the body panels there on Wednesday after dark.

Benny and I arrived at the shop with the panels. Seeing no paint booth, Benny asked, "How are you going to paint the panels?"

"You'll see," said Reds, the shop owner.

An hour later, we heard a loud roar about three blocks away. Looking out the front door, we saw members of the Hell's Angels motorcycle gang approaching on their Harleys with immaculate paint schemes. In their saddle bags they were carrying painting equipment and supplies.

Inside, Benny showed them the new Viceroy body panel paint scheme. The leader then organized the other four. They hung plastic in an open area in the back of the shop and put newspapers on the floor to create a paint booth. Then they quietly began preparing the body panel surfaces for a primer coat. Watching them work as a team through the night was amazing.

When the primer had dried, the paint crew dried the final two colors by taking two large tables and stacking them on top of each other. Then, as each panel needed drying, a crew member would hold the panel over his head and fan it in front of the heating unit. When he got tired, another would take his place. If the paint was drying too slowly, the leader would turn up the shop heat.

Around 4 a.m. the Hell's Angels painting crew had finished. They put the shop back in perfect working order. The shop personnel heading to work that morning would never know they had been there. Finished, the leader and his crew roared off on their cycles with a shifting roar that expressed their satisfaction with a job well done.

At daybreak I called our crewmembers and asked them to meet us at the track in Riverside that afternoon at five o'clock. We had to get the car back together by the first practice session on Friday morning.

At the track office we met Les Richter, who managed the facility. Les was a breath of fresh air after our contentious encounter in Monterey. He took us out to a barnlike structure where track equipment was stored and gave us the cleanest section to work on the car all night. In true Richter fashion, he outlined his rules: don't broadcast what you're doing here to others, and don't wander outside the building after the gates are locked. He didn't want any insurance problems. With those instructions, we reassembled the Lola, working through the night and finishing in time to take a breakfast break. But by this time, the media were reporting that the Black American Racers Lola had blown a motor, and it was doubtful that it would race.

Later that morning we checked all the nuts, bolts, and fittings. Because Benny missed the qualifying round for the race, he had to start in the thirty-fourth starting position out of thirty-five cars. When the flag dropped, Benny began smoking his way through the backmarkers. Then he began picking off faster competitors with ease, until his motor's ignition system went away at the far end of the course on lap six. Through the fire drill of reassembling the car and double-checking everything after breakfast, we forgot to check the cable clamp to the battery to see if it was tight enough. The battery cable came off completely as Benny charged through the field. He finished twenty-eighth. We had a long ride back to the East Coast.

In June the team journeyed to Lime Rock, Connecticut, where Benny placed sixth and kept in the top ten point standings with no trouble. This was the first time Ron Hines, Benny, Lenny, and I had ever seen Wendell Scott on a road course. He was driving for Lem Cammack, a successful black real estate broker from Willingboro, New Jersey, who had a big-block '69 Camaro that ran in SCCA.

Cammack being on a tight budget, unable to bring any welding equipment or spare nuts-and-bolts or other universal fittings and hoses to the track, put Wendell at a big disadvantage. Wendell came over and asked our team if he could use our welding equipment and anything else he might need. Since Wendell was our hero and friend, we were more than happy to give him anything he needed.

You can't know how good a driver Wendell was unless you observed him driving a car that was unprepared to race. Cammack's car had the most horrific oversteer problem I'd seen in years. Coming down the hill under the bridge, Wendell had to lean on all his years of experience to keep the rear of the car from leading the way onto the front straightaway. Wendell manhandled and fought the car like a ship's captain trying to get through a storm at sea. After practice he came over to Ron Hines and me and said, "Len, this is the worst car I've ever driven in my life, and I've driven a lot of bad equipment."

Ron, John Zeitler, and I went over to look at the car. It had the wrong springs, shocks, and transmission gears, and worn-out brakes. We recommended to Lem and Wendell that they not race the car. Like the true racer he was, Wendell said he hadn't come all the way to Connecticut to stand around. He was going to try to qualify the car. I can't remember what happened in the race, but I did give Lem a good piece of my mind for reducing Wendell to a level that insulted all his fellow black racers and his brilliant career.

At this race, Rose kept asking me to introduce her to Paul Newman. I had met Newman several years earlier through Carl Haas, so he knew me by sight. Almost all the racers in the pits gave him breathing room, without hounding him for autographs. He enjoyed racing almost more than acting, and most of the people in the pits were glad he ventured out among the public instead of hiding behind bodyguards and private enclaves.

Before the Formula Super Vee race I spied Newman walking through the pits. Like Wendell Scott, he almost always had a towel draped around his neck in the pits. Catching up with him, I said, "Paul, I'd like to introduce you to my wife, Rose."

"Hello, Rose," he said.

Coming face to face with one of her movie idols, and seeing those light blue eyes, Rose froze in her tracks. Having encountered the same situation thousands of times before, Paul Newman just walked away, smiling to himself. It took a full two minutes before Rose came down from the stratosphere and was able to speak.

Between the Lime Rock and Watkins Glen races, Benny found out about a new Bosch ignition system that was going to be given to five Formula Super Vee Gold Cup teams. We received this secret information only because we were a top-ten team in the series, privy to another level of research and development information. After Benny's photo finish at Laguna Seca, a series insider whispered to us that Robert Bosch had developed five racing ignitions for the Formula Super Vee Series through their research group. Four of the five ignitions had already been given out to the top teams in the series.

When one race team receives new product, large or small, from a series sponsor, every team wants the same product. While among the a top-ten in the series, our team had the Champion Spark Plug Company as an associate sponsor. To complicate things further, we were the only team in the series that was to be sponsored by Champion. Like many associate series sponsors all over the world, Bosch paid the first-, second-and third-place cars at each race prize money if they used the company's ignition systems, including spark plugs. Since Champion and Bosch were direct competitors in the sale of ignition products, we did not carry the Bosch decal on our car; but Champion agreed to pay the team the prize money. In NASCAR and other sanctioning bodies, teams that for various reasons don't want their cars cluttered up with numerous decals pay the sanctioning body for not having them on their cars.

I caught up with Wolfgang Husted, the Robert Bosch motor racing representative, and gingerly asked him whether we could be given the fifth and last ignition setup. Wolfgang listened to my pitch and countered by asking what would happen if Benny won a race. How was Robert Bosch going to get credit for our new and advanced ignition? I told him that I'd have to run the scenario by Jim Young at Champion.

I made a number of round robin calls to both Champion and Robert Bosch, and ultimately worked out a compromise. If Benny won a race, Robert Bosch would mention in its press release that he had used their new advanced ignition system. Champion would identify the spark plugs as theirs. Such a compromise between competing companies very seldom bears fruit, but in this case the caliber of both Jim Young and Wolfgang Husted as racing representatives allowed one to be reached. We realized later that the ignition was far better than the one we had been using.

The next race was at Watkins Glen, New York, on 13 July 1975. Lenny, Rose, and Stephanie all accompanied me to the track. Ron Hines rode with us, with his personal tool chest in the trunk.

When not performing gopher duties for the team, Lenny would wander over to the Formula 5000 teams housed in the garage and watch as their crews worked. In the years he attended the Glen, he went out of his way to observe the Penske, Roush, UOP Shadow, and Roman Brio teams. The Penske teams made the most impression on him. He accompanied me to one of Penske's trailers one morning when I had to borrow a Smith's tachometer cable. He said, "Dad, Penske can make a race when other teams have to go home!" I replied that that is why you have to be sponsored to run up front, unless, of course, you have illegal funds or you're a fool and race beyond your means.

For the most part the race weekend was uneventful. Tom Bagley, a racing friend, led from start to finish and won the race. Benny finished fifth.

Viceroy was so satisfied with the BAR sponsorship program and Benny's much improved performance as a driver that they allowed us to develop a Formula 5000 racing program. On 17 September 1975, Benny stepped into the most highly sophisticated race car he had ever driven, a Lola T-332 Formula 5000, at the Indianapolis Raceway Park, embarking on a new phase of his career. In 1975, the legendary driver Dan Gurney and other insiders declared the new Formula 5000 cars to be faster than the European Grand Prix cars of that era.

Formula 5000 racing was not altogether new to Benny. He had raced in three Formula 5000 events sanctioned in 1972, in what were known as Formula A cars, under SCCA as part of the Vanguard Racing effort. To conserve funds earmarked for track rental fees, Grant King, our internationally known chief mechanic and ally, chose to shakedown the car between the SCCA E cars practicing for the weekend National race.

When Grant King and his crew rolled the new high-dollar Lola

T-332 onto the straightaway, most of the SCCA drivers and crews stopped to take a look. This was one of the first Lola T-332s that Carl Haas had imported to the U.S. After taking a dozen shakedown laps, Benny knew he was handling much more horsepower than his Lola T-324 Formula Super Vee. He also found out that the throttle response was a lot faster and different from the McLaren M10-A formula car he had driven in 1972.

When a team and its sponsor are moving a driver up to the top series in any major sanctioning body, they must have paid advisors to overcome the driver's inexperience. Jumping from a car with a fourth-gear speed of 158-mph on a straightaway to one with a fourth gear speed of 210-mph on a straightaway, with hundreds of shifts in between, is a lot to handle for a new driver moving up in the middle of the season with no track time. For this inaugural test session, Benny had an abundance of reliable advisors: Grant King, versatile chief mechanic and car builder; Skip Barber, veteran world-class driver who, over the years, became a racing friend of the highest order; John Martin, a driver with excellent skills; and Mo Campbell, vice president of Black American Racers, Inc. After every series of laps, they huddled around the cockpit of the Lola.

The early conversations were of the typical test session nuts-and-bolts variety. Is the car pushing? Is the rear end loose? Too loose? Are the brakes grabbing? Is the oil pressure staying up around eighty or ninety pounds? The group encircled the cockpit and made a change after each practice session, based on Grant's and Benny's directions. After each change, Benny's laps became faster.

Towards the end of the afternoon test session, the advisors gave Benny the go-ahead to take some hot laps around the track. Skip Barber and John Martin flagged him in after two sideways slides out of turn fifteen, the flat sweep at the head of the long straightaway. The second lap had the advisors' hearts in their mouths: Benny skidded off the track at over 125-mph and went nose first under the guardrail, stopping within three inches of his helmet. If the car had continued under the guardrail, he would have been decapitated. Both Skip and John conducted high-intensity instruction conferences with Benny, while the crew—rushing to prepare the Lola for one final session—implored Benny to concentrate on smoothness, to which he complied by recording his best laps of the day.

The most memorable marketing meeting during the summer of '75 was Mo Campbell's meeting with a vice president of Pep Boys, the aftermarket auto parts retailer. While researching Pep Boys, Mo and I had discovered that blacks made up 52 percent of its consumer base; yet none of the chain's advertising, marketing, or public relations programs were geared to the black community. Mo thought Pep Boys could mount an effective PR program in the black community. But the vice president immediately dashed his hopes, saying in harsh terms that he had the colored market sewn up and didn't have to reach out to the black community for anything, and that he was interested only in increasing the white market share.

Mo then proposed that Pep Boys use the racing team in print ads in black weekly newspapers. The executive retorted that black newspapers published dated materials. The ads placed in daily and Sunday newspapers blanketed the colored community, so Pep Boys had it covered. He wasn't wasting any time giving any money away to the colored press just to be nice. Finally, he said poor urban colored people needed Pep Boys more than any other racial or ethnic group in Pennsylvania, because most of them had broken-down rattletraps that needed fixing all the time so they could get back and forth to work. "Those poor colored folk will line up early Saturday morning before our stores open to buy fan belts, alternators, starters, and other items," he said. "In fact, I'm not afraid of the NAACP or any other civil rights groups picketing or boycotting our stores, because the poor blacks are going to buy our products anyhow. They need to get to work."

After that, I made it a point to ride past their stores on occasion, when I was in Philadelphia on Saturdays. The executive was right. At some stores there would be half a dozen or more black men lined up at the door before opening time. By midday, the parking lots were filled with black men of all ages with their hoods up, changing oil and repairing cars. Since 1975, I have stepped inside a Pep Boys store only once. If our team had participated in the Indy Racing League in the 1990s, when Pep Boys was the series sponsor, I would have paid a fine before wearing a Pep Boys patch.

Mo Campbell and I went out of our way to search for black

mechanics during the 1974 and 1975 racing seasons. We hired Elliott Platt from Boston, who was willing to move to Indianapolis to work under Grant King's tutelage. Although Elliott's intentions were probably good, it seemed impossible for him to come to work early and leave late every day. Plus, he really wanted to be a race car driver. Just before the inaugural Long Beach Grand Prix, we had to let Elliott go. He returned to Boston, and we never heard from him again.

Whereas the 4 May 1975 Volkswagen Gold Cup race weekend was the worst racing experience I'd ever had, the inaugural 23-28 September 1975 Long Beach Grand Prix race weekend of, and the events leading up to it, were among my very best racing experiences. The team and me led by Grant King and Mo Campbell worked in perfect harmony. Although driving to the limit of his abilities, Benny was relaxed and caught up in all the prerace activities.

Chris Pook, the race promoter, had taken an American racing event up to the Formula 1 world-class level. There were really no backmarker teams invited. The drivers were world-class, and the fans were of the Mid-Ohio mode: race-savvy, polite, and well behaved. Benny and I also relished the weekend because the event was totally free of racial problems. Among the fans who came up to us were aspiring black driver Willie T. Ribbs and his father. Seeing Benny in a world-class Formula 5000 race car that day fueled Willie's ambition to become a professional race car driver.

Most of the world's best race car suppliers were also in attendance. When all the cars were displayed in a large parking area with their teams standing around in the background, the suppliers looked at all sixty cars like biologists dissecting frogs in a research lab. Bill Simpson rushed around counting the number of drivers who were wearing his Simpson driver suits. Manufacturers scampered about looking at every motor or chassis in sight, including fasteners, hoping to see their own products. Joe Hunt of Joe Hunt Magnetos came over and saw his magneto on our Formula 5000 Lola and gave a sigh of relief. We were the first team he'd seen with his magneto jutting out above the motor compartment.

Successful inaugural events of the Long Beach Grand Prix caliber are a happening in every aspect. Early in the week, as the vendors were setting up, car owners, drivers, significant others, and family members bought up everything that might become a collector's item. Dan Gurney advised me to buy the brass belt buckles. He had limited edition numbers 001 to 005. I learned that week that even at the memorabilia level there are insiders and favorites. The name car owners and drivers had the inside track on the low-numbered belt buckles. The vendors saved the buckles for them, looking for a favor in the future or simply because they were fans. To buy belt buckles for Lenny and myself, I went to the back of the vendor's trailer with Dan Gurney early in the morning, before the vendor was officially open for business.

Being on board the *Queen Mary* was a delightful experience. The entire team stayed on the ship as it was docked in the Long Beach harbor for the entire week. All the festivities were marvelous, but, again for me, the most memorable was Mother Unser's on-deck chili party one evening as the sun was setting. Mother Unser was from the old school of racing mothers. She genuinely viewed the guests at her parties as extensions of her family. Mo Campbell and I felt honored just being there. Plus, I've always liked to talk to Bobby Unser, because over the years, he has provided me with obscure details about black racing history.

There were two preliminary heat races. The top twenty-eight cars in the two heats were gridded for the main race on Sunday, 28 September. The layout of the street race was a two-mile configuration with sixteen turns. The only other street course at that time was the Grand Prix in Monaco on the French Riviera, where some of Long Beach participants had also driven.

Benny gridded twenty-fourth. Both Viceroy and the entire BAR team were floating on cloud nine. With less experience than any of the drivers in the field to make the race, this was a Herculean achievement. Grant King's car preparation was first rate, especially in the brake department. The car was capable of 200-mph down the back straightaway, with a little reserve in the tank. The T-332 Lola was the equal of or better than an Indy or Grand Prix car in many respects.

The race started out with a roar that reverberated off the surrounding buildings. Benny stayed out of trouble, and everything seemed to be okay, when on lap seven he pitted unexpectedly. Unbuckling and getting out of the car, he said, "The clutch is gone.

We're through for the day."

A fifteen-second, three-way conversation ensued.

"Your call, Len," said Grant.

"Benny, get back in the car," I said.

"Why?" asked Benny as he got back in the car.

"Ram shift."

"Transmission won't take it."

"A Hewland will."

During the week, Carl Haas had introduced me to Mr. Hewland, the British inventor of the Hewland transmission, who was up in years. He had watched Benny in practice and said, "My transmission is almost bulletproof. You can shift without the clutch."

"Ram shift by sound and landmark," I told Benny.

"Gotcha," he replied.

"Brake real hard off the long straightaway to give the motor revolutions a chance to allow you to downshift," added Grant, and off drove Benny.

This brings me to another story. Chris Pook had to satisfy churches, businesses, and residents along the road course route for being inconvenienced during the race. The members of one church were black and mad as hell that their services had to be canceled because of a race. They complained to Pook's staff that blacks should not support the devil's work on Sunday nor a lily-white sport. When the church leaders were told Benny Scott and Black American Racers were participating in the race, their resistance melted. They were offered free tickets behind our pits in the grandstand. About twenty-five of them, mostly women, came to the race and sat behind our pit dressed as if they were going to church, big hats with flowers around their hat bands and all. As Benny pulled away, out the side of my eye I noticed that the black church women looked relieved. I knew their expectations were high, and that they wanted the black driver to stay in the race.

At the track Benny began identifying certain landmarks in relation to his shift patterns. For example, one shift point was at the Linda Lovelace *Deep Throat* sign on the front of a movie theater along the course. The triple X area of the sign could be seen clearly at high speeds. Another shift point was at the equal scales of justice monument on the hill, and so on.

Two-way radios weren't prevalent at the Long Beach Grand Prix in 1975, but Black American Racers did have a complete set to talk among the crew except in the race car. I had an illegal radio frequency programmed in our sets that only I knew about. I had a hotshot electronic technician program in NBC's and CBS's radio frequencies on separate channels, because ABC was televising the event. This eliminated other teams or fans eavesdropping on us. As a result, no one really knew what was wrong with the car.

That afternoon, I learned why a corporate sponsor loves to have more than one car in a race. Viceroy had three in this one. Al Unser went out early on, then Mario Andretti, leaving Benny as the only Viceroy car left. Although Benny, far less experienced than Unser or Andretti, was driving without a clutch, he drove at his limit safely all afternoon. Once he got into a shifting pattern, when not in heavy traffic, he clicked off his laps within ticks of each other. He also kept from being swallowed up by England's Brian Redman and David Hobbs, Australia's Vern Schuppan, Canada's Eppie Wietzes, and New Zealand's Chris Amon. Benny also had to contend with the foreign drivers working together, as they had done at Pocono International Speedway three years earlier. When the checkered flag dropped, Benny was in eleventh place. He had a great day, considering he'd had to shift without the use of his clutch.

The black church group came out of the stands after the race to shake Benny's hand. Several took pictures with him. As a mix of racing crew and fans were talking to Benny, *ABC Wide World of Sports* commentator Jane Costaine showed up wanting a live interview. At that exact moment, the Valvoline's West Coast representative emerged from the crowd to put a Valvoline patch on Benny's uniform. I removed the patch. In the background, the TV crew was saying two minutes to go. The Valvoline rep said he'd write a check on the spot for a thousand dollars.

"You gave a select few drivers five thousand, and we want the same thing," I said.

"Twenty-five hundred," said the Valvoline rep.

"Thirty seconds to go," said the TV crew.

"Write the check for five thousand dollars now," I said.

He did. Then he slapped the Valvoline patch on Benny's chest with Velcro, just as Jane Costaine was about to go on the air live.

Everyone connected with the team was elated with Benny's performance, except Skip Barber. Getting me to the side, Skip said, "You know why the new clutch failed?

"Benny was slipping the clutch," I replied. "You're right. Call me when I get back to Connecticut."

After the race, the drivers all mingled around and talked to each other without any animosity, then left the course. A small group of drivers from Europe were seen by us for the last time. Their small airplane went down in England as they returned home from Long Beach.

In October 1975, the team entered the Formula 5000 race at Laguna Seca. Benny and I hoped we would not have to face the racial problems we had encountered in May and, thanks to the efforts of Assemblyman Willie Brown and John Bishop, we didn't. But Benny got in a bad shunt with Mario Andretti in a qualifying heat that put us out of further competition because the monocoque was bent.

Since we were through racing for the weekend, Bunny, Willie Ribbs' father, came over and borrowed major pieces from the car to enable the Levi's-sponsored team to make the race. In order to have a chance to continue with their sponsorship in 1976, it was critical for the Levi's team to qualify. While several Levi's race team crew members were removing parts from our Lola, Grant King broke into a smile, sniffing the aroma wafting through the pits. "Do you smell that?" he asked me.

"Yes, it smells like sweet potato pie," I replied.

"That's black folk and Southerners all the way," said Grant. Then he asked an official: "Who's selling the sweet potato pie?"

"A colored lady up on the hill," said the official.

I hurried toward the place where the woman was selling the pies, and I spied her sitting in a little shack that looked like an 1850s outhouse on a Mississippi plantation, with the front door cut out so she could hand the pies out to her customers. She had a bandana on her head like Aunt Jemima on the pancake box. I could not believe what I was seeing! In northern California, near a racetrack where very few blacks could be seen let alone live close by!

I went up to her and asked all the questions a black person would ask: who, what, when, where, and why? She had baked over 175 pies, she told me, and she was sold out. She said she didn't know a black driver and a black-owned team were in the race. I told her my wife, friends, and chief mechanic all had been raised on sweet potato pies.

"I know that, honey, but the white folk got here first," she said. "I'll save you a pie the next time you're here."

I walked away, disappointed. First, a $60,000 Formula 5000 race car had been destroyed. Then, I couldn't even buy a $2.50 sweet potato pie. Another bad day at Laguna Seca. We left the track early, smelling the incongruous combination of race car fuel and sweet potato pie.

From a financial standpoint, Mo Campbell and I were not worried about the almost-totaled Formula 5000, because we had it insured by Lloyd's of London on a race-by-race basis. With calculations based on the number and severity of past Formula 5000 crashes, the team had to pay a $1000 cashier's check to Lloyd's of London a week before each race. There was a $2500 deductible clause.

When the Lloyd's of London man looked at the mangled T-332 Lola at Grant's shop in Indianapolis, he was sick. This was only our second race under the negotiated insurance payment plan. Lloyd's paid Black American Racers, Inc. $45,000. Carl Haas air-shipped a new monocoque and a few vital pieces over to us in record time, enabling us to be ready for the October Formula 5000 race in Riverside.

That was another happening. All of southern California's beautiful people turned out. Beautiful women of all ages, the fan who always appeared at major races with the extravagantly large mustache, even a man with a leopard cub on a leash. We were garaged next to the well-known mechanic George Bignotti, who told the man with the leopard cub to keep the hell away from him or he'd run him over with a pit cart. I was glad George said it, because if he hadn't, I would have. Benny, however, brooked no distractions when it came to getting his head ready for a race.

While both teams were preoccupied with the leopard, someone stole Benny's new $1200 Viceroy driver's suit off the front seat of the truck. This was after Simpson had moved mountains to make the suit ready for Riverside on an impossible schedule. Of course, the first thing the Viceroy executives asked when they visited us in the garage area was, "What happened to the new suit?"

George Bignotti had advised me in 1971, when visiting Red Oliver at his shop: "Dyno every motor before it goes in your race car, no matter what level you're racing. Know where you are at all times." George focuses on two considerations only: putting his driver on the pole—or at least as close to the polesitter as possible—and winning the race. On that weekend in Riverside, he was trying to do just that for Gordon Johncock, who had won the Indy 500 in 1973 and would win it again in 1982.

While Grant King was making minor chassis adjustments to the Black American Racers Viceroy Lola, George was going through one motor after another. In all, he ended up installing five motors in Johncock's car. Between installations, he began discussing the situation with Grant King. After the main bearings went in the fourth motor, he found the problem, an obscure one: In certain turns, the oil suspended itself on the side of the dry sump tank just long enough to interrupt the flow to the motor, resulting in main bearing loss. I've always appreciated the motor geniuses who are willing to share information or to explain a problem even to those—individuals or teams—with whom they have no affiliation.

The season ended on an amusing note. On returning home to Trenton, I received an emergency call from Nevada. On the line was a local Trenton politician who, until that moment, I had always believed was a God-fearing, Bible-toting Christian. He even said grace in public. He was calling from the Cottontail Ranch, at that time the most famous legal house of prostitution in the United States.

"I just got finished getting my pipes cleaned out, when I looked out the window and I saw your Viceroy truck parked out front," he said. "You better have it moved now. You don't want a reporter to take a picture of it here."

I said to myself: "Either it's Hosea Williams and his civil rights group picketing around our Viceroy truck in Atlanta, or it's the truck sitting in front of the best little whorehouse in America. Never a dull moment!"

I asked my political friend how he wound up at the Cottontail Ranch.

He said, "I was so caught up in racing that I didn't know what was going on."

"What?"

"I learned from other married men: Always volunteer to go with your wife to Las Vegas," he said. "While the wives are playing the slots, us married guys go to the Cottontail Ranch and get our pipes cleaned out. Now, promise me you won't tell anyone where I've been."

I promised never to tell on him. As for myself, I smile every time I've heard our local politician, back in Trenton, praise the Lord for his health and happiness.

Returning to the business at hand, I asked him to give me the telephone number, and then called the madam of the establishment and explained the problem. She got one of the crewmembers to the phone just after he had finished the infamous Mamie Stover four-minute sexual encounter. Losing my composure, I started yelling at him over the phone about how dumb he was. Then I ordered him to move the truck immediately, with no clothes on if necessary. By the time the first crewman moved the truck, the other two had finished "getting their pipes cleaned out," and they drove down the road wearing big smiles on their faces and with no harm done.

Because the team met Viceroy's sponsorship goals on and off the track, we had no doubt that we'd be racing under the Viceroy banner in 1976. It was not to be. Viceroy slipped from tenth to eighteenth in cigarette sales in 1975, causing worker layoffs at its factories. Viceroy's senior management staff tried to retain BAR for another year, but when the union heard the news, a group at the Louisville plant went on a wildcat strike. They would not return to work until our team's contract was terminated. Their premise was that the money going to the race team could be used to rehire a number of laid-off workers. The company capitulated, and that decision pushed black racing development back 20 years.

Understanding the union's point of view, I took the bitter pill without malice. Benny all but quit racing. The abrupt cancellation of the Viceroy sponsorship practically put the team out of business overnight. Returning from California, I had to freeze all spending immediately. Grant King stored the Formula 5000 at the garage he used at the Indianapolis Speedway, and I sold the Lola T-324 Super Vee and spare parts back to Carl Haas within a month, thanks to his consideration of the team's plight.

When a race team is suddenly without sponsorship in October, it's almost impossible to secure one in November or December, unless a team functions on the Roger Penske level. Even Penske's organization would be hard pressed to defy the odds against obtaining race team sponsorship within such a time frame.

Mo Campbell tried a desperate marketing move to keep BAR, Inc. alive, which almost worked. He attempted to entice Linda Lovelace, the star of the triple X-rated movie *Deep Throat*, to accompany us to sponsorship presentations at corporations. Mo was doing PR work for Linda in regard to a Broadway-type play she was appearing in Philadelphia. Sponsorship presentations would have been easy to come by. Linda was agreeable, but serious personal and financial problems involving the IRS led to her sudden flight to Europe.

In November 1975, two morale builders occurred that kept both Benny and me going despite the sponsorship setback. Around Thanksgiving both Dan Gurney and Carl Haas called and asked me if Black American Racers, Inc. would be interested in becoming a member of the North American Grand Prix Association that was being formulated to race the Formula 5000 cars. Gurney explained that initially only twenty-four teams would be admitted into the association, and that he would welcome BAR as one of them on the basis of our professional track record.

Within two weeks of Dan and Carl's calls, D. Parke Gibson, Viceroy's marketing consultant, informed Benny and me that we would be honored at the Third Annual Black Athletes Hall of Fame banquet to be held at the New York Hilton in March. Charley Mays, the founder of the Black Athletes Hall of Fame, made certain every year that he paid tribute to nationally and internationally accomplished blacks from around the world who participated in sports, not just baseball, football, basketball, and boxing but in all sports. Gibson's call raised our spirits somewhat and gave Benny and me something to look forward to during the winter of 1976.

Chapter 9
Black Athletes Hall of Fame, 1976

T he excitement of being honored at the Third Annual Black
Athletes Hall of Fame banquet raised my spirits, despite the
lack of a racing sponsor. Benny, being a true race car driver,
didn't care one iota about being inducted into any hall of fame. He
was only interested in whether he was driving a race car in 1976.

Charley Mays, the founder of the Black Athletes Hall of Fame,
was a visionary. His goal was to develop a museum in an urban setting that would attract both white and black visitors. He hired Larry
Johnson and Harvey Myers, black architects from Princeton, New
Jersey, to develop architectural renderings of a proposed building.

Charley, Harvey, and Larry shopped the concept around to several cities and settled on negotiating with Las Vegas. Statistics suggested that enough black tourists visited the city to make a black
sports museum viable. Charley also wanted a facility that would
hold receptions, meetings, and small banquet events. The city was
interested in making the project become a reality, but the casino
industry was against it. It's alleged that the hotel industry in Las
Vegas discouraged the building of a black museum with banquet
facilities, because it would have reduced their market for the same
services. Since Dr. Martin Luther King and others removed race as
a criterion for denying blacks hotel accommodations, hotels that
otherwise would have gone out of business in the early 1970s stayed
afloat because black organizations rented their meeting rooms and

banquet facilities on the weekends, when the white community's use of these marginal hotels was on the decline.

Several members of Mays's inner circle suggested that he ask black athletes and entertainers for seed money to get the project off the ground. As a personal friend of the architects, I watched as a bystander as Charley tried to do just that. I noted that either these celebrities were living beyond their means or that their finances were almost totally controlled by white agents. The black athletes' agents (who for the most part had no interest in promoting black economic development with their clients' money under any circumstances) totally thwarted any attempts by their clients to donate or invest in the project. Furthermore, the sports agents actively sided with Las Vegas business interests for their own personal gain.

From a racial viewpoint, I observed that the agents viewed the athletes more as pets than as clients. From an economic viewpoint, I observed that the agents' loyalty to the white business community behind-the-scenes enabled them to obtain room perks, gambling markers, family vacations, free limo service, food, and knowledge of sweetheart business deals. Having no support, the project failed. To this day, Charley Mays's dream has yet to become a reality.

When the word got out about Benny and me being honored in New York City, nearly two hundred relatives, friends, hangers-on, and status seekers wanted VIP credentials or tickets to the banquet. Benny and I were allocated a total of twenty banquet tickets. Benny didn't have anyone accompany him because of the cost of traveling from California. Time permitting, Rose and I automatically took our children to most major events affecting our family. So, counting Lenny and Stephanie, Benny, my brother Bruce and his wife Evelyn, seven tickets were spoken for. Kenny Wright, the driver of the Miller Brothers drag racing station wagon Mr. Diplomat, and his wife Libby got the next two tickets.

Selecting the rest of our guests became a nightmare right up until two weeks before the ceremonies. Hangers-on, pretenders, and acquaintances became outright pests. The people we knew least well were the worst. They were willing to pay up to $500 a ticket to be included in the entourage. The final nine people we selected were friends only, because we were determined to have a relaxed evening without being surrounded by two tables of people trying to impress Benny or me. Those we invited were Sylvia Proctor, Mr. and Mrs. Howard Rogue, Tom and Lillian Cooper, Ernest and Fay Smith, and Donald Cogsville and his son Donald.

The Black Athletes Hall of Fame induction ceremony being the world-class international event that it was meant to be, Benny and I couldn't arrive in a Checker cab. Most of our group gathered at our home in Lawrence Township, New Jersey, a suburb of Trenton. All the men wore the latest tuxedos in style, because we knew boxing promoter Don King would be in the most up-to-date fashions. We didn't want to look like hayseeds at such an event.

The limousines selected had to be the latest year and model. Fortunately the A-1 limousine service had two new stretches available for the evening. One driver, whom my wife and I had used on a number of previous occasions, even had his autograph book ready. He volunteered to be the last limo to return so he could get as many autographs as possible. He had Benny Scott sign the first autograph of the evening.

With two stretch limos and two cars, we headed to New York City as a small caravan, arriving on time at the New York Hilton. There were about twenty limos in line for drop-offs, blocking the entire corner. As celebrities alighted from them, they were almost crushed by reporters and TV cameras. We didn't have that problem. As Rose, Lenny, Stephanie, and Benny Scott stepped out of our limo, the reporters and TV cameramen paused. I heard a reporter say, "Who are these people?" Another answered, "Who the hell knows? Skip 'em." We walked into the hotel with plenty of breathing space and up to the private reception without our clothes getting mussed up or crushed by autograph seekers.

The evening was typical of high-energy, black-centered events. You could feel the electricity in the air. The stick-and-ball athletes exhibited unbridled manchild attributes that gave the evening a carnival atmosphere. (The only other festivities I've attended over the years that even come close are those put on by the Italians. Their events, like those of blacks, are lively and exhilarating.) With nine hundred in attendance, there were five hundred people, mostly men, between six and seven feet tall. One could feel the underlying bravado in the room. I had already made up my mind about what to do in case any age-old hostilities happened to break out during the evening: I was going to take up my position behind boxing legend Joe Frazier.

Rose was a little uncomfortable at the private reception because the athletes undressed every woman who entered the room with their eyes. Both of us noticed that the white women got the edge on attention from the black athletes over the black women. I, however, was completely comfortable, because I knew a number of the honorees and guests on a first-name basis.

The highlight of the VIP reception for me was talking with ABC sports commentator Howard Cosell again. I noticed that Cosell communicated with people through his mental radar screen, centered around both sight and time per individual. Muhammad Ali could talk with Cosell for up to four hours anywhere, any time, on a one-to-one basis.

I was at the other end of the spectrum. Cosell allotted me two minutes in person or by telephone. The only media personality in auto racing who comes remotely close to Cosell's basic reporter demeanor, in my experience, is TV broadcaster Chris Economaki. The difference is that Economaki, unlike Cosell, is considerate and not arrogant.

I first got on Cosell's radar screen on a telephone interview in the early 1970s to discuss blacks' participation in racing. I informed him that Jack Johnson, the great former heavyweight champion of the world, had been the first black to obtain a professional race driver's license—in 1910. Just as Economaki would have done, Cosell immediately looked up the information himself and found it to be true. Thereafter, he would give me two minutes of his precious time without hesitation. In reality, I had wanted to sucker him into a $1000 bet on whether the Jack Johnson story was true.

While I was being endowed with my undivided two minutes at the VIP reception, a no-name Denver Broncos cornerback butted in, sticking out his hand and introducing himself. Cosell looked down at the cornerback's outstretched hand with disdain. Then, in a raised voice so others nearby could hear, he said, "How dare you interrupt me while I'm talking to Miller! You come back and introduce yourself to me when you are famous, not until." Then he said, "How dare he interrupt my train of thought." Then, after hearing one more black racing fact, he said that if there was anything he needed to know, I should call him. My time was up.

As we were lined up in the hall to be introduced one by one on the dais, by happenstance Don King, Paul Robeson, Jr., and I were grouped together. Robeson introduced himself and began telling us how he was going to defend his father's human relations and racial equality principles to the point of defiance. Cosell came over and said to Don King, "Don't sugar-coat anything in boxing. And Miller, you've got to let the world know where blacks stand in racing. This is your only chance to get your message out." Then he walked away.

By the time Charley Mays introduced, the White House representative Arthur Fletcher, Paul Robeson, Jr. was motivated to speak the absolute best and truth on his father's behalf. I discarded my bland prepared address and instead decided to center my remarks around the 1975 racing incident at Monterey, California. Don said he would ad lib his remarks, but they would be penetrating.

Fletcher's greetings from the president set the tone for the evening. Art and John Wilks, who also worked at the White House, were in my opinion, the fairest and most forthright black Republicans nationally known during the Nixon years. Fletcher exhibited his forthrightness in his opening remarks, giving an accurate picture of the status of black Americans in sports without resorting to distancing himself from black America on principle, as too many black Republicans I've known over the years do unnecessarily.

After Art Fletcher's forthright speech set the tone the emcee, actor and comedian Bill Cosby, tried to inject humor in his casual but very effective way. Before the program really got going good, he began to mock the prim and proper Jamaican soccer and rugby players who were being inducted. Being very British, they took offense. When several of them accepted their silver bowls and Olympic-style ribbons, they unleashed a haughty tirade against Cosby, inducing him to check his usual barbed humor the rest of the evening.

With the Jamaicans' biting acceptance speech, the stage was set for the "thunder and lightning" batting order to come later in the program. The leadoff speaker was Paul Robeson, Jr. The second speaker was Don King. I was third. Howard Cosell was speaking cleanup.

Robeson spoke in stark fashion about his father's refusal to compromise his principles, summarized his feats as a college football player, NFL player, singer, actor, and political activist, and reminded us that, because of his political convictions, he had been denied entrance to the College Hall of Fame. His portrayal of the U.S. government's treatment of his father and others left the audience stunned. His brutally honest portrayal of his father's mistreatment resulted in feeble applause from the blacks in the audience and almost none from the whites. When he returned to his seat next to me, he was visibly relieved. Saying what had to be said had enabled him to make peace with himself on his father's behalf. His speech delivery reminded me a lot of Malcolm X. Years later, on 29 May 1998, I read in *The Trenton Times* that the New Jersey State Assembly had finally passed a resolution, sponsored by Speaker Jack Collins and Assemblyman Joseph Charles, to mark the 100th anniversary of Robeson's birth.

Don King batted second. Like the great NASCAR promoter Humpy Wheeler, Don used light cavalry in his remarks with a mixture of self-promotion and his vision of the future in terms of black economic empowerment in sports promotions and business ventures. His extensive wit kept everyone fearful of going to the restroom in his or her seat. He had not yet developed the "Only in America" speech, so his specific remarks were less than memorable, but he received a great ovation from the audience.

I was third in the batting order. My remarks were a cross between Robeson's heavy artillery and King's light cavalry charge. I laid down a steady machine gun barrage with several high-altitude artillery bursts, centering my remarks on the 4 May 1975 racial incident at Monterey.

I summarized in strong terms how all types of discrimination had hindered Benny's development as a driver. You could have heard a pin drop. For most of the eight hundred or so blacks in the audience, this was the first time they had ever known that blacks were in racing and that they actually could see a real live black race car driver in person. I noticed a number of women wiping tears from their eyes. To avoid becoming too militant or graphic I abruptly stopped, to thunderous applause. As I accepted my silver bowl and ribbon, Bill Cosby whispered, "Good, young man, good."

Several recipients later our cleanup hitter, Howard Cosell, came to the podium. True to his word, he also took an advocate's speaking posture. He delivered his penetrating remarks in the mode of General George S. Patton. His delivery was somewhat arrogant, brutally honest, penetrating, and effective. His remarks centered around Jackie Robinson; how proud he would have been if he had lived to see Frank Robinson become the first black manager in major league baseball. He said sports would have to be integrated at all levels before black Americans' dreams could be realized. When he finished, the applause was even more thunderous than when I had spoken. After Cosell sat down, I reflected how, under his tutelage, the four of us as a team had kept the audience sensitized to what needed to be done. The rest of the evening was composed of Jeff Gordon-type remarks, "Thank you Mom, thank you dear, thank you everyone," then the recipient sat down.

Afterwards, before the private party started in the revolving Presidential Suite overlooking Manhattan in a 360-degree circle, our whole party except Benny, Rose, and me left in one of the stretch limos and the two cars. I wouldn't realize until many years later that the Black Athletes Hall of Fame experience had both a positive and an expansive effect on Lenny, giving him the confidence to handle himself in any situation unintimidated by famous people.

At the break of dawn, when the party concluded, Rose, Benny, and I came down the private elevator to our waiting limo. Near the elevator we saw the usual: roughly twenty camp followers milling around—swinging college students, go-go dancers, call girls, nymphomaniacs, con artists, and transvestites. The ratio was 9 to 1 white. This was the first time Rose had ever witnessed such a scene, and she was thoroughly disgusted and showed it as she entered the limo. The limo driver was pleased with the evening. While waiting for us he had gotten thirty autographs and had shaken hands with several of his sports heroes. We arrived back home at dawn—relieved but gratified.

Chapter 10
Miller Days, 1976-77

After the Black Athletes Hall of Fame event, I immediately returned to the overwhelming task of seeking sponsorship dollars for the 1976 season. While it is well nigh impossible to obtain sponsorship money from scratch after October of the preceding season, I had the added problem of finding sponsorship for Benny on par with the white drivers. Except for our former prime sponsor and the associate sponsors such as the Champion Spark Plug Company, Valvoline, and Goodyear, corporate America turned a cold shoulder to our efforts. The motorsports departments could bring themselves to sponsor Black American Racers only at the $5,000 level, expecting us to produce on and off the track at the $300,000 level. In short, they looked on us as a charity case.

With time running out, Benny bought a used Formula Super Vee to run himself on the West Coast until I could obtain sponsorship money. This relieved a great deal of the pressure on me. In the midst of the "silly season" uncertainties, Tommy Thompson, a black SCCA Formula Ford club racer and a member of the BAR Association, said he was interested in running under the Black American Racers, Inc. banner to keep the road to Indianapolis project alive. Tommy lived twenty-four miles from my home with his significant other, Carol Johnson, who was an avid road racing fan and general motorsports enthusiast.

Tommy was an even more private person than Benny Scott. He

never bragged about his skills or accomplishments. Although he was in an interracial romantic situation, he was race-neutral in his dealings with everyone he came in contact with. Unlike a number of successful black male athletes, he never flaunted his intimate relationship like a prize trophy on his arm. He was a quiet person quietly going about his racing capabilities. His demeanor was similar to that of Al Unser, Sr., the great Indy driver. He never raised his voice, he quietly drove his race car to the best of his ability, and he never openly complained about anything at any time, on or off the track.

With Benny I shared my plan to sell all the team's racing equipment except the Formula 5000 in order to raise enough money to buy a new Lola T-620 water-cooled Formula Super Vee, later known as a Mini-Indy car. Benny agreed, because it shaved $15,000, off the overall racing operating budget. Benny further agreed that we should keep the Formula 5000 until we were certain we could not operate it on at least a partial schedule.

Having ensured that the BAR team would be in business in 1976, I looked forward to the North American Grand Prix Association meeting. Toward the end of February, Carl Haas called me to report that the association had been officially organized on 19 February 1976, and that a meeting would be held just before Easter at the Circus-Circus Hotel in Las Vegas.

Because racing constituted only 40 percent or so of my daily activities, "Miller Day" evolved. Rose dreaded the Miller Day. Lenny and Stephanie grew up within the Miller Day environment and didn't know any different. In their thirties and early forties now—at the time of writing this book—they have even done me one better and have graduated to the "Super Miller Day."

Typically, the Miller Day heading to the North American Grand Prix Association meeting in Las Vegas, started at 5 a.m. at the Quality Inn Philadelphia Airport transporter stop at Exit 7 of the New Jersey Turnpike, where I met Mike Frusco, who worked for me at Dynamic Programs, Inc., my management consulting firm. We had to go from Philadelphia to Albany on the first flight of the day to collect the $40,000 that the New York Department of Transportation had owed me for over nine months of government consulting.

In Albany at 8 a.m. it was snowing. We met with NYDOT officials for an hour and received the check, then headed back to the airport in a taxi. By this time it was snowing very hard, with an accumulation of nine inches. The cab got stuck at the entrance to the airport. Mike and I had to get out and push the cab out of the rut. Ultimately, we had to walk to the terminal to catch our plane. The return flight to Philadelphia was the last flight of the day; after our take off, the airport was shut down. Back in Philadelphia at last, at the airport I gave Frusco the check to deposit in the bank. I then hurried over to the United Airlines gate for the noon flight to Los Angeles to meet Benny Scott in the airport. It was about 3 p.m. West Coast time when I arrived at LAX in winter clothes. The temperature was in the high 80s.

After discussing a number of racing-related business problems with Benny and eating dinner, I hopped a flight to Las Vegas at dusk. As the plane neared the city, the pilot announced that we were being put in a holding pattern, and that the Las Vegas Airport was temporarily closed, because of a severe sandstorm. We flew around for an hour and a half until we were permitted to land. I finally arrived at the Circus-Circus Hotel and Casino around 10 p.m.

While I was registering at the Circus-Circus, I began to feel tired and was looking forward to going to bed. On my way through the casino, I ran into Dan Gurney playing the one-dollar slot machine, the one with the big lever that stood in an open area. He told me a lot of the fellows were around.

When I returned from putting my bag in my room, Dan was over $100 to the good. "You should try the dollar machine and see if you have racer's luck," he said. This was the first time in my life that I'd ever played the dollar machine. After about half an hour, Dan was ahead by $200, and I was ahead by $50. He said, "Let's quit and see what the others are doing." It was then about 1 a.m. Las Vegas time, and I had been up since 4 a.m. East Coast time.

We went over to the bar and ran into several wealthy businessmen who were interested in joining the North American Grand Prix Association. They had not been invited to that morning's meeting, but had come to hang around its edges as business "camp followers." One was a coal mine owner from back East who wanted to buy a Formula 5000 race car. Hearing this, I immediately decided to sell him the Black American Racers Formula 5000 Lola, because we needed cash. After ten minutes of discussion, I sold it to him for $30,000 on the spot. He was as good as his word. One week later he wired $30,000 to me in Trenton, and I had Grant King release the car.

As Dan and I headed back through the casino, we ran into Vel Miletich, Parnelli Jones's partner, playing blackjack. We stopped to watch. As he lost hand after hand, I asked another bystander how far behind he was. "Twenty thousand," said the bystander. I whispered the figure to Dan, who said, "That's about enough to complete my motorcycle project."

As tired as I was, I couldn't bring myself to go to bed. Concentrating on Vel's strategy, I noticed he held at 16. The blackjack players I hung around on the East Coast almost always held at 17. Being naïve and out of my element, I asked Vel why he didn't hold at 17. He almost bit my head off. "Leonard," he said, "if you think you know more about blackjack strategy than me, you sit down and play, or shut up!" I shut up and stood behind Vel while he lost a total of $50,000 before I went to my room at 5 a.m. That was the end of what I now call a Miller Day, traveling long distances to a number of places in a short period of time.

After sleeping several hours, I woke up, not knowing where I was. I finally got my bearings and went to the North American Grand Prix Association meeting room. All the founders were present and sitting together: Dan Gurney, Don Markland, A. F. Budah, whom I didn't know, Vel Miletich, less his blackjack money, and Carl Haas with his eternal unlit cigar. Donald J. Regan, later to become a key person in the Reagan White House, was the legal counsel present; he facilitated most of the meeting.

With Regan's assistance, the founders developed an excellent set of by-laws that almost guaranteed world-class racing events equal to Formula 1. Each invited participant had to pay an initiation fee of $4000. The number of cars per race was limited initially to twenty-four. The by-laws stipulated that "new participants may be admitted to the association only if eighty percent (80%) of the participants approve the admission of such new participant, the number of racing cars may then exceed twenty-four (24)." The participants' manual was well prepared and fair to all potential members. Volunteers with no ownership or participating capital expense involvement were not permitted to be in decision-making positions that could adversely affect the association's overall success.

When we broke for lunch, the group somehow ended up at the bumper cars. Anyone who has been around race car and aviation types knows that spells trouble. Carl Haas offered to pay for one round of bumper car tickets, which totaled eighteen. Dan Gurney and Parnelli Jones divided the group into two teams of nine, with Dan and Parnelli as team captains.

The demolition derby that ensued was devastating. As every youngster and adult knows, you're told not to hit another driver head-on in a bumper car for safety reasons. That rule went out the window. In addition, some bumper cars were faster than others. The 360-degree spins and sideway moves put on by the two teams were so remarkable that more than a hundred people crowded around to watch. Some were avid racing fans and began recognizing the drivers.

When finally the manager of amusements stopped us, two bumper cars had been totally destroyed, subrails were bent, and static electric rods on cars were also bent, totally immobilizing them. Carl Haas had lost his cigar after three bumper cars hit him at once hard enough to cause a mild concussion.

The amusements manager was livid as he surveyed the damage. While he was yelling and screaming, a number of us tried to make a quiet exit off the floor. That didn't work, because fans and autograph seekers blocked the exit gate. At this point the manager didn't know what to do, so he stopped yelling, quietly turned off the lights in the bumper car area, and posted an "Out of Service" sign until further notice. We all, including Carl, went back to the meeting room and roared with laughter.

Flying back across the country that night and reviewing the goals of the North American Grand Prix Association, I knew that Dan Gurney, Carl Haas, and the directors were on the right track in providing and developing an American world-class formula series equal to or better than Formula 1, and at a lower cost. It was not to be however. The Formula 1 hierarchy in Europe fought vigorously through the Fédération Internationale de L'Automobile and its friends in formula racing to head off any direct competition to its series. Later, CART tried to fill the American void in formula racing, but failed in its ultimate goal of capturing the Indy 500 as its premier event. Now its series is filled with foreign-born drivers who have cut their teeth almost solely on formula racing, thus giving them an experience edge over up-and-coming American drivers.

Returning from Las Vegas, brought me back to reality. Decisions for the 1976 racing season had to be made based first and foremost on financial considerations. Benny was on the West Coast, and most of the Mini-Indy races were in the East and Midwest. If Benny ran the team from California, travel expenses would be prohibitive. If he flew to each race, with the car based in New Jersey, transportation expenses would also be prohibitive, especially in the absence of a major sponsor.

After reviewing the budget many times by telephone, we decided a creditable top-ten effort in the Formula Super Vee Mini-Indy Series was not in the cards. During the last several conversations, I mentioned to Benny that Tommy Thompson, whom he had met in 1974, was willing to step into BAR's Lola T-324. To maximize any motor racing effort on any level, proper planning and goals must be established at the beginning of the season. Tommy and I decided to enter Formula Super Vee races at sanctioned SCCA events in the Northeast during the 1976 season for three reasons. First, the series was soft. The level of competition was not as intense as the USAC Mini-Indy Series. This would allow Tommy to step up a class and to get good experience without the danger of crashing every time he raced. Second was the budget. To be competitive in the USAC Mini-Indy Series would cost an additional $40,000. We agreed that each of us would utilize his personal financial resources to buy equipment and parts. Tommy's girlfriend, Carol, also contributed. The third consideration was our proximity, living only about twenty-four miles from each other. Tommy lived in Somerset, New Jersey, and I lived in Lawrenceville. This cut down on long-distance calls and extra travel expenses, and made us both readily available for moving equipment, shagging parts, and performing emergency tasks.

After we formulated our game plan, I approached Ron Whitney

of R & W Enterprises for the purpose of building a motor. Ron had been building motors for the team off and on since 1974. Ron was key to our formulations because the only way he knew how to build a motor was correctly, taking into consideration the latest motor development research. Also, R & W motors had proved to be durable. In fact, the only motor failure we've ever had from Ron Whitney was in 1980, when I gave him some used parts to put together a dirt track motor. On this occasion Ron agreed to put together a state-of-the-art motor at the best possible price.

Now that Tommy and I had our racing program in place, I reapproached Jim Young of Champion Spark Plug Company and Leo Mehl of Goodyear, to tell them about BAR's plans for getting back on track towards Indy in 1976. Champion agreed to put in dollars and product, and Goodyear agreed to supply a limited number of tires for the racing season.

After we finalized the season's budget, we had enough money to pay a chief mechanic, provided I stayed home from most of the races. I secured a road racing mechanic, an acquaintance from Trenton who agreed to prepare and maintain the car for the season. He was fired within two weeks. Much to my surprise, Tommy had better setup skills than many mechanics working on the professional formula road racing teams. Tommy's ability to bump steer, string and use caster and camber gauges, transfer weight, and do tire management was equal to four average mechanics on a NASCAR team and two professional CART mechanics on a top-five road racing team. His natural and self-taught skills were amazing. Some nights while working on the Lola T-324, he would effortlessly set up Formula Fords as if they were toys for his group of friends.

Tommy compiled an impressive record in his first year with the team. He entered a total of fifteen races, won four, placed second five times, and finished third twice, set a track record at Bryar, New Hampshire, and set lap records at Bryar, Summit Point, West Virginia, and Bridgehampton, New York—all with one Ron Whitney motor and his own suspension setups. Tommy was the first black driver in SCCA history to win a division championship, the first black driver to win four SCCA-sanctioned races in one season, and the first black driver to enter fifteen road races in one season.

Everyone associated with Tommy in 1976 was elated by his accomplishments. I tried to use them as a basis for a second conversation with Tom Shropshire, a high-ranking black executive at Miller Brewing Company, for a sponsorship opportunity. Shropshire turned me down cold. I then had Ernest Green talk to him about how opening racing up to blacks would increase the number of mechanic, welder, auto body, and motor builder opportunities for our youth. Shropshire turned down Ernest Green too. He never told me why until 1998. He said that, except for Willie T. Ribbs, he placed black civil rights, fraternal, and select community organizations first on his list of sponsorships. Grants and black racers came in last.

Black American Racers began the 1977 season by moving up to the USAC Mini-Indy Formula Super Vee Touring Series. To stay competitive, Tommy and I each invested $25,000 in the operation. Every unsponsored team since the dawn of motor racing faces this dilemma time and time again: Does a team run old equipment and become a backmarker every week and lose its zest to win, or does the team sit out races until it can race competitively? We chose the latter.

In the spring of 1977, Tommy bought a crew cab dual-wheely and camper for traveling across the United States. I bought a Lola T-324 motor from Ron Whitney and a twenty-eight-foot tag-a-long trailer. While Tommy raced the Lola T-324, I continued to look for sponsors. During the mid-to late 1970s, I kept in contact with Jim Cook. At the time Jim became for us what Tom Cotter of Cotter Communications, the best auto racing PR man in the U.S., would be in the mid-to late 1990s. Jim recommended that BAR enter the Mini-Indy 100-Kilometer race on 24 September at the Trenton Speedway, as part of the 150-mile championship race for Indy cars. He also said he would give Tommy as much publicity as possible, because many major sponsor representatives would be present. The International Association of Machinists and Aero-Space Workers sponsored the race. *The Trenton Times* newspaper used the race as a benefit event for its Christmas Appeal, which received two dollars for every ticket sold. This type of project would guarantee Jim Cook an extra 8-10,000 in ticket sales.

I mentioned *The Trenton Times* benefit event to the president of the local chapter of the New Jersey State Federation of Colored Women's Clubs. After several meetings with the executive committee and the state president, the federation agreed to provide the tires, the fuel, and all entry fees for the team that weekend. Jim added the New Jersey State Federation of Colored Women's Clubs to the funds allotment list, along with the Deborah Hospital in Browns Mills and *The Trenton Times* Christmas Appeal. The federation's Trenton chapter did an excellent job selling tickets to people in the black community who had never been to an automobile race, nor seen a race car at a show or exhibit. Then, on the day of the race, a promoter's worst nightmare surfaced. It rained most of the day— by the bucketful. It was a nightmare for me too. When you introduce a corporation or individuals to racing for the first time, you don't want the race rained out, the car performing poorly, or the driver crashing at the beginning of the race.

Trenton Speedway was part of a state fairgrounds complex and had covered grandstands down most of the front straightaway to turn one, plus an enclosed area under the grandstands where food was served. This type of structure kept fans from leaving too fast, because they could find a number of dry areas at the facility. The members of the federation and their guests, including a group of needy children for whom Jim Cook and George Hamid, owner of the speedway, had provided tickets, stayed huddled under the grandstands for several hours. Finally, the group went home, never to return to a motor racing event again. At last, the race was called off. All the team's momentum, not to mention our attempt to introduce new fans to racing, was totally lost. When the skies finally cleared, Tommy crashed in practice. We canceled going to Watkins Glen and instead saved our money to race in 1978. I was not to know until then just how pervasive the Trenton jinx was to be.

Chapter 11
Lowest of Lows, 1978

T he 1978 racing season turned out to be the lowest of low
points in my entire racing career. To start, the Lola T-324
air-cooled Formula Super Vee was rendered obsolete.
Luckily, I sold it to Certainteed Corporation, which turned it into a
show car. I immediately ordered a Lola T-620 from Carl Haas.

When Tommy tested the car at Bridgehampton, his home track,
he immediately discovered the car wasn't the best Lola ever built. Its
frontal area was bulky and broad, covering the wheels. The idea was
to cut the wind-force better than the T-324 and to change the down
force dynamics, but somewhere along the line the chassis engineers
had missed something. The car wasn't cutting edge. At best, it was
an average-performing race car.

Again, this is where, all other things being equal, well-heeled
sponsored teams ability to buy better equipment automatically gains
five to ten finishing places in any given race. We decided to enter five
races, with help from the Champion Spark Plug Company. The five
races were in Milwaukee, Wisconsin; College Station, Texas;
Ontario, California; Watkins Glen, New York; and Trenton, New
Jersey. Besides the financial factor, Tommy had only so much vacation
time from his regular job.

As most racers will agree, it is important to enter the first race in
any touring class to gauge the competition and start earning points
immediately. We had to forego this plan, skipping the first three

races of the season but entering the next five.

The Mini-Indy race at the Milwaukee Fairgrounds on 18 June 1978 was the highlight of the season for Tommy. Because of continuous rain during qualifications, the drivers had to draw for starting slots. Tommy drew twenty-eighth—dead last. With Carol Johnson and me assisting, Ron Hines worked until grid time to make the car as near perfect as possible. Having the car dialed in correctly, Tommy might be able to drive it into the top ten or even to win the race, because Milwaukee was flat and known as a driver's track. There was only one yellow flag the entire race, and the competition was above average. Tommy finished ninth.

The Mini-Indy double-header race at Ontario Motor Speedway was the most eye-opening race for me and Ron Hines that season, until the Trenton race. Before going to California, I received a call from the Champion Spark Plug Company asking what we needed in order to go faster. After a lengthy discussion, Champion volunteered its research and development camshaft-grinding facility at Long Beach to help us develop a cam for the Ontario race.

This was the first time we'd ever heard of companies outside the Big Three automakers having "skunk" works. Through this experience, I learned that Goodyear had an extensive clandestine race motor building operation for the purpose of improving the success of certain select sponsored teams of its own. This revelation reminded me of a comment a CIA operative had made to me in the 1960s: "Anything that you imagine is possible in beating a system has already been done, or will be done in the near future." After meeting Dick Jones at Champion's secret Long Beach facility in 1978, I said to Ron Hines that we'd never run as a backmarker in a touring series race just to be out there on the track. Front runners and their blood relatives coming up through lesser series at the same time have access to hidden resources of all kinds that ensure them more racing success than unsponsored teams might ever imagine.

The week we spent with Dick Jones and his technicians at the unmarked Champion R & D facility was like a week in a candy store. The facility was state-of-the-art, with the most up-to-date cam-grinding equipment available at the time. When Jones's technicians were busy with other secret projects, Ron Hines and Tommy, under

Jones's supervision, would assist with motor assembly and dyno tasks. Over a five-day period, seven different cam configurations were developed and dynoed at great expense to R & D, just to get a three-horsepower gain in the midrange. As with both previous and subsequent motors that Ron Whitney and son built, the installed cam passed the most extensive testing processes and was still the correct grind for the Ontario race.

Black American Racers appreciated Champion's concern as a sponsor to reevaluate the motor-related areas where they had world-class expertise. Working under the tutelage of Dick Jones and his technicians for five twelve-hour days increased the team's knowledge of camshaft configurations a hundredfold.

After our experience at the secret Champion R & D facility, we knew our problems were not in the motor area. The problem was in the slow-working Lola T-620 chassis. We later heard that Gary Bettenhausen and Herm Johnson had each spent between $15,000 and $20,000 to make extensive changes to their Lolas to make them more competitive with the Ralt chassis.

The Ontario Mini-Indy race was a doubleheader. The first nine cars finishing in the first race would be inverted for the second race. Tommy finished ninth in the first race and thus was on the pole for the second race. Even though Tommy's pole had been won through an inverted start, Ron Hines and I noticed more photographers than usual taking pictures of Tommy and the Black American Racers Lola. The foreign press afterwards played up the fact that a black driver and team were on the pole. Tommy finished seventh in the second race. We and Champion were both happy with the two top-ten finishes and the worldwide positive press they had generated.

The Ontario race weekend was the second time the team came into contact with Willie T. Ribbs. We found him to be the exact opposite of his father, Bunny Ribbs. Willie seemed to resent the fact that another black driver was trying to go to the Indianapolis 500. He spent the weekend standing on the fringe of our open garage area, bad-mouthing Tommy's driving ability. He openly exhibited the crab-in-the-barrel syndrome that many blacks, including me, detest—criticizing another black person who is trying to be successful. The unnecessary and unwarranted loud criticism Willie heaped on Tommy and the team that day provoked Ron Hines to reproach him directly about it. Willie replied that he was the best black driver in America, and that we were wasting our time trying to go to Indy or anywhere else.

When Ron relayed this brief conversation to me, I decided I had heard enough. Seeing Willie and his two white friends heading to the infield refreshment stand, I went over to him. But as I approached him, he hurried away. Some time later, I mentioned my displeasure with Willie's arrogant and harsh attitude toward other black racers to his brother. After that weekend I spoke to Willie only twice in more than twenty years, and that by telephone, until Doc Watson, a racing friend, made peace between us in 1998.

Because we were staying up in the points standings, Tommy and I decided to dig deeper in our pockets and enter the Texas International Speedway event at College Station, Texas. We enlisted Ron Hines and Kenny Wright, who had always made himself available ever since I first started drag racing in the mid-1960s. After a long tow from New Jersey, Tommy crashed in practice and damaged the car beyond trackside repair.

In time for the Texas race, a new and larger wing was approved for use by USAC for the Mini-Indy cars. We had been lucky enough to obtain one of the first wings of its type. The new wing was not damaged in the crash. When Robert Fitzpatrick, a fellow car owner whom I had gotten to know on the circuit, saw that the wing hadn't been damaged, he asked to borrow it. The wing on his car was the old type and provided less down force. After the team let Robert borrow the wing, a small group of car owners came over to me and asked why I would have the nerve to lend the latest cutting edge wing to a "faggot." I was taken aback, because I had not even been thinking along the lines of whether Robert was gay or not. One owner said, "Look over there, Len. The whole team looks like a bunch of faggots. We all should agree not to lend those freaks anything."

I said, "You're discriminating against another team owner for reasons having nothing to do with racing." Tommy walked away in disgust.

At the evening chili contest, I was still being ribbed about lending the wing to the Fitzpatrick team. Finally weary of it, I said, "I'm not into gay-bashing, because I look at the situation from a black point of view." They all walked off scratching the backs of their necks. To this day, I don't think they understood my comment.

As we faced the long tow home, we didn't realize that the crash in practice at the Texas International Speedway was only the first dark cloud to form over Black American Racers in 1978. As Tommy, Kenny, Ron, and I headed back to New Jersey in silence, we didn't in our wildest dreams imagine that soon, one of us would never be riding in Tommy's crew cab truck again.

When September rolled around, Tommy was twelfth in the Mini-Indy Series nationally. Black American Racers was also ranked twelfth as a team nationally. The points fund paid out to twelfth place, and the top rankings, as far as publicity and background information for potential sponsors, were centered around the first twelve drivers and teams who ranked twelfth or better in the national Mini-Indy standings.

The team looked forward to the 23 September 1978 Mini-Indy race at the Trenton Speedway. It was our home track, plus I knew everyone of importance within a hundred-mile radius on a first-name basis. So promoting Tommy, BAR, and the Champion Spark Plug Company was a snap.

George Hamid, owner of the speedway in the 1970s, constantly tried to find ways to increase black awareness of racing events. But no matter what he tried, the events always attracted fewer than twenty-five blacks, most of them men. Late in August 1978, Jim Cook (who was contracted to promote the September 23 race), George Hamid, and I met at the speedway to discuss how we could increase black attendance at the race. We decided to embark on an awareness program that would involve preteens and high school-aged black children.

I contacted the Trenton YMCA and scheduled Tommy and the car to arrive at a large group gathering on Fowler Street in Trenton on a Saturday morning early in September. When Tommy, Ron, and I showed up with the car, the youngsters seemed to think we were from another world. Not one of the sixty or so children there had ever seen a real race car before. I could see Tommy go into quiet shock when the youngsters started jumping into the driver's seat.

Living the life of an honorary white man in a safe and secure suburban, middle-class community had totally shielded him from rough-and-tumble inner-city kids. He literally didn't know what to do. Ron and I quickly restored order, and our demonstration began to go smoothly thereafter. During the question and answer period, several teenagers asked the big question: "Where can we see you race?"

As a result of the successful experience, Jim Cook authorized 300 free tickets for distribution to the Trenton YMCA. He also allowed the Y to distribute tickets to other worthwhile groups serving inner-city kids. The tickets were for seating in the open grandstand between the covered grandstand area and the back gate to the infield.

Because the Trenton Speedway was the team's home track, and because of the open-door policy Jim Cook afforded us, Tommy and I were around the track while the New Jersey State Fair was in full swing. One day after practice, Tommy decided to take a bumper car ride. Unknown to him, a group of good-looking young black women had been watching him in practice. As he was maneuvering the bumper car around, one of them ran across the floor, dodging other bumper cars, and jumped into his car in a flash.

Using the king's English, Tommy asked her to get out. She refused and grabbed the wheel. Tommy grabbed the wheel back, steered the bumper car over to the edge of the rink, and politely asked her to get out. She looked at Tommy and said, "You look like a black man, but you act like a goddamn white man." Then she jumped out of the car as fast as she had gotten in and went off with her two girlfriends. The last word I heard her say was, "Shit."

The day of the race was sunny. About a hundred paying black fans were in attendance, a minor record. The YMCA kids and their chaperones were in the open grandstands anxiously awaiting the start of the race. Track announcer Bill Singer, a friend and ally, was at his best revving up the crowd.

When Bill announced it was two minutes to grid, the blackest racing cloud the team had to face began to form. When Tommy started the Lola T-620, there was no oil pressure. Ron checked and found the new hi-capacity trick Bertils oil pump had malfunctioned.

Jim Cook stalled the start of the race for several minutes to give us a chance to correct the problem. When he saw we were not ready, he sent a USAC official over to us to see if we could make the race. Ron told the official he needed a few more minutes. Tommy stood silently by the car with nerves of steel.

After several more minutes, Cook had to start the race. Prior to the green flag lap, Tommy caught the rear of the field. He was twenty-eighth—dead last. It looked like Milwaukee all over again. The black kids in the open grandstands gave a yell of approval after seeing Tommy catch the field.

The race was fast, with only a few caution flags. Bill Alsup, the points leader, was determined to clinch the 1978 Robert Bosch Volkswagen Gold Cup before the last race of the season. Geoff Brabham, a second-generation driver from Australia, wanted to continue his success in the United States by winning the race. Bob Cicconi, who later won some exciting sprint car races on ESPN's *Thursday Night Thunder* in the 1980s, was equally determined to win his first Mini-Indy race of 1978.

The race went nicely for Tommy. He moved up from twenty-eighth place. On the last lap, racing's lowest of lows turned a bright and cheerful Sunday afternoon at the Trenton Speedway into a bellowing cloud of smoke coming out of turn four.

People always remember who was next to them during a catastrophe, a disaster, the darkest hour of combat, or racial persecution. On 23 September 1978, the person standing by me was Lou Cicconi, a racing friend before and since that day that will remain etched in my memory for the rest of my life.

Lou and I were standing behind the pits on the last lap. Ron Hines and Kenny Wright were at the pit wall. I took my eyes off Tommy for a split second to watch Bob Cicconi try to pass Geoff Brabham at the finish line. In fact, Lou's crew and friends started running toward the finish line from where they were standing behind pit row. It was at this minute that Lou grabbed my shoulder hard and pointed down the track. My senses shifted into slow motion. I couldn't believe what I was seeing.

I saw Tommy go two stories in the air, with the car breaking into three parts. The motor and rear subframe completely broke away from the monocoque. The front tires, wheels, and suspension went everywhere. He had flipped after running over a wheel on John Barringer's car between turn four and the open grandstands. If Tommy had been propelled back any further, he would have landed on top of the parked cars behind the track fence. Both Barringer and Tommy were taking evasive action to avoid hitting Nancy James, who suddenly slowed in front of them when her car lost its electrics. It was alleged afterward that Planters Peanuts had promised Nancy $25,000 in sponsorship on condition that she finish the race. She coasted diagonally over the finish line, causing mayhem behind her.

Before Tommy had landed, I was off running toward him. My brother Bruce, who was in the A grandstand with Lenny and the rest of my family, took off running too. As Tommy went up in the air, Johnny Rutherford, who had been entered in the Indy car event that day by First National City Travelers Checks, was coming through the back gate. Rutherford got to Tommy first. He looked for fire and for whether any jagged metal that might have pierced Tommy's body. Neither problem was apparent.

By the time I and others got to Tommy, the rescue squad and firemen had arrived. They had to use metal cutters called the Jaws of Life to separate him from the cockpit. It took twenty minutes, but it seemed an hour to me. One of the rescue workers that I knew whispered to me, "It looks real, real bad, Len." Because John Barringer had good vital signs, he had to wait for the Jaws of Life. He had two badly broken legs, and the front of his car was totally mangled.

While the rescue squad and the firemen were trying with great care to extract Tommy from the monocoque, I noticed some of the YMCA kids had tears in their eyes. Tommy had gone airborne at the edge of the open grandstands. It was the worst possible thing they could see at a racetrack, and this was their first exposure to motorsports. I doubt whether if any of those kids ever returned when they grew older.

After twenty minutes of intensive rescue work, Tommy was transported to St. Francis Hospital in Trenton. I wasn't allowed to ride in the ambulance. When it left the track, I ran back to the trailer. By this time, Ron and Kenny had everything loaded.

As Ron and Kenny were loading the trailer, the tow truck

brought what was left of the car. While we were loading the final pieces of the car, a crewman from another team brought over one of the Goodyear tires he had found across the track, carrying it as if it were a piece of gold. "You can sue Goodyear," he said. "Blame everything on the tire." Then he hurried away. After what Goodyear, especially Leo Mehl and Lee Guag, had done for the team over the years, suing them didn't even cross my mind. After getting everything loaded, I crossed the track to meet my family. My wife and Mae Lee, a friend and neighbor, offered to go to St. Francis Hospital with me. Mae's husband Wendell volunteered to take Lenny and Stephanie home. Carol Johnson had not arrived at the hospital yet.

No sooner had those logistics been settled, Bruce came running around from behind the grandstands, saying he had to talk with me about something in private. I told him I was overwhelmed and didn't have time for a private conversation. He then said he'd gotten into a fistfight behind the open grandstands. When he said "fistfight," everyone within hearing distance tuned in. I said, "What happened?"

"I heard a young, tough-looking white turkey say as he was watching Tommy being cut out of the race car, that's one less nigger we have to worry about," said Bruce. "I went over and hit him. The cops separated us, and the turkey ran out into the parking lot."

My feelings at that point turned from hurt and despair to black rage. Mae Lee said, "Leonard, you and Bruce aren't going to jail. We have to go to the hospital, now!"

Rose, Mae, and I went directly to St. Francis Hospital. Several doctors who could hardly speak English greeted us. After a heated discussion with them, I barged into the emergency room area where Tommy was being worked on. Another doctor who could hardly speak English was looking Tommy over. When I looked over at him, while the doctor was trying to hold me back, all hope for his survival drained out of me with a rush. He was bleeding out of every bodily orifice. I stopped pushing the doctor, turned around, and walked out, while Mae was pushing to get in the room.

I told Mae and Rose in the corridor that Tommy's condition was as bleak as it could get. We went to the waiting room to wait several hours for Carol and Tommy's parents to arrive from north Jersey. While we were waiting, I checked to see how John Barringer was doing. After checking on his progress I returned to the waiting room, where Tom Bagley and his wife were waiting for me.

Tom had just driven the Kent Oil Special in the Indy car race that afternoon. In the early 1970s he became friends with both Benny and me when he was participating in the Formula Super Vee Series. Seeing Tom and his wife was an instant morale booster for me. When you know death is at the doorstep, the room seems to get darker, the hospital gets quieter, and meaningful conversation dissipates to nothing. Tom and his wife helped us all get through the next hour, by showing they truly cared about Tommy and everyone connected with him.

Tommy's parents arrived late in the evening, after Rose and Mae had gone home. Carol got the Thompsons and me together and spoke to us as if we were a group of slaves on a Southern plantation, with no rights to speak about anything. Mr. Thompson started out by saying he would like to have the American flag on his coffin if Tommy didn't survive. Carol told him in no uncertain terms that since coming back from Vietnam, Tommy had never wanted to have a flag on his coffin. The Vietnam issue didn't bother me, because in those days the entire nation was split on it. What bothered me was Carol talking to Tommy's parents as if they were little children. Then she turned to me and said that neither I nor Black American Racers would have any participation whatsoever in the funeral. Finally, she said we could all go home.

As I headed out of St. Francis Hospital that night, I felt like a Native American who has had his sacred burial grounds desecrated by the U.S. Cavalry. By 1978 I had seen many interracial marriages where the black man volunteered to become or was made into an "honorary white"—without the privileges. In only a few instances had I seen the cultures, attitudes, and mores blend together from such racial unions. I went home alone, totally upset as well as grieving from all the day's events.

But when I got home around 10 p.m., my day still wasn't over. When I told Rose that Tommy had been put on life support, she unleashed all her pent-up emotions on me. She said I should quit racing, that it was a white man's sport, that the black man could be successful in sports only on an individual basis, that I was trying to reach an unrealistic goal. Stop, stop, stop!

After Rose settled down, Lenny knocked on the bedroom door to ask how Tommy was doing. I told him it looked like he wasn't going to pull through. Then Lenny quietly said, "I'll drive the race car for Black American Racers." Hearing that, Rose went ballistic. The neighbors must have heard her up the street. She said she'd divorce me if Lenny was put in a race car, after the state she'd seen Tommy in at St. Francis Hospital.

On Monday afternoon, Ron Hines and I went to the hospital together around 4 p.m. We felt totally helpless looking at Tommy on the life support system. We felt one of his ankles to see how cold it was. We repeated the ritual on Tuesday and Wednesday. Each day we felt one of his ankles. On Wednesday, they were ice cold. Carol called me on Thursday to say Tommy had been removed from life support. "I'll be in touch with you when the funeral arrangements are finalized," she said. I offered to have S. Howard Woodson, the pastor of Shiloh Baptist Church in Trenton, preach the funeral. Carol said again that she didn't need any help from me at all.

At the funeral Jim Young from the Champion Spark Plug Company, Ron Hines, Kenny Wright, and I sat together. It was a strange feeling, being ostracized as we were. I felt like an intruder. The minister started out by saying that he had not met or known Tommy, but he knew Tommy had bought the farm. Then he went on to make the standard religiously correct statements always made at a funeral where the minister doesn't know the deceased. During the minister's nice but bland remarks, my thoughts strayed to the kind of funeral service Reverend Woodson might have conducted. He, at least, had known Tommy slightly and knew what Black American Racers was all about.

After the funeral we journeyed to Nyack, New York, for the burial ceremony. Ron and I had to stand on the edge of the crowd gathered for the internment. I thought at least Ron should have been a pallbearer. The burial site was on top of a hill, in beautiful surroundings. But it was a strange feeling to have to stand at the edge of the internment ceremony like a house slave and observe a group of "corn pone" people gathered under and around the tent while the minister read from the bible.

As Ron and I headed down the hill to our car after the graveside ceremony, he said, "Len, what did you think of the funeral?"

"When we met Tommy he was an upper-middle-class, honorary white man without credentials," I said. "When he went into the ground today, he was an upper-middle-class black man with universal credentials."

We rode back to Mrs. Thompson's house in silence. The strain of the past two weeks was finally taking its toll, and the racial politics surrounding the funeral had added an extra level of stress on both of us.

At the repast, Mrs. Thompson took me aside and asked me what BAR was going to do now. I told her that, like her, I was at a loss. She grabbed my arm and looked me straight in the eye, the way only a battle-weary black mother can do, and said, "You can't stop now. If you do, Tommy will have died in vain. Keep trying." Mrs. Thompson's words touched me so deeply that I got hold of Ron and we quietly left.

Reporters were very sympathetic and supportive about Tommy's tragedy. As most race teams can attest, the motor racing press doesn't concentrate on exposés for news. The entire Eastern Motor Press Association was supportive and I still have a personal note from Ernie Saxton, EMPA's president, in my files. Other names such as, Harry Blaze, Jay Dunn of *The Trenton Times*, Chris Economaki, Bill Shand of *National Speed Sport News*, and Bill Singer, the announcer at Trenton Speedway, come to mind.

Within days after Tommy's funeral, Joe Gerber, president of the Sunoco Race of Champions, called. I relayed to him what Mrs. Thompson had said to me. Joe said that was why he was calling. No matter how bad it gets, said Joe, real racers finish the season. With Joe's encouragement, I called Benny Scott and asked if he was available to enter his car under Black American Racers on 28 October at the Phoenix International Raceway. Benny finished high enough in that race for Black American Racers to maintain its national twelfth-place ranking, last in the points payout. As Joe Gerber predicted, most of the top officials in the USAC and others in the racing community, including Wendell Scott, were glad we hadn't sat out the last race out of self-pity.

Chapter 12
Starting from the Bottom Again, 1979-81

A s 1979 came in, Kenny Wright had quit his involvement in racing. We had been through many tragedies together since we started out racing at Atco Dragway in 1969. Ron, too, said he had to take a break for a while. Except for moral support from friends in the racing community, Black American Racers, Inc. was now me. But just when I thought my motor racing days were finished, a lucky turn of events occurred. During a Democratic party function in Trenton, Albert "Bo" Robinson, who later became a highly visible Trenton city councilman, casually mentioned to me that his son Albie was interested in driving a race car. "Tell him to come around and see me," I said.

After several meetings with Albie, I told him BAR was willing to try him in dirt track racing. Flemington Fairgrounds, only thirty minutes away, was the dirt track nearest Trenton. After I was certain Albie was serious about learning to drive a race car, I contacted Les Katona, a local racing hero who had just opened Lawrence Engineering, primarily a supplier of dirt track racing parts. After meeting with Les and his daughter Gloria, who also aspired to be a race car driver, I agreed to rent Les's K3 Jr. Sportsman dirt car, provided he would maintain the car and coach Albie. Working with Les and Gloria on and off the track was like working with Grant King years earlier. We never had any serious disagreements, and under Les's tutoring Albie's driving skills improved each week. Also, Les and

Gloria's participation with BAR nearly eliminated racial hostilities at the track.

Albie was entered in the Rookie Sportsman Series, a class for beginning drivers at Flemington Speedway. Les and Gloria met us at the track each Saturday night during the rookie season, which ran until 14 July, after which the rookies ran with the experienced dirt track Sportsman racers. This was an excellent training system, allowing drivers new to racing to learn the track lines and running wheel-to-wheel first, without having to learn how to race while running against experienced racers and causing needless crashes and mishaps.

Les started Albie in his K3 Jr. on 2 June. We had to start racing six weeks into the season because Les and Gloria were busy opening their new business, and I had to establish a personal racing budget that I knew I could live with without owing money to Les at the end of the season.

On that day, Les and I started Albie in Sportsman heat race 1, after practicing all afternoon. Because the gear shift lever was located between his legs, shifting gears was awkward at first for Albie. To our surprise, against more experienced drivers he went from twelfth in heat race 1 to sixth at the finish. Encouraged, we entered him in heat race 2. He started in fourteenth place: dead last, to gain more track experience. He finished eighth. In the Sportsman feature race, he started twentieth out of thirty cars **and was** black-flagged halfway through for running too slow. Now fatigued and racing against much more experienced drivers, Albie was beginning to slow down almost one second per lap, which could lead to a serious crash when the leaders began lapping the field late in the race. After the Sportsman feature was over, Les, Gloria and I huddled in the infield discussing Albie's driving potential. We concluded that he was coachable. What we liked best about his driving that night was his patience.

Early the next week I went exuberantly to his father's office at United Progress, Inc. (UPI), Trenton's local poverty program organization. Bo Robinson was Trenton's most colorful political character from the late 1960s to the early 1990s. He took great pride in the respect "street people" gave him. He took even greater pride in socializing with street people when time permitted. I discussed with Bo both Albie's progress and his potential. I asked him to come out and support him on Saturday nights, whenever he had spare time. Leaning way back in his chair, Bo told me he had me at the track to support his son. Furthermore, he said, he wasn't going up to Flemington and sit in the grandstand with a bunch of northern rednecks. "I trust you," he said. "You take care of Albie."

As I drove away from the UPI office, I couldn't help wondering how a black leader like Bo Robinson could spend so much quality time with the street people and none with his own son. I immediately called Albie's mother, Jane Robinson, and later met with her to explain what we were doing at Flemington. She was very supportive. Her main concern was about the possibility that Albie might be injured. She was especially concerned because Tommy Thompson's death was still fresh in her mind. Jane showed up at every race, sometimes with Albie's sister, Kim, who also was very supportive. I was very disappointed with Bo, because I could not imagine putting socializing with street people ahead of supporting one's own family. To know why he did this, you had to know Bo personally.

For the next three weeks, BAR entered Albie in the rookie feature races. He started twenty-seventh, twenty-eighth, and twenty-eighth. He worked his way up through the field each week and finished thirteenth, eleventh and eighteenth. On 30 June Albie started fourteenth, in the middle of the field for the first time in the season. He finished eleventh. Then, on 7 July, he started sixteenth and finished seventh.

Les decided to go all out and improve the suspension setup and go over the motor. The improvements made a big difference. On 14 July, Albie started seventh in the rookie feature, but racing luck turned against him. He got caught in a big pileup in the front pack, and though it wasn't his fault, the car was unable to continue. When he got out of the car on the first turn and took off his helmet in typical race driver disgust, the fans noticed for the first time that he was black. A small group began to heckle him and call him a "dumb-ass nigger." Like a knight of King Arthur's Round Table, Albie bowed in jest and walked back to the pits. The hecklers were left confused and speechless. Albie's mother, who was sitting in the stands nearby, thought he had handled the situation very well, without becoming combative. That night I was glad Bo hadn't been at the race; he would have single-handedly started a riot.

Les, Gloria, and I were satisfied with Albie's progress. His mother was happy he had not gotten hurt nor had to face continuous racial remarks from the fans. But after the rookie series concluded on that day, Albie suddenly decided he was going to move to Texas. Unbeknownst to him, he was part of the first wave of young blacks to migrate back to the South and Southwest because they thought there were more employment opportunities there than in Trenton. I was totally disappointed that Albie was leaving. When I asked why he was moving to Texas, he said he was going to get a mechanic's job. Before he migrated to Texas, he bought the K3 Jr. dirt Sportsman. In 1997 he sold it, after keeping it in storage for fifteen years. Years later he moved back to Trenton and tried to become a male model.

As soon as Albie exited the scene, Bruce Driver, then twenty years old, immediately contacted me to ask if he could drive the car. I knew several of his uncles, including Sonny Driver, so Bruce wasn't a complete stranger to me. He had been raised around go-karts and race cars all his life. His father, Corky, was one of only a few blacks ever to hold a season ticket at the Flemington Speedway.

When Bruce came to my office for our first meeting, he was very impressive. He was outgoing and radiant, the right age, in excellent physical condition, and determined to drive for Black American Racers. The meeting was the beginning of a love-hate relationship that lasted through the next two racing seasons. I immediately contacted Les Katona and asked him to put Bruce in the K3 Jr. for the last race of the season. Bruce drove the last race of the small-block Modified division at Flemington without driving over his head or causing any problems on the track.

We had a hunch that Bruce was going to be a better-than-average driver. So I went into high gear and touched base with Humpy Wheeler at the Charlotte Motor Speedway, who said, "Direct your efforts from now on towards NASCAR. That is where motorsports is going to explode over the next twenty years." Wendell Scott agreed. Jim Young at Champion said his company would help with sponsorship, spark plugs, and related parts. Leo Mehl of Goodyear was glad I hadn't given up on my dream and said he'd supply tires. Valvoline agreed to supply oil and lubricants. If Champion, Goodyear, and Valvoline had turned their backs on me, Black American Racers would not have been able to mount a winning effort in 1980.

Rose and I owned a garage beneath our office building in downtown Trenton, so space wasn't a problem. It was large enough to work on one car. Bruce found an almost-new AMC Gremlin dirt track chassis that conformed to Flemington's Sportsman class specifications. After buying the car, trailer, and spare parts as a package, Bruce and I worked out a deal with Frank Mangone, owner of Central Jersey Welding, to update the car. Mangone had built the car in the first place. His chassis was competitive at the Flemington, East Windsor, and Bridgeport, New Jersey dirt tracks.

While I was in the process of organizing the team again for a serious effort on the local level, I met and discussed both my short-term and long-range plans with my friend and confidant Ron Hines. We needed him to maintain the motor at the track every week. Ron Whitney and Ron Whitney, Jr., who continued their very close relationship with me, were always comfortable with the fact that Ron Hines was maintaining the motors they built for the team, so they were on board.

Except for watching Albie race several times in 1979, Ron Hines sat out the entire year. Tommy's death affected Ron almost as deeply as it had Tommy's family. Tommy was the second black driver he had worked with to die in the past ten years; the first had been Byron Milton, a personal friend who had died in a crash in the early 1970s at the U.S. 30 Drag Strip in Gary, Indiana. By 1980, Ron had already visited Tommy's grave twice. He put Tommy's steering wheel from his fatal crash over his fireplace mantle, where he could see it each day. For my part, I put Tommy's picture in a red frame and hung it over my desk at home, where it remains today. Although other racing pictures have been rearranged over the years, Tommy's picture has not been moved from its original spot.

After a month of much discussion, Ron Hines agreed to work with the dirt track effort at Flemington every weekend during the 1980 season and to maintain the motor between races. Bruce did not finish the first two rookie races, because he tried to perform too many race preparation tasks himself. After failing to finish the second rookie race, he had me meet Mark Blackwell, a white childhood friend of his. Mark was the eldest son of a wealthy family and an avid dirt track and motor racing enthusiast. He had a basic knowledge of race car setups, motors, and finances, and he understood Black American Racers' goals. He blended in well with the team. His brother, Tommy, also helped out on occasion.

After having been in the higher echelons of racing, running in local races was a piece of cake because of the experience, resources, and finances available to the team. First, Ron Whitney found a 1968 camshaft configuration that was perfect for Flemington's 5/8-mile track. Second, Goodyear supplied tires so we could put on four fresh ones each week. Third, thanks to Frank, Mark, and Bruce, the chassis worked well on the track each week. Ron Hines took care of the motor like a doting parent would take care of a baby.

Success came quickly. Bruce won the rookie main event at Flemington Speedway on 10 May 1980, leading for almost the entire race. Two weeks later, he made dirt track history by becoming the first black driver to record two wins at the track. This feat prompted me to call Bobby Merritt, a cinematographer and friend who had traveled with me from one racetrack to another since 1976. I told him we needed to develop a video of Bruce for sponsorship-bid presentations.

Bobby began coming from New York City to Flemington most Saturday nights to take video footage of Bruce. Ace Lane, Jr., the son of one of the most famous race car photographers who ever lived—and black—took the still pictures. When Bobby and his assistant appeared on the scene one Saturday night, I noticed Bruce seemed very uncomfortable but never said anything. I didn't realize it at the time, but this was the beginning of our love-hate relationship.

On 30 May 1980, Bruce won his third rookie feature of the season, bringing the crowd to its feet by diving under the race leader with a strong inside move. Bill Singer, the regular track announcer at Flemington, was ecstatic over the public address system. He gave Bruce, Black American Racers, and everyone connected with the team great postrace coverage in the booth and down in the winner's circle. The team was in the clouds—but I kept sensing that something was amiss.

On the way home I told Lenny, who often sat in the fourth turn stands by himself when I was in the pits, that I knew what was wrong. When being interviewed by Bill Singer or Paul Kuhl, the track owner, Bruce never uttered the words "Black American Racers." I also noticed that Bruce was very uncomfortable if more than two blacks were around him at any one time. Later Mark, Bobby, and Ron Hines all made the same observations independently.

The following Saturday Bruce, Ron, and I were set to go to the Flemington Speedway, when Bruce and I got into the worst disagreement over blackness that I've ever had with another black person—as intense as the one-time feud between Judge Leon Higginbotham and Justice Clarence Thomas. As we were getting ready to load the car up, Bruce lashed out about the Black American Racers logo on the car. He felt that as a person he was beyond Black American Racers, Inc. Furthermore, he felt he didn't need to be identified with Black American Racers anymore because, halfway through his first racing season, he had already won three races. He finished by saying he didn't want Bobby Merritt around him taking pictures.

Ron and I both were in shock over Bruce's outburst. Quickly recovering, I said, "We are not racing today."

"I am going to race, because I have a chance to win the rookie championship," said Bruce.

I went to the front of the garage and slammed the overhead door down so hard that one of the hinges broke, then locked the door, and went around to the front of the building, where Bruce and Ron were standing by the trailer. As I approached Bruce, he continued to lash out at me uninhibitedly. When he paused for a minute, I said again, "We're not racing today."

He said that he was becoming one of the best dirt track drivers in New Jersey and didn't need me. He didn't relate to black people, he said, because he was really white on the inside. "We're going to lose any chance at the rookie championship!" he protested.

"Jackie Robinson would turn over in his grave if I went to the track with you today," I said.

"He didn't understand what I was getting at."

"That's the point."

By this time, the telephone was ringing. The track office wanted to know what had happened. I said we weren't racing that day. Mark Blackwell wanted to know what had happened. I told him in general terms about my conversation with Bruce. "Oh shit," he said, and got off the phone. It took all week for both of us to calm down.

By 21 June, the last week of the rookie series, the love side of our love-hate relationship surfaced again. Bruce won the final rookie feature with a vengeance, though we lost the rookie championship. Bruce very graciously congratulated Darryl Carmen, the rookie points champion, during the winner's circle celebration, with both of them holding the checkered flag.

Up to this point, Black American Racers had no formal contract with Bruce. I decided that one would have to be drawn up, or we'd have to stop racing for the rest of the year. Bruce's arrogance and demeanor were leading to serious problems. When I informed Bruce that I had a contract for him and/or his selected legal counsel to review, he showed up with his father Corky. Corky was typical of what black sports agents in all sports have to face endlessly. He was like NBA star Dennis Rodman's father: one who is never helping when he should be, but shows off and acts supercaring in public for the purpose of getting on board and superficially sharing only in his son's success. Bruce's mother was the exact opposite. She bought his uniform and other driver accessories for him from time to time.

Corky's review of the contract was an insult to my intelligence. After listening to him for several minutes, I immediately surmised how Bruce had acquired his manchild attitude. Also disturbing was the way his father attacked me in a way he would never have attacked a white team owner in the same situation. If I had been white, he would most likely have made Bruce sign the contract without review and left the meeting with a watermelon grin. I walked out of the meeting and returned to my office, leaving Ron to go over the contract provisions. Ron reviewed the contract, and Bruce signed it, but not before Ron said Bruce could hire his own lawyer to review it. Bruce's father declined; it would cost them money. So, we got back to racing.

Bruce's success on the track and his warm personality by now had attracted a number of female admirers, both single and married. One white, upper-middle-class, snotty Princeton young woman took a serious liking to Bruce. It quickly became evident that she had never had any real exposure to black people like Ron, Bobby, Lenny, and me. She was somewhat more comfortable with Mark Blackwell, until she found she couldn't turn Mark against Ron or me. She poisoned Bruce's mind against me all season, telling him behind my back that he didn't need me, that I was a jerk, that I had made him lose the rookie championship, and so on. What she didn't realize was that the people she confided in didn't like her dating a black man. As a result, only Bruce ever really believed her negative comments about me.

Becoming an overnight local racing personality made Bruce, in his mind, bigger than the team itself. He thought he could do as he pleased. He had been told before the season started that all racing parts bought for the team had to be approved beforehand by me. One day, he decided to order $4000 worth of parts on his own from Les and Gloria Katona. When they order on their own, many drivers order too many parts. Bruce was no exception. Les asked Bruce if I had given him permission to order for Black American Racers. Bruce said no. Then he signed for the parts personally and promised Les that he would pay for them. But he didn't. About forty-five days later, Les filed papers at the Mercer County Courthouse for collection. The sheriff started chasing Bruce down for the money. Since he couldn't pay the bill, he offered his share of the car's ownership to Mark if he paid the bill in full. Mark paid the $4000 and became part owner of the car. Bruce's girlfriend now hated me even more.

Mark becoming part owner of the car led to a strategy meeting at his garage in Pennington, which Bruce refused to attend. In addition to Mark and me, Lenny attended the meeting. In the best interest of the team, we decided that Mark would deal with Bruce on and off the track, and I would take care of everything else, including budgets, sponsors, public relations, and monitoring the racial climate at the track, which from week to week was fair at best.

Mark's full commitment to putting Bruce in the winner's circle and keeping harmony on the team paid off on 7 August 1980 the day that Bruce Driver, for the first time in his life, really knew what black men have to put up with at the worst possible moments in America. At the drivers' meeting before the 100-lap Sportsman feature race, it was announced that all yellow caution laps would count. (At the weekly races, yellows didn't count.) If yellow laps were not counted and it was a bad crash night, the 100-lap feature would not conclude until the wee hours of the morning. This, in turn, would be costly to the track and cause fans with children to leave before the race was finished.

This was the biggest dirt track race of the season in New Jersey. The race was for the state championship, plus a guaranteed starting position in the nationally recognized Sportsman race held at the New York State Fairgrounds in Syracuse on Sunday, 12 October. This was a high-stakes race. All of New Jersey's best Sportsman racers and hotshoe invaders from tracks all over the Northeast started the race before a sellout crowd.

Mark and Ron Hines had the car ready to go with an excellent pit crew that included Mark's brother Tommy. Ron Whitney had freshened the motor, and the 1968 cam configuration was still in the motor. Bruce's racing focus was 100 percent plus. Rose, Lenny, a number of our family friends, and Bruce's father were in attendance and anxiously awaiting the start of the race. It began at a torrid pace. On the third lap Billy Cannon, who was vying for the track's point title with another local hard charger named Jimmy Brenn, got into an early mishap on the third lap. Cannon's car was so badly damaged he quickly lost three laps, and when he finally exited the pits his motor was sour.

As the race wore on, Bruce worked his way up through the field the same way A.J. Foyt had done years before in a race at the Reading Fairgrounds. The only difference between Foyt and Bruce was that Foyt could pass cars on both the inside and outside grooves with the same power. Bruce passed only on the inside, even when he had the power and an outside groove to work with. I made a mental note of the difference for future reference.

With four laps to go, Bruce took the lead. Several hundred of his fans started yelling, "Bruce, Bruce." With three laps to go Bruce didn't want to tax the motor or spin out, so he let Billy Cannon by because, according to the team's scoring, Cannon was at least one or two laps down. When the checkered flag came out Bruce wheeled his car into the winner's circle, with all of us heading there to congratulate him on his great victory. Billy Cannon wheeled his car into the pits and started to get out of the car. What followed was a repeat of what Wendell Scott had endured at a NASCAR race in Florida in 1963.

As the celebration was about to begin, Billy was told to drive his car into the winner's circle, because he was the winner. Confusion set in. Neither Bruce nor Billy knew what was going on. Mark and I did. I left the winner's circle looking for Paul Kuhl, the track promoter. Mark went running up to the scorer's booth looking for Al Tasnady, Kuhl's right-hand man. He found Tasnady on the roof by himself, looking out over the track with his arms folded.

"What's going on here!?" yelled Mark.

"Mark," replied Tasnady, "we ain't sending no nigger to Syracuse to represent our track."

Mark later told me it was the first time in his life that he really knew how badly blacks could be treated based solely on race. After a short tussle, with Mark almost shoving Tasnady off the roof, Mark rushed into the scorer's booth. When he opened the door, he saw the scorers erasing the charts and doctoring the results. With the stroke of an eraser, Al Tasnady had put Bruce's racing career back five years.

The track officials were smooth in committing racial fraud. First, most of the officials in the winner's circle really didn't know what had transpired. They just did what they were told. When I spoke with Paul Kuhl, he claimed he had taken the scorer's results verbally. I still insisted that Cannon had not won the race. Kuhl just politely let me ventilate and continued on with the winner's circle ceremony.

While the ceremony was in progress one of the officials told Mark, who now had returned to the winner's circle, to keep his driver away from the track ceremonies. When the officials finally announced Billy Cannon as the winner, many of the fans threw beer cans and drinking cups onto the track and booed for several minutes. Meanwhile, Bruce was standing on the back of a competitor's truck yelling, "I've been cheated!" with a growing crowd around him chanting, "Bruce, Bruce."

I told Mark to load the car up and to take Bruce home. In the parking lot behind the fourth turn grandstands, our friend Jack Tannenbaum asked me what I was going to do. "I don't think I'm going to do anything," I said. Jack, who had known me for fifteen years, was taken aback. I explained: "If it was Wendell Scott, Benny Scott, Tommy Thompson, Coyle Peek, Kenny Wright, or Alex Baynard, Flemington would have to bring me to my knees or I, with assistance from the black civil rights hierarchy, would bring Flemington Fairgrounds to its knees. Bruce has no idea of the gravity of what happened tonight, because he has no understanding of racial politics. I would hate to see the civil rights community waste its efforts defending a black driver who would turn his back on them as soon as the case was settled." We all went home feeling totally disgusted, fatigued, and racially violated. Several local reporters were brave enough to tell the truth in their columns the next week.

For his part, Bruce was thoroughly upset. Neither I nor Ron Hines nor Mark Blackwell could truly reach out to him. Bruce was in the same state as a fourteen-year-old having motion sickness without knowing the real reason why. To Lenny and Ron, I remarked that it was a pity to see a black man not really understanding why he was upset over a serious racial incident. Bruce was so beside himself about being robbed of the New Jersey State Championship that he drove too aggressively and erratically the next week and crashed the car.

By 5 September, Bruce had settled down and won his first Sportsman race at East Windsor Speedway. He won the race on the last lap, bringing the crowd to its feet. Ron Hines, Mark, Lenny, and I always looked forward to going to East Windsor Speedway because it was a racially neutral track. The fans there were from the Trenton area's white middle and upper-middle-class. A good number of state civil service workers and their families attended the races, along with teachers, small business owners, contractors, and volunteer firemen. We never heard Bruce or anyone being called a nigger, and the track officials treated Bruce and the team fairly at all times.

Despite the love-hate relationship that developed between me and Bruce, and the steady diet of racism encountered at the Flemington Fairgrounds that year, he was just short of sensational for a rookie driver. Bruce won five feature races and built a solid fan base.

But another incident also confused him. Mark's father was working on getting a zoning variance through Pennington's local zoning board. One night during this process, Bruce drove the race car at full bore out of the Blackwells' garage complex and down the side street beside their property. Local residents jammed the police station's switchboard with complaints about the deafening noise. The next week, the board turned down Mr. Blackwell's request for a zoning variance, referring to the incident in its ruling. In a fit of rage, Mr. Blackwell yelled out in the meeting, with about fifty residents in attendance, "That fuckin' nigger driving a race car down the street cost me $35,000!" Mr. Blackwell later apologized to me, after I read his remarks in the local newspaper. Bruce stayed out of Mr. Blackwell's line of sight for several months afterwards.

Despite Bruce's antics, Mark and I continued to improve the car during the winter months, and Ron Whitney built a new motor that proved itself in the 1981 season. Mark and I discussed everything we wanted to accomplish that year. We decided to run East Windsor Speedway on Friday nights and Flemington on Saturday nights, the same as in 1980.

The only blowup over the winter was when Bruce called the Champion Spark Plug Company behind my back and said he wanted the sponsorship transferred to his name. This caused an upheaval. Champion wanted to know if Black American Racers had gone out of business. Was Bruce now driver and team manager? After several telephone conversations, I got the sponsorship support back on track for 1981. Bruce "snipping" me behind my back with the team's most loyal sponsor was completely disloyal and intensified the hate side of our relationship even more.

The 1981 team operated out of Mark Blackwell's garage in Pennington, New Jersey. In addition to his brother Tommy and Ron Hines, Mark enlisted Todd Randson and Johnny Begnosky as regular crew members. Everyone worked together exceptionally well on and off the track. This team, with Bruce driving, went to the winner's circle five times that season. I now sat in the stands by myself, because Lenny was away at Morehouse College in Atlanta.

Flemington's racial incidents continued. The first one occurred on the day Bruce won his second Sportsman feature. When Bruce and the team went to the winner's circle, a group of toughs in the covered grandstand yelled out, "Send that nigger home! We don't want to see him in the winner's circle any more this year! He's won too many races already!" Hearing what they said, Bruce bent over in the winner's circle with the checkered flag in his hand pointed to his posterior and yelled, "Kiss my black ass!" The toughs lurched from their seats, ran down the aisle, and started climbing the tall fence in front of the covered grandstands, yelling, "Nigger, we're gonna kick your ass first!" The police had to pull them off the fence while the victory ceremony was quickly completed. Many fans clapped when the toughs were pulled off the fence. Mark loaded up our equipment as quickly as possible and got Bruce off of the track.

The second major incident occurred in the summer. Lenny was surrounded by a large group of backmarkers, relatives, and friends who had been racing at Flemington for years and had never won a race. After Bruce won the feature, they surrounded Lenny in the open grandstands in the fourth turn and said, "You niggers need to go back to Trenton. We're tired of that nigger driver of yours winning here."

Although Les Katona was not officially working with the team in 1981, he continuously discussed with me Bruce's early apexing, that is turning too early in the turns. Early in the season, I called Skip Barber to arrange for Bruce to attend Skip's driver's school. After several phone conversations, we decided to send Bruce to Lime Rock, Connecticut, to attend the three-day racing school held there periodically. The head teacher at the location was Bruce MacInnes, with whom I had had an excellent relationship since the early 1970s. I always tell people that Bruce MacInnes is the only driver I've ever seen on the track who could make a Formula Ford sound like it had an automatic transmission.

Ron Hines, Bruce, and I traveled to Lime Rock together for a place that Ron and I always loved to visit. Both Benny Scott and Tommy Thompson had had excellent finishes at the track in the 1970s. A group of professional, semiprofessional, and amateur drivers, and several racing school specialists, showed up for the three-day driving course.

Bruce's real knowledge of race car driving became apparent

immediately. He didn't concentrate or take heed to the different driving techniques that MacInnes and his assistants demonstrated on the track or in the classroom. Realizing what was happening, I asked MacInnes to lend me a car. With Skip Barber's okay, I began participating in the school's racing activities. I was forty-seven years old at the time, and at the conclusion of the three days, I was actually driving better overall than Bruce. This result confirmed my worst fears: Bruce was solely an oval track racer, with a tendency to early apex.

On the way back to New Jersey, I began a discussion with Bruce about his overall potential to go to the Daytona 500 or the Indy 500. I centered my comments on his being a black driver accomplishing these goals. But, before we could even begin to discuss driving a race car at the higher levels of racing, I felt the racial aspect had to be addressed.

"You have the problem, under your own admission, that you are really a white man with a brown skin," I said. "I understand your point of view. But the rowdy fans at Flemington Speedway see you as a 'nigger.' Using the premise that you are black in a white man's sport, that means you will be judged by a double standard. You have to be almost as good a driver as Mario Andretti or Dan Gurney to be successful in motor racing. You have to be able to turn left, turn right, go uphill and downhill. In short, be a complete driver. Benny Scott and Tommy Thompson could do all these things, and neither ever attended a driving school. Being a local driving hero is nothing compared to being a national driving hero."

Later, with Mark Blackwell, Les Katona, auto racing promoter Joe Gerber, and Wendell Scott I discussed where I thought Bruce's potential might lie in the future. With a lot of work, I said, he had the potential to run America's short tracks with the best hotshoes in the country. It would take a miracle for him to run the superspeedways and the major road courses and eventually win races at that level, because he had a tendency to turn his car into the turns on the racetrack too early.

The most positive change at Flemington Speedway in 1981 was having free access to the Purple Room, a VIP refuge that Paul Kuhl had set up for track insiders. The top team owners and sponsors got into the Purple Room by invitation only. Lenny and I looked forward to going there after the races because they had excellent food and all you could eat. Also, track insiders got to know us as human beings instead of as a bunch of "monkeys" coming to the track making the white drivers and teams look bad.

As the season wound down, a young man from the New Jersey shore area approached either Mark Blackwell or me every Saturday night at Flemington, wanting to buy our race car. Mark and I, for a number of reasons, were seriously thinking about buying a car from Grant King in Indianapolis for the next season. At the end of the '81 season I asked Grant to quote Black American Racers a price for a dirt Sportsman racer. During the season Grant had given Mark excellent setup tips, and a car Grant had sold to Ken Brenn, Jr., a fellow racer, turned out to be a winner at Flemington.

At the end of the '81 season the young man, Steve, made us an offer we couldn't refuse. When we accepted, Steve drove his truck and trailer to Mark's garage to pick up the car. That same night, Bruce came by the garage and noticed the car wasn't there. When Mark said we had just sold it, Bruce went into a rage. He accused Mark and me of leaving him high and dry with no ride for 1982, and he stormed out of the garage. Bruce did not speak to Mark for three years, though they lived in the same town.

Bruce called me the next day, still in a rage, accusing me of conspiring with Mark to leave him without a ride. Before I could explain our plans for 1982, Bruce began screaming through the telephone, using every curse word known to man and trying to humiliate me in the process. At one point I had to hold the telephone away from my ear, Bruce was yelling so loud. After Bruce hung up, I called Grant King and canceled the order for the new car.

Chapter 13
Bad Times, 1982-88

I n the early 1980s, dark financial clouds began to appear throughout the black business community nationwide. According to a Democratic holdover I knew who still worked in the Reagan White House, there was a big push to decimate the minority business programs and the labor unions. Furthermore, the "soft" manpower consultant projects in which I participated at the departments of Labor and Housing and Urban Development would be reduced to minuscule levels.

In 1981, my company, Dynamic Programs, Inc., was grossing $6 million per year. By 1984, it was grossing less than $1 million a year. As a result, I had to liquidate all my racing possessions except my complete set of *Automobile Quarterly* books. I could have gotten at least $2000 for the set, but I was determined to hold on to it. Ron Hines took all my vintage car parts, rare car books, tools, and equipment to the automobile flea markets in New Jersey during the year. Everything eventually sold except my rare Grand Prix chassis construction book, because I refused to accept less than $150 for it.

In an attempt to stop the continuous flow of red ink at Dynamic Programs, Inc., I tried to obtain a large telecommunications contract in Lagos, Nigeria, through, my friend Joe Bear, who was an economist and well connected to Nigerian officials. With the help of Gogo Hassan, a Nigerian computer consultant and ex-IBM employee in London, we set our sights on winning the $10 million contract to computerize all the personnel records at the national telecommunications agency. Hassan had seen Bruce Driver race at the East Windsor Speedway in 1981 and took a personal interest in my quest to build a competitive black-owned race team. But before we could consummate the contract, some unknown persons blew up the agency's high-rise building in Lagos one night to conceal book-keeping and personnel irregularities. If we had completed the contract, there would have been enough profit built in to continue racing and clean up all my mounting debt.

During the severe business downturn, Lenny graduated from Morehouse College and Stephanie entered Howard University. My money was so depleted that I had to go through my contacts in Sigma Pi Phi fraternity. At the time it was America's top black male secret organization. Every member was highly successful in his chosen field. One member had worked with Robert Oppenheimer on the Manhattan Project—the making of the atomic bomb. Another member and personal friend was Colin Powell's mentor in the U.S. Army. In certain circles we were unofficially dubbed W.E.B. Dubois's talented tenth. My contacts assisted me in briefly delaying both children's tuition payments. They allowed me to pay when I could, which Rose and I eventually did to the last penny. Friends voluntarily came to the rescue during this period. John Wilks, a leading black Republican; James Blow, Hamilton Bowser, Bobby Bryant, Joe Britt, Jim Felton, Jim Jackson, Kerry Kirkland, Herb Riley, Fred Vereen, Jr., and others helped me survive by providing me with contracts or free office space for several years. Walter P. Lomax, Jr., M.D., the best friend a person could ever have, and William Losch, senior vice president of Hunterdon National Bank, kept me going through the difficult financial times. Tommy Matthews, his father Joe, Sr., and his brother Joe, Jr., of M & M Sunoco in Washington Crossing, Pennsylvania, allowed me to run up gas and repair bills for six months at a time. Senator Wynona Lipman, through her influence in the New Jersey legislature, was instrumental in keeping my business telephone service on during my darkest days, while Ernest Green contacted a number of influential blacks to see if they would participate in keeping the racing project alive.

In the midst of the financial chaos facing me, Lenny started taking flying lessons, because he had to release his pent-up desire to drive race cars. He had been introduced to airplanes when one Sunday afternoon in 1975, I took him along with me to Mercer County Airport in New Jersey to make a speech about blacks in motor racing before the local chapter of Negro Airmen International. Their president, Paul Mitnaugh, was an advocate for black participation in the aviation industry. Lenny had been taken that day to the twelve airplanes that landed, flown by black pilots and co-pilots, several of them being among the renown Tuskegee Airmen. Unknown to me, Lenny asked a pilot named Bob where he could take flying lessons. Bob told him to schedule an introductory flying lesson with him at Trenton-Robbinsville Airport.

I thought that Lenny, being just fourteen, would be somewhat passive during the introductory lesson. I was completely wrong. Bob, after getting the Cessna 150 airborne, let Lenny take the controls for a minute. With the wings dipping, Lenny flew the plane like a grasshopper in the air. He didn't want to give up the controls and hated to come down. When Bob got out of the cockpit he said, "Both the Tuskegee Airmen and the Negro Airmen are going to be proud of him someday. Don't kill his urge to fly."

We were very excited on the way home. When I told Rose what had happened, she said Lenny had to concentrate on his school work, and she didn't want her only son to get killed flying an airplane. After Tommy's death at the Trenton Speedway in 1978, she had become even more adamantly against Lenny taking up flying. It wasn't until his last year at Morehouse that Lenny began secretly taking flying lessons at the Peachtree Dekalb Airport in Atlanta. I was the only person who knew about it. We didn't tell his mother until two years later, when I took her and his sister to the Peachtree Dekalb Airport to see him demonstrate his skills. Although Rose had fought hard to keep him from flying, she was nevertheless proud of his accomplishments and fully expected him to become an excellent pilot.

When Lenny graduated from Morehouse, he returned home to begin his pilot's career. Lenny and his friend Arnold Purnsley worked their way up through the commercial pilot ranks, although they were assigned the worst routes and schedules more often than the white pilots. What Arnold and Lenny put up with would have made most blacks in comparable situations quit. They used me as a sounding board on how to cope with the racism they faced. When Arnold temporarily dropped out of aviation out of frustration, I introduced Lenny to Jim Brame, one of the first black top-gun naval air fighter pilots and a commercial airline captain, and retired General James Hamlet, one of the best combat-in-arms generals and infantry soldiers who ever lived. General Hamlet had fought side by side with Vernon Baker, the black Congressional Medal of Honor winner, and was an Aviation Hall of Famer and mentor to General Colin Powell. Lenny also received wise counsel from Lee Archer, a renowned World War II P-51 Tuskegee Airman fighter pilot.

Jim Brame taught Lenny the path a black pilot must take to fly for a major commercial airline as well as the fine art of flying. General Hamlet instilled in Lenny the need to aim for perfection and reminded him that when he had accomplished his goal, he must not turn his back on black people. The general expected him to teach and to mentor other black pilots in the future. Lee Archer taught Lenny to fly the plane to the ground, especially if it's propeller driven, not to panic, and never to give up. "White folks think blacks are always scared, as depicted in television commercials," he told Lenny. "Never give in to this stereotype."

Implementing their advice, Lenny became more than qualified to apply for a commercial pilot's slot at a major airline. He took the test—and was notified that he had failed. I knew immediately that something was amiss. I sought out Leroy Jenkins, a black attorney in Washington, D.C., who knew all the civil rights laws. Leroy informed Lenny that twenty-four black pilots had filed a class action suit against the airline for blatant discrimination. In the 1970s and early 1980s, most black pilots were hired by Federal Express and United Parcel Service, because they flew cargo only and at night. There was an unwritten understanding within the airline industry that black pilots were not to be involved with flying white passengers, because of their presumed incompetence flying sophisticated aircraft and also because, if hired, they would be working in close quarters with white female flight attendants.

Knowing I was in financial straits, Leroy recommended that I have Lenny join the class action suit winding its way through the Equal Employment Opportunities Commission (EEOC). Lenny agreed to this plan of attack. When the class action suit reached the office of the commission chairman, it was thrown out. Lenny and I were told that the chairman disapproved of the black pilots using a government agency for legal redress, and that he felt that, individually or collectively, the pilots should sue the airline directly. The chairman's name was Clarence Thomas.

I immediately called John Wilks, the former deputy assistant secretary of labor in the Nixon administration and author of a series of affirmative action regulations, whose opinion I held in high regard. I asked him whether he knew Clarence Thomas and where he had come from. "He's a black man that got in the short line," said John, meaning that Thomas had joined the far-right wing of the Republican party because there were so few blacks there that he would be in the short line for recognition and choice political appointments.

Several days later, after talking over the situation with Lenny, I called Leroy Jenkins to tell him that Lenny would file suit against the airline individually, even at the risk of being blackballed, and to ask for the names of the other pilots in the class action suit. Leroy gave me the names, and Lenny and I called them, splitting the list in half. We told them that if they each contributed $500 toward Leroy's attorney's fees, I would pay the remainder. All declined outright. Some were afraid of being blackballed from the airline industry for life. Others thought the EEOC should fight their battles. A small group even said they were not going to spend one dime of their own money to sue the airline, because they had other things to do with their money. But having grown up in the pre-Dr. Martin Luther King, Jr. era, I was used to forging ahead on what was right, even if I had to stand alone. It did not matter whether Clarence Thomas closed off an easier path of legal redress.

Part of Leroy's strategy was to bring Lenny's predicament to the attention of Congresswoman Cardiss Collins, chairwoman of a transportation subcommittee that had oversight over the airline industry. She assigned her chief counsel, a hotshot black attorney named Warner Sessions, to meet with us.

As the appointment neared I was flat broke, no cash at all. We had to take Amtrak to Union Station in Washington, D.C. Lenny had enough money for one round-trip ticket on the regular train, plus a large wine bottle full of loose coins. He obtained coin wrappers from the bank and wrapped the coins into rolls, which took almost four hours. After turning the wrapped coins in at the local bank, we had just enough money for one more ticket. We also learned from this experience that a large wine bottle holds about sixty dollars' worth of coins.

The day arrived for us to visit Congresswoman Collins's office. We drove to Trenton to catch the train. I knew of a side street where we could park to avoid paying for space at one of the lots surrounding the train station. We had no money for food, so we had to pretend not to be hungry; a tough thing for me to do, but no problem for Lenny because he never ate much of anything.

When we exited Union Station, we walked across the street and started up the open green space in the direction of the Capitol building. Halfway there, my knee gave out on me. I took one of the horse pills that Joseph Torg, M.D., the Philadelphia Eagles team surgeon, had given me for a badly swollen knee and, with my arm around Lenny's shoulder for support, continued on toward the Capitol in great pain, doing my best to mask it so as not to alarm Lenny. As I saw the flag waving over the Capitol building, I said to myself that it was flying that day for Lenny and the other black pilots, beginning with the Tuskegee Airmen. My parents' example had taught me that neither Clarence Thomas nor the mightiest airline in the world was going to deny Lenny employment solely on the basis of race.

We went to the wrong congressional office building. As a result, we had to walk another long block and down several long corridors to Congresswoman Collins's office, where Warner Sessions and Leroy Jenkins were waiting. Sessions led us down into the bowels of the building. When I sat down, Warner jokingly mentioned that I was sitting in the same chair that Oliver North had sat in during his congressional interrogation. Before he could finish I jumped up, pain or no pain, and moved to a different chair. The last thing I needed was bad luck rubbing off on me.

After an extremely productive strategy meeting, we were directed to the underground tram that ran between the congressional buildings. The tram cut down our walk back to Union Station considerably. Late that evening we arrived back in Trenton, hungry but full of hope.

After two years of legal battles, Leroy Jenkins won the case. Lenny had passed the flight test, but it had been thrown away. The alleged culprits had supposed that, like most black applicants, Lenny would be intimidated by a major airline's legal department and wouldn't contest the rejection letter. During the legal battle, I had to sell my prize 1965 Volvo PV-544. The car was in such excellent condition that the Volvo Wizard, a Volvo enthusiast from Connecticut, bought it on the spot and drove it home. Rose cherished that car. It was so reliable that she had driven it to Virginia Beach on vacations with Lenny and Stephanie and my mother-in-law when the kids were little, and we drove it all around New Jersey for thirteen years, with not a minute of trouble. When the Volvo Wizard drove the car out the drive, Rose couldn't look. Lenny and I looked at the money and were happy we could continue the legal battle.

In 1985, Billy Thompson, whom Lenny had met at Morehouse, expressed an interest in driving race cars. Billy was an avid race fan and acted out his dreams by racing everyone he could on the streets of Hampton, Virginia. His mother could do nothing about his yearning to race cars. Billy introduced me to his mother at their home in Hampton. Over lunch, I explained to her the steps to becoming a race car driver. Since Billy had no previous experience, I strongly recommended that he attend a racing school.

Billy signed up for the Skip Barber Race Driver's School weekend at Moroso Motorsports Park in Palm Beach Gardens, Florida. I was glad he had selected that school. As a novice driver, Billy would be exposed to two excellent race car instructors, Bruce MacInnes and Walt Borhm. Lenny and I were forced to take Amtrak's Silver Meteor to West Palm Beach and back, because the three-day school was held during Easter Week, and all planes to the area were booked. Billy met us at the train station when we arrived.

The weekend was a disaster for Billy but fun for Lenny and me. The first thing we noticed was that most of the drivers attending the school, including Robby Unser, Bobby Unser's son, were semiprofessionals. Obviously, Billy had not listened to MacInnes's instructions, but instead tried to impress Lenny and me. He bonzaied the car—floored the gas pedal—every time he went out for his practice session, and carried too much speed both into and out of the corners, causing him to end up on the grass.

After it had showered several times, Billy bonzaied the car in the rain, keeping the dry track line instead of driving the car up higher, out of the groove near the marbles, the loose track particles usually found on the edge of the high track driving groove. Billy kept driving the car into the wrong groove and didn't appear to have learned enough from the classroom instruction to improve. Lenny and I decided to forget about Billy ever being a race driver and started walking around the paddock to see what else was happening.

That weekend at Palm Beach a vintage car race and display of antique cars in pristine condition were being held. In and around the paddock area, we noticed every type of rich person known to us—the stuffy bluebloods, eccentric inventors, wine-and-cheese-circuit types, flamboyant new-money types, pompous pretenders, encyclopedic fountain-of-youth types with young beauties, and the self-sponsored drivers who raced for free because of their business interests. In the midst of the fine array of vintage race cars, I spied a Cadillac Allard, a limited-production hybrid race car that I had always liked, originally been drawn to it as a youth in 1951 because the emergency brake was on the outside of the driver's cockpit. It was a postwar racing car that looked like a brute machine out of the 1930s.

Before Lenny and I went over to look at the car, I asked several people about the man sitting in it. The nearby car owners said the owner of the Cad-Allard was very eccentric, and that most of the regulars left him alone. He never mingled much during the vintage car weekends, they said, but he had one of the best specimens of a Cad-Allard in the United States.

Having been raised in the back door of Philadelphia's Mainline blueblood community, I was not in the least intimidated going up to the eccentric multimillionaire and asking him about his magnificent car. Lenny and I proceeded over to look at it. As we did, the man got up and asked us if we were familiar with the car. I told him we were.

He proceeded to put me through my paces. When I mentioned that there were other motor applications for the Allard, I got his undivided attention. Then, in his eccentric manner, he asked whether I was colored or Hispanic.

"Colored," I said.

"I wouldn't have thought a colored man would ever have known what a Cadillac Allard was," he said, with a rich man's arrogance.

Then he invited us over to his estate in Palm Beach to see his thirty world-class concourse cars of all types. The cars, he told us, were kept in a climate-controlled garage and shown only twice a year at parties that he and his wife gave, and on other rare occasions. We wanted to go over and see the cars, but we had to catch the Silver Meteor back to Trenton. He didn't like being turned down.

While Billy was taking us back to the train, he asked me what I thought of his driving potential. "Nothing," I said. "Stick to being a lawyer." With that, Lenny and I rode back to Trenton on the train, with me telling racing war stories the whole way.

Chapter 14
Our Dirt Track Winner Reappears, 1989

I n 1988, I stopped the flow of red ink in my consultant business
and wiped out $250,000 of debt, because my immediate fami-
ly, friends, business associates, and federal, state and local
government officials kept me afloat. As my financial fortunes were
improving, one evening Bruce Driver called me out of the blue.
"I'm building a Modified car, and I want you to come over and see
it," he said. "I'm building it at a friend's farm about twenty minutes
from your place."

The car was in the corner of the barn in the midst of his friend's
1960s-era muscle cars, motorcycle and car parts strewn around on
the floor. Bruce explained his current situation: He had gotten married and his wife Linda loved racing. Looking things over, I estimated that Bruce needed $50,000 to complete the car, including a new
motor.

Bruce and I had several more meetings to air out our previous
differences. Once we settled these we met with Linda, who was
wonderful to work with. She was one of the few wives I had ever met
in an interracial marriage who was truly racially neutral. Linda was a
breath of fresh air after Bruce's previous girlfriend, who had exacer-
bated the tension between Bruce and me in 1980 and 1981.

By happenstance John Simon, president of the United Minority
Enterprise Association, asked at one of our meetings how the auto
racing was coming. I told him Bruce was building a Modified car.

John, a close ally, mentioned to another friend of mine, Herb Jones, that I needed financial backing to get Bruce started racing again.

Herb Jones was a very successful black steel erection contractor, and his firm, Coastal Steel, was one of a handful of black union contractors. His father had been the first black union member in Philadelphia's Iron Workers Local, joining in 1929 and paying dearly, as did other members, on its picket lines in the 1930s. Because of his father's dedication to the union during its darkest days, Herb had been made a second-generation cardholder and had many of the best workers from the union hall to work for him. These workers helped to catapult Coastal Steel to $30 million a year in revenues.

I took Herb to meet Bruce and to see the car. Like many before him, Herb liked Bruce's outgoing personality immediately. Returning to my house, Herb said, "Len, I'll help you get the car out of the barn, because we need young black men participating in all types of sports."

Bruce, Herb, and I formed BDM Racing, Inc. BDM stood for Bruce Driver, Miller. The idea was to move away from advertising that gives importance to racial identification. With the country becoming more conservative, the name Black American Racers, Inc. was now becoming a liability. Besides, Bruce was more comfortable with a racially neutral team name. We decided to run at a NASCAR-sanctioned track, where prerace car inspections were standardized, and where we could work our way up through a nationally recognized touring series. Herb relied on Bruce and me for our racing expertise and underwrote the fledgling operation with meaningful financial support.

Bruce found a construction company where we could house the car in Morrisville, Pennsylvania. Timmy Elonis, who was familiar with Bruce's gutter and downspout installation business, ran the company. Timmy, built a structure between two storage trailers to house the race car, and his two brothers helped on and off the track whenever they had time. It was interesting to note that Timmy's father was a die-hard Wendell Scott fan, a favorite because, in the 1960s, Wendell had demonstrated that an independent racer with an exceptionally competitive spirit could be successful in Grand National stock car racing.

Bruce and I decided to compete in 1989 at the nearest NASCAR-sanctioned track, where Modifieds ran on Saturday nights. We selected Shangri-La Speedway in Owego, New York. Herb and I hired Ron Whitney to build motors that would be competitive there. Finally, I called racing promoters Joe Gerber and John Simon to tell them that Bruce and I were racing again, with sponsorship from the region's leading black-owned steel erection company.

This time around Bruce and I could dispense with the love-hate relationship, because Bruce had matured having married a very supportive wife and becoming a father, and he finally recognized when he was being discriminated against because of his race. Timmy also supported our effort, financially, technically, and any other way that was needed on or off the track. Mark Blackwell, Ron Hines, and the 1980-81 pit crew had either gone on to other ventures or refused to crew for Bruce ever again. Lenny and I were the only carryovers from the successful 1980 and 1981 seasons.

The team's first Saturday night at Shangri-La during the spring of 1989, Bruce competed in his first heat race at the track against Jimmy Spencer, "Mr. Excitement," who later became a national NASCAR star. Every track promoter in the Northeast loved to have Jimmy Spencer compete at his track. He took no prisoners, and his aggressive driving-style kept the fans on the edge of their seats.

Bruce started out driving in the heat as if he had just won a race the previous week rather than eight years earlier. Jimmy Spencer and Bruce went wheel-to-wheel at a blistering pace for most of the heat race. The crowd was on their feet cheering for both drivers, and the announcer was yelling over the loudspeaker that it was the best heat race between two drivers he'd ever seen in his life.

Bruce held his own until the white flag lap, when Spencer forced Bruce to the outside. That was the best move Spencer could have made, because Bruce's outside moves were the weakest point in his driving skills. When Spencer and Bruce got between turns two and three on the back side of the track, Bruce ended up going at high speed down the bank and out of sight. There was a hush over the crowd until the track announcer told them Bruce was okay. What we didn't learn until after the season was that the rear end of our race car was misaligned by one inch, which allowed Spencer to inch past Bruce, because Spencer's car was set up almost perfectly for the track. As all the old-timers used to say, both car and driver have to be almost perfect when competing against the best in any given series.

After several races at Shangri-La, we noticed that we were having excessive tire wear. Also, we were settling in as a seventh-place car. From previous experience, I knew we needed a Modified chassis expert to go over the car and to help the team out from time to time at the track. Joe Gerber found an expert race car mechanic with a garage in Binghamton, New York, who agreed to go over the car and prepare it for Bruce each week at a very reasonable price.

Herb and I liked the idea. This would save six hours of towing to and from Owego each week and allow Bruce more time to run his gutter and downspout installation business. But Bruce rejected our idea outright, because he didn't want competing teams to know our secrets. (I hadn't known we had any.) This decision forced us to buy $4000 worth of additional racing tires, because the rear end alignment problem wasn't detected until after the 1989 racing season.

By the middle of the season the tire problem had become so acute that team supporters such as Winston Bryant, Jr., M.D. and Vernon Hammond, as well as Lenny and my brother Bruce, had contributed to the cost of buying tires for the team. If not for their support, Bruce would not have been able to finish the season. Larry Shirley, an avid race fan and engineer, also helped the team out, doing odd tasks from time to time.

The most interesting characters we met in 1989 were the Zacharias family. The father and his many sons were fixtures at the track. One of them raced in every class, and they were not kind to outsiders encroaching on their territory. As the season progressed, Bruce made his presence felt with solid top ten finishes. This annoyed the Zachariases, especially after Bruce bumped one of the brothers one Saturday night.

After the bumping incident, the entire family, their friends and pit crew, surrounded Lenny and Bruce in the pits. Several had large adjustable wrenches and jack handles in their hands. As they yelled insults at Bruce about his tenure in New Jersey, someone blurted out, "You niggers need to stick to basketball." The security guards had to break the group up, and I had to call Dale Campfield, the track promoter, to tell him to stay keenly alert to any crowd surrounding Lenny and Bruce in the future, which he did.

Bruce became the 1989 Rookie-of-the-Year and finished in the top ten in points. During the racing season everyone at the track, including the Zacharias family, grew to like Bruce and to accept the team. Once everyone got to know us, it was easier to concentrate on racing instead of worrying about whether someone in the pits is going to come over and attack you. Like Chris Woods a few years later, Bruce was a popular recipient of the Rookie-of-the-Year award in Shangri-La's Modified division, winning it in his first year of asphalt oval racing. His efforts earned him an invitation to the NASCAR Winston Racing Series National Invitational showdown at Volusia Speedway Park in Barbersville, Florida. This invitational race is held every February on the eve of the Daytona 500 at nearby Daytona International Speedway.

But after the successful racing season at Shangri-La, Bruce informed me and Herb that Linda was expecting a second child, and that he had to spend more time operating his gutter and downspout installation business. It was impossible for him to travel to Shangri-La every week. After several discussions, Herb and I bought Bruce's share of the equipment. Later, Bruce and Timmy Elonis returned to Modified racing at the Flemington Fairgrounds, which had become a NASCAR-sanctioned track and had been paved with asphalt since Bruce had last competed there in 1981.

Chapter 15
Changing of the Guard, 1990-93

T he 1990 racing season began with Herb Jones and me
having enough basic equipment to continue competing in NASCAR-sanctioned Modified racing. Halfway
through the season we had decided to sell the car and equipment and
abandon our goal to develop black drivers in motorsports, when Joe
Gerber called us one early summer night in a state of great excitement.

Joe said he had been at the Riverside Park Speedway in
Agawam, Massachusetts to present the trophy and check for the
winners of the Sunoco Race of Champions Series qualifying race for
the Modifieds and Street Stocks. When the winner of the Street
Stock race came to the winner's circle and took off his helmet, Joe
was surprised to see that he was black. Immediately after returning
home to Glenside, Pennsylvania, Joe phoned to tell me to go up to
see the driver.

Because of my busy schedule, I had to fly up to Agawam to see
this driver, whose name was Chris Woods. My friend Hank Henderson, president of Henderson Industries, owned a twin-engine
airplane. Hank's oldest son David pressed his father into lending his
private plane and pilot to fly to Massachusetts the next Saturday.
Hank came out to the Teterboro Airport in New Jersey to see us off,
and said he hoped we'd finally found a black stock car driver with the
potential to go to NASCAR's Winston Cup division.

After landing at the small county airport, we rented the only station wagon available and proceeded to the speedway, which was an extension of an amusement park, in a scenic area off the Westfield River. David Henderson and his brother Kenny accompanied by his son headed to the stands. I bought a pit pass and went looking for Chris Woods and his number 2x Street Stock. Since there were only four blacks in the pits, he was easy to spot. One of them was Booker T. Washington Jones a retired Modified driver I had known since 1970. The other two were crewmen who looked at me like I was from Mars.

Meeting Chris Woods was a new racing experience for me. Here was a black man driving for a white team, with an accent like John F. Kennedy, and a member of the only black family in Boyleston, Massachusetts. According to several residents of that town, after his family left him homeless at thirteen he had been raised by the Coleman and Fuller families, with support from the Boyleston community at large. He had learned his racing skills mainly from Bobby Fuller, the oldest brother of Rick and Jeff, both top Modified drivers on the NASCAR Featherlite Tour.

As I watched the crew busily prepare the car for the heat races, their demeanor reminded me of *The Brady Bunch* of the popular '70s television series. They were good examples of the sort of young suburban white men so prevalent in America in the '60s. On recognizing me as a motorsports figure, they introduced themselves. They spoke with confidence and were unabashedly blunt in their questions. They surrounded me as though I were a coach giving instructions at a high school football game. I informed them, Chris included, that I had come to see Chris race and evaluate his driving ability. The group said fine with them and went back to work preparing their number 2x Street Stock for the heat races.

I wished Chris luck and went around the track to the main grandstand to watch the heat races. Chris started from the back row in his heat race and wasn't able to qualify for the main event. As a result, he had to win the consolation race to get one of the two remaining positions for the Street Stock feature. Before the consolation race, Chris came up into the stands to apologize to me for his driving so poorly in his heat race, and to say that he would do his best to win the consolation race, which he did.

In the Street Stock feature race of the evening, Chris started in the last row of the full field of cars and worked his way up to fourth place by the time the checkered flag fell. After the race, the Hendersons went to the pits with me to congratulate Chris on his good showing. I told him I'd keep in contact during the season.

On returning to Pennsylvania, I immediately went to see Herb Jones to tell him what had happened in Massachusetts. Based on what I had seen, I told him, I felt we should keep our Modified race car a little while longer and not quit racing yet.

As the 1990 season progressed, Chris won two Street Stock feature races and six heat races. In the middle of the season I journeyed to Boyleston to find out more about his background. Bobby Fuller was kind enough to let me stay at his house for several days to keep my expenses down. It was during this trip that I got to know Bobby better and met Ralph Wagner, a local businessman. Wagner was the epitome of the successful "small-town-USA" businessman, the sort who participates in all aspects of his town's daily life. Wagner and I hit it off immediately, because we shared similar experiences, such as dirt track racing and street rodding, in the early 1950s.

Wagner had a vintage-looking gas station in the middle of town that he let Chris and the Brady Bunch use to keep and prepare the 2x Street Stocker for the Saturday night races at Agawam. He also helped to support the team financially. I told him what Herb Jones and I were trying to accomplish by training black drivers in auto racing. He said he thought Herb and I had a good idea, and that I should keep him informed on what we had in mind for Chris.

It was during this visit that I learned about Chris's background. His family had left him homeless when he was in junior high school. According to the recollections of several people I met, he came home from school one day to find his family had gone. His father had deserted the family earlier, and while left sitting on the front steps of his house, this time the Coleman family took him in for a while, even though their own family was large.

After staying with the Colemans until they couldn't stretch their food budget any further, Chris went to live with the Fullers. He began serving on their pit crew on weekends, because he had no other life. His family had been the only black family in town, and the nearest blacks were in Worcester, many miles away.

Chris, having been taken in by the Colemans and then the Fullers, did not surprise me one bit. Massachusetts had a proud tradition of helping blacks since at least 1776. It started with Crispus Attucks (the black martyr who was the first patriot killed in the Revolutionary War, at Bunker Hill) and continued with a strong underground railroad network for runaway slaves, the Massachusetts 54th Infantry Colored Regiment during the Civil War, and civil rights leaders, including the great Frederick Douglass—expounding their messages there without threats of being killed because of their race. Within this historic framework, Chris Woods had been given a boost to finish high school and to obtain a job to which most black teenagers in America's inner-city neighborhoods would not have had access. But Chris's upbringing in somewhat liberal racial surroundings proved to be an impediment to his success in North Carolina a few years later.

Several months after my visit to Boyleston, Herb Jones and I both returned to the track at Agawam to meet with Chris and converse with Joe Gerber who was promoting the Sunoco Race of Champions qualifying race that evening. We told Chris we had a Modified that he could try first at a quarter-mile track in his general geographical area in 1991. Chris suggested that Bobby Fuller be his chief mechanic, and Bobby agreed to get Chris going in the Modified when we were ready. Herb and I decided to turn the car over to Chris the next winter.

Chris drove for the Brady Bunch in twenty-six races in 1990. One of his two feature wins was the qualifying for the Sunoco Race of Champions Street Stock race held at Pocono International Speedway in Mt. Pocono, Pennsylvania. Every good running Street Stock in the Northeast, and a few from the South, descended on Mt. Pocono every year. There were 163 entrants. Chris qualified twenty-second, finished eighth, running the last ten laps with no brakes, and was named Rookie-of-the-Year. His driving style in the race was almost as exciting as one of the Zacharias brothers had been at the Shangri-La Speedway.

At the end of the season, Herb and I decided to let Chris drive the Modified car in between driving the Street Stock in 1991. I then told Bobby Fuller and Ralph Wagner that Herb and I would pay the expenses to operate the Modified for a total of ten races. Fuller agreed to maintain the car at his shop and to teach Chris how to drive it, if Herb and I would send all our racing equipment to him in Boyleston. We agreed.

Ron Whitney developed the motor for the car, and Bobby Fuller did everything else, with help from the Brady Bunch. He strongly suggested that we enter the first quarter-mile race at Monadnock Speedway in Winchester, New Hampshire. The track was the ideal size and configuration for Chris's Modified racing debut. As a rookie, Chris had to start twenty-eighth—last—in the starting lineup. The only practice he had had in the car was that weekend. He learned the track racing line by following and being instructed by all the Fullers—Bobby, Jeff, and Rick. Their tutelage and Chris's focus bore fruit.

Seeing high-powered, hi-bred, low to the ground Modifieds begin a race on a quarter-mile asphalt oval is like seeing and hearing a million bumble bees fly through the air in a close squadron formation. There were no scheduled pit stops, just out-and-out, wheel-to-wheel racing.

Just before the race, Herb felt faint and went to sit in the truck. When Chris had moved from twenty-eighth place to fifteenth halfway through the race, I ran back to the truck to get Herb to watch his progress. By the time Herb and I returned to the grandstands, Chris was running in the top ten, behind both Fuller brothers. When the checkered flag came out he was seventh, just behind Rick Fuller.

Everyone was elated—though Bobby Fuller reminded us not to get too elated, because Chris had a long way to go in racing. Like Grant King years before, Bobby was easy to work with. He had a thorough understanding of how to make a Modified chassis perform on the racetrack. He understood how geometry, physics, and arithmetic combine to make a race car a legitimate contender on any given weekend afternoon. Bobby's abilities created a learning situation that set the goal for Chris to improve his driving ability and catch up to the race car setup, instead of the setup catching up to his driving ability.

The winning race car setup preparation showed itself later in the season when Rick Fuller asked to borrow the car at an Agawam race. Rick had wrecked his car the week before. He was in the middle of the hotly contested Modified Tour points race that season, and he didn't want to sit out the race and lose ground to his competitors. Chris, Herb, and I agreed to lend Rick the car, and Rick's chief mechanic fine-tuned the chassis. When the green flag dropped, Rick drove the car up through the field as if the other cars didn't exist. Past the halfway mark, he had moved into second place. Once he was solidly in second place, the race leader began blocking the track, lap after lap so that he couldn't pass.

Seeing that he wasn't going to be able to pass the leader, Rick bumped him so hard the leader's car climbed the fence, bounced violently back onto the track, and stopped. At this point the officials announced over the public address system that I was to report immediately to the trackside office. There I was informed that our car was being black flagged because of Rick Fuller's rough-riding driving tactics. After the race Rick said, smiling, "We could've won, Chris. You've got a good driving car there. It drives on the racetrack like a Cadillac."

Although Bobby Fuller prepared the car flawlessly and Chris improved his driving skills with every race and stayed out of trouble on the track, the season was relatively uneventful—except for one event, at Thompson, Connecticut that a number of us will never forget. As Bobby and the crew were making last-minute adjustments to Chris's Modified, one of the crew members whispered to me, "Here comes Chris's mother. There's gonna be trouble; Chris hates his mother." I looked up the hill toward the grandstands and saw a small, feisty-looking black woman coming towards us, with a physically challenged older white man who looked like a character out of a *Frankenstein* movie. As the woman neared our pits, Chris looked up and saw her, then ran and hid between the trailer and the back of the truck. She shook her cane at him and yelled, "Don't run from me! You don't know nothing about life and never will! You're so innocent that when white folks take advantage of you and are racist, you're too dumb to know it! You need to hide behind the trailer!"

Here we were, preparing the Modified for a race on a beautiful

Connecticut Sunday afternoon. As Chris's mother went through her tirade, with the grotesque-looking older white man looking on, the crew kept working on the car, pretending she wasn't there. When she had finished her tirade, I introduced myself. She said, "You'd better look out for his personal and racing interests, because Chris is very naïve about racial matters. He's so naïve that he wouldn't recognize a Ku Klux Klansman with his hood on."

It took me several minutes to coax Chris out from behind the trailer. When Chris spoke to his mother, she settled down and said she was rooting for him. With that, he put his helmet on and began getting in the car. As his mother departed, she yelled: "Mr. Miller, remember what I said. Chris trusts white people more than his own mother, for the wrong reasons. They're going to be his downfall." It turned out to be a prophetic statement. When Chris moved to Concord, North Carolina, several years later, he began associating with the wrong white people for the wrong reasons, to the detriment of his racing career.

By the end of 1991, Chris had competed in thirty-two Street Stock races with the Brady Bunch crew and the support of Ralph Wagner. He competed in ten NASCAR Modified Tour Series events with the support of Herb Jones and me, with Bobby Fuller serving as chief mechanic and the Brady Bunch as pit crew. Although Chris competed on a limited schedule in the NASCAR Modified Series, he finished in the top fifty in national points. He was making such good progress that we sent him to the Buck Baker Driving School in Rockingham, North Carolina, to see if he had the potential to drive on NASCAR's larger tracks.

A group of us journeyed to Rockingham as observers. Chris's performance at the school rejuvenated Lenny to the extent that he felt we should make an all-out effort to market Chris as a NASCAR driver. While Lenny, Joe Gerber, and I did just that, Chris competed in twenty-four NASCAR Late Model races at Riverside Park Speedway in Agawam. He won three feature events and placed in the top ten fourteen times. Because of Chris's success at the Buck Baker Driving School, a NASCAR insider tried to lure him away from us that winter.

As 1993 approached, the Brady Bunch started to break up. As

members of the crew grew older they changed jobs, developed other interests, got married, and had children. Because of their individual time constraints, they put pressure on Chris to maintain a high degree of involvement on weeknights in preparing the car. Chris also was maturing and had developed a white love interest that he didn't want the Brady Bunch to know about.

Because he wasn't putting in enough time with the rest of the team on the preparation of the Street Stock, Chris raced it only twice in 1993. In his first race, Chris finished second at New Hampshire International Speedway on 18 April. He won his second race, at Thompson International Speedway on 25 April. But, after the Thompson race, the Brady Bunch fired him and selected another driver to drive the Street Stock, keeping it secret from me for several months.

I asked Chris why he hadn't told Lenny or me that the Brady Bunch had fired him. He said he was embarrassed, and that he thought we'd fire him too. When I asked why he didn't help work on the car anymore, he said he had developed a relationship with a local white girl, and that he could only see her while the crew was at the garage working on his car.

Late in the spring of 1993, Lenny told me and Herb that he felt the only way the team could grow was to move south. Racing continuously in any stock car series in the Northeast was fine if we intended to be part-time racers. If we aspired to be a professional stock car racing team, we had to establish a base in North Carolina. After being fired by the Brady Bunch, Chris was ready to move south.

Unprompted by Herb or me, Lenny began developing marketing concepts to present to potential sponsors and contacted Tom Cotter of Cotter Communications for an appointment. Lenny and I met Cotter at his office near the Charlotte Motor Speedway in Harrisburg, North Carolina, in late spring of 1993. This meeting proved to be the clincher for deciding to move south. Cotter said, "We could not sell marketing concepts based around a black driver without a shop facility, personnel, and racing equipment." He also told us that we needed to run Chris weekly at a difficult short track such as the Concord Motor Speedway.

Lenny made an appointment to see Yvonne and Henry Furr, the owners of the Concord Motor Speedway, and traveled again to North Carolina to meet with them. Lenny and the Furrs hit it off immediately. This meeting, and Cotter's advice, allowed the team to establish itself in the right location with track owners who truly gave us the right advice, including how to successfully defuse potential racial problems.

Lenny had Herb Jones and me accompany him to Concord to meet the Furrs, Tom Cotter, and Todd Moore, a member of Cotter's staff, at the Construction Company, a favorite eatery with a strictly NASCAR décor complete with photos and other memorabilia. At some point during any visit to Charlotte, most race fans, owners, insiders, and sponsors eat at least once at the Construction Company.

In December 1993, Chris said he would move to North Carolina the next year, if Lenny could find him a job. A week before Christmas, Lenny called a meeting with Herb and me concerning the need for us to establish a motorsports shop in Concord with all deliberate speed. Herb asked who the team manager would be. "I will be the team manager and obtain a job for Chris in North Carolina," said Lenny. Without reservation, we voted Lenny president of the racing team.

Then Herb said he had gotten the "horse out of the barn" and that he would cease any further financial commitment to the team. Herb had decided to remarry and to begin winding down his main business interests in Pennsylvania. He said that Lenny, with his youth and extensive racing knowledge, was now the key to black drivers reaching the higher echelons of NASCAR racing. Potential sponsors were not going to listen to two senior citizens about their future racing plans.

As of 1 January 1994, Lenny and I and Chris Woods were now the racing team; R & W Enterprises, John Carberry, Bob Merritt, Joe Gerber, and my brother Bruce were our only "hands on" team boosters left. As the new team president, Lenny focused on establishing a presence in Concord. Herb Jones exited the scene knowing there was a new generation in place to continue the development of black race drivers into the twenty-first century.

With Lenny's perseverance and the continued counsel from

Al Anderson and Joe Gerber, our silence on the racetrack exploded into thunder when Dr Pepper became the primary sponsor of our Chevrolet and Pontiac NASCAR Late Model Weekly Racing Series stock cars.

After years of being kept out of the winner's circle, our 2001 driver Morty Buckles—with Rick Townsend, co-owner of Townsend Racing Products, serving as crew chief for Miller Racing Group—won the Late Model race at Coastal Plains Speedway in Jacksonville, North Carolina, on 7 July 2001, with Dr Pepper emblazoned on our car.

The win almost erupted into a minor disturbance. As Morty and the team stood alone in the winner's circle, competitors in the pits waved rebel flags at us in defiance. While the sheriff and track officials gave us protection and genuine support, a boy about seven years old, his nose pressed against the catch-fence in front of the grandstands, yelled repeatedly, "You people go home!"

As Lenny and I left the track, I said, "Wendell Scott was declared a winner in 1963, but he wasn't awarded the trophy until all the fans were long gone. In 2001, we're going home as winners with our trophy in front of the fans. We're starting to make some progress."

A

82nd Airborne (U.S. Army), 20, 21
A Team, the, 76
ABC Wide World of Sports, 108
Absher, Michael Kenneth, 23
Accurate Carburetors, NYC, 37
Africa, 27
African Americans (blacks)
  attendance at racetracks, viii, 28,
    138-141, 178
  attitude toward motorsports, vii,
    2, 9, 28, 42- 43
  discrimination against, 5, 7, 31,
    91-98, 155-156, 164-167,
    174-175, 186
  in motorsports, vii, 31, 33, 112-
    113
  social life, vii, 7, 28, 42-43
Agawam, MA, 177, 179-180, 182
Airport Hilton Hotel, Chicago, 55
Akron, OH, 51
Albany, NY, 124
Ali, Muhammad, 54, 118
Allison, Bobby, 77, 90
Alpha Phi Alpha fraternity, 17, 95
Alsup, Bill, 75-76, 83,139
Amon, Chris, 108
Amtrak, 37, 166-167
Anderson, Al, 78, 88, 186
Anderson, Alfred "Chief", 19
Anderson Communications, 78,
  87, 89
Andretti, Mario, 71, 83, 96, 108,
  109,159
Archer, Lee, 164
Ardmore, PA, 18
Arkansas, 21
Armageddon Soul Band, the, 85
Armstrong, Billye Jean, 65
Ashe, Arthur, 49
Atco Dragway, NJ, 29, 33, 40,
  41,145
Atlanta, GA, 37, 112

Attucks, Crispus 180
Aunt Jemima, 109
Aunt Lonia, author's aunt, 38
Australia, 139
Automobile Quarterly, 161
automobiles and automobile parts
  (by model)
  American Motors, (AMC) 80,
    149
  Buick, 3, 14, 50
  Cadillac, 1, 5, 7, 9, 68, 168-169,
    182
  Cadillac Allard, 168-169
  Chevrolet, 3, 33, 37, 40, 41, 44,
    86, 186
  Chrysler, 45
  Cord, 2, 39-40
  Dodge, 45
  Duesenberg, 1
  Ford, 1, 4, 5, 7, 8, 9, 11-15,17,
    20, 61, 62, 86, 93, 129, 158
  Jaguar, 37
  Jensen, 91
  Lincoln, 1, 7,9, 13
  Lola, 82-83, 87, 90, 96, 102-103,
    106,110-111, 113, 124, 128-
    130, 133, 135, 138
  McLaren, 53, 103
  Mercury, 7, 13
  Oldsmobile, 67, 68
  Packard, 1, 7
  Pontiac, 186
  Porsche, 55
  Plymouth, 8, 10, 11, 19, 30,
    41-43
  Studebaker, 8
  Stutz Bearcat, 2
  Volvo, 24, 25, 29, 30, 33, 167

B

B/S money division (NHRA), 44
BDM Racing, Inc. 172
Babbich, Mike, 50, 51
Bagley, Tom, 142

Bahamas, the, 89
Baker, Vernon, 164
Baltimore, MD, 68
Barber, Skip, 103, 109, 158-159
Barbersville, FL, 175
Barringer, John, 140, 142
Barringer High School,
    Los Angeles, 31
Barris, George, 8
baseball, 113, 121
basketball, 23, 113, 174
Bass, Leon and Mary, 89
Batmobile, 8
Baynard, Alex, 32, 41, 44, 46, 156
Bear, Joe, 161
Bear Brake and Alignment, 81
Bedford-Stuyvesant (Brooklyn),
    45, 66, 67
Begnosky, Johnny, 157
Beirut, 67
Bell, Leo G., 85
Benny Scott Racing, 78
Berlin, 67
Bertils oil pump, 138
Bethea, Randy, 73, 74, 76-78
Bettendorf, IA, 50
Bettenhausen, Gary, 135
Bignotti, George, 69, 110-111
Binford, Tom, 86
Binghamton, NY, 174
Bishop, John, 97, 109
Black American Racers
    Association, 61- 65
Black American Racers Day
    (Atlanta), 87- 88
Black American Racers Day
    (Englishtown), 66- 68
Black American Racers, Inc.
    (BAR), 56-57, 61-63, 79, 94, 96-
    97, 103, 107-108, 110-112, 135,
    137, 142-153, 157, 160, 172
Black American Racers Yearbook
    (1974), 69

Black Athletes Hall of Fame, 113,
    115
Black Athletes Hall of Fame
    banquet (third annual, March
    1976), 115-121
Black Berry River Inn, CT, 82
Black Mafia, 45, 68
Black Mafia List (FBI), 68
Black-owned businesses, 57-58
Black Republicans, 119, 165
Black Volkswagen Club
    (Milwaukee), 81
Blackwell, Mark, 150-157, 159,
    160, 173
Blackwell, Mr. (father of Mark and
    Tommy), 157
Blackwell, Tommy, 150, 154, 157
Blaze, Harry, 144
Blow, James, 162
Blue Lantern Hotel, Monterey,
    CA, 92-93, 97
boat-tail racing cars, 1
Bob (pilot), 163
bootleggers, 21
Bordentown State Reformatory,
    NJ, 20, 28, 39
Borhm, Walt, 167
Boston, MA., 105
Bowling Green, VA, 15
Bowser, Hamilton, 162
boxing, 113
Boyleston, MA., 178, 180-181
Brabham, Geoff, 139
"Brady Bunch" (Chris Wood's pit
    crew), 178-79, 180-181, 183-84
Brame, Jim, 164
Braselton, GA, 87
Brenn, Jimmy, 154
Brenn, Ken Jr., 160
Bridgehampton, NY, 129, 133
Bridgeport, NJ, 149
Brink's Armored Car Service, 57,
    58

Britt, Joe, 162
Broderick, Bill, 85
Brooklyn Heavy, 61-62, 66-68
Brower, Brock, 23
Brown, Dick and Gloria, 89
Brown, Assemblyman (later
    Mayor) Willie , 96, 98, 109
Brown & Williamson Tobacco
    Company, 72, 75, 92, 94
Bryant, Dr. Winston Jr., 174
Bryar, NH, 129
Buck Baker Driving School, 183
Buckles, Morty, 186
Bucks County, PA, 30
Budah, A.F., 126
Bunker Hill, Battle of, 180
Burlington Country Jail, NJ, 68

C

California, 7, 36, 55, 65, 77, 79, 84,
    90, 109, 113, 116, 133
Call, Joe, 24
Camden, NJ, 23
Camel cigarettes, 91, 94, 96, 97
Cammack, Lem, 99-100
Campbell, Mo, 71-73, 76, 78-80,
    89, 103-06, 110, 113
Campbell, Willie "Camrod", 66,
    67
Campfield, Dale, 175
camshafts, 30, 134, 135, 150
Canada, 46
Cannon, Billy, 154-155
Carberry, John, 185
carburetors, 11, 13, 37, 39-41, 95
Carling Black Label Beer, 59, 60
Carmen, Darryl, 152
Caroline County, VA, 1, 11, 15
Casey, Ethan, ix
Cecil County, MD, 40
Central Intelligence Agency (CIA),
    25-28, 30-31, 37
Central Jersey Welding, 149

Certainteed Corporation, 133
Cessna, 163
Champion Spark Plug Company,
    53, 94, 133-35, 137, 143, 149, 157
Championship Auto Racing
    Teams, (CART) 77, 128
Charles, Assemblyman Joseph, 120
Charlotte, NC, 83, 98, 185
Charlotte Motor Speedway, 79,
    148, 184
chassis, 47, 135, 174
Chavis, Ben, 32
Chicago, 32, 55-56, 74
Chicago Expo, (Operation PUSH)
    56-59
chrome, 4, 5
church people, 107-108
Cicconi, Bob, 139
Cicconi, Lou, 139
Circus Circus Hotel and Casino,
    Las Vegas, NV, 124
Civil War, 180
Clappsaddle, Butch, 5-6, 9-10
Coachman, Alice, vii
Coastal Plains Speedway, Jack-
    sonville, NC, 186
Coastal Steel, 172
Cogsville, Donald, 117
Coleman family, 178-180
College Station, TX ,133, 136
Collins, Congresswoman Cardiss,
    165-66
Collins, Speaker Jack, 120
Concord, NC, 185
Concord Motor Speedway (Con-
    cord Motorsport Park), 23,
    184-85
Congressional Medal of Honor,
    164
Connecticut , 76, 82-83, 90, 99,
    100, 109, 158, 167, 183
Construction Company restaurant,
    185

Cook, Jim, 40, 131, 137-39
Cooper, John, 87
Cooper, Tom and Lillian, 117
corporate sponsors and
    sponsorship, vii, 47, 49, 51, 55,
    58, 60, 69, 71-75, 86-87, 101,
    104, 108-109, 112-113, 116,
    123, 129-131, 134-135, 138,
    140, 148, 172, 185-186
Cosby, Bill, 119, 121
Cosell, Howard, 118-121
Costaine, Jane, 108-09
Cotter, Tom, 130, 184-85
Cotter Communications, 130, 184
Cottontail Ranch, 111-112
Craftsman Truck, 86
custom cars, 5-8
Custom Cars magazine, 4

D

Danville, VA, 48
Darlington Speedway, SC, 22
Daytona, FL, 73
Daytona 500 159, 175
Daytona International Speedway,
    22, 87, 175
Deborah Hospital, Browns Mills,
    NJ, 131
Deep Throat (film), 107, 113
Defending the Spirit (book by
    Randall Robinson), 20
Delaney, Lump, 6
Deliverance (film), 13
Dell, Graighill and Fentress, (law
    firm), 49
Dellums, Ron, 90
Delpy-Neirotti, Lisa, viii, ix
Democratic Party, 145
Denny (young mechanic), 55
Denver, CO, 54
Denver Broncos, 118
Desimone, Larry, 6
Detroit, MI, 3, 68

Deutsch, Richard, 50, 53-54
Direct Automotive Field Support
    Unit (45 Ordnance Battalion,
    U.S. Third Army, Ft. Bragg), 21
dirt track racing, 145, 151, 154
Disco 9000 (film), 55
Donohue, Mark, 83
Douglass, Frederick, 180
Dover Speedway, DE, 63
Dr Pepper, 186
drag racing and drag racers, 11,
    13-14, 29-30, 32-33, 35-47, 49,
    65-66
Dredge, Bill, 85
Driver, Bruce, 148-49, 150-160,
    162, 171-75
Driver, Corky, 148, 152
Driver, Linda, 171,175
Driver, Sonny, 148
Dubois, W.E.B., 162
Dunn, Jay, 144
Durham, Malcolm, 61, 66, 69
Dynamic Programs, Inc., 56, 65,
    124, 161

E

Earnhardt, Dale, 22, 25
East Coast Drag News, 42
East Windsor Speedway, NJ, 149,
    156-57, 162
Eastern Motor Press Association,
    75, 144
Eastern State Penitentiary, 8
Ebony magazine, 62-63, 73
Economaki, Chris, 75, 118, 144
Elkhart Lake, WI 80, 82-83
Elonis, Timmy, 172, 175
England, 61-62, 93, 109
English, 23, 30, 138
Englishtown, NJ, 38-40
Englishtown Raceway Park, 38-40,
    66, 68
Equal Employment Opportunities

Commission (EEOC), 165
Essex, County, VA, 11
Europe, 93, 109
Ewing Drive-In Theater, Trenton, NJ, 48

F

Fat Sam, 92, 94
Fauver, William, 24
Federal Bureau of Investigation (FBI), 67-68
Federal Express, 164
Federation of Internationale de L'Automobile Committee, (FIA), 98
Felton, Jim, 162
Fentress, Lee, 49, 53
First National City Travelers Checks ,140
Fitzpatrick, Robert, 136
Flemington (Fairgrounds and Speedway, Flemington, NJ), 145, 151, 156-160, 175
Fletcher, Arthur, 119
Florida, 167, 175
football, 29, 113, 120, 178
Ford Motor Company, 86
Formula 5000, 102, 105, 109-110, 113, 124
Formula A cars, 49, 53, 54
Formula Atlantic, 61
Formula Ford, 61-62, 93, 129, 158
Formula Super Vees, (Mini-Indy cars) 55, 59, 72, 74, 76-77, 79-80, 82-83, 87, 89, 91, 93, 95, 100, 101, 128, 130, 133-37, 139
Formula 1, 77 , 82-83, 98, 127
Formula 1 World Drivers Championship, 83
Formula V, 48
Fort Apache, The Bronx (film), 45
Fort Bragg, NC, 20, 23
Fort Jackson, SC, 20, 21

Fort Ord , CA, 98
Foyt, A.J., 86, 154
France, 26
France, Bill Jr., 87
France, Bill Sr., 87
Frankenstein, 182
Frazier, Joe, 118
French Riviera, the, 55, 106
Frusco, Mike, 124
Fuller family, 178-180
Fuller, Bobby, 178-183
Fuller, Jeff, 178, 181
Fuller, Rick ,178, 181-82
Furr, Yvonne and Henry, 185

G

Gadson, Dr. Eugene, 56, 65
gambling 7-8, 44-45, 116, 125-126
gangs, 31-32
Garcia, Chino, 31-32
Gary, IN, 149
gasoline and racing fuel, 5
Gazaway, Bill, 63-64
gears, 33
George (author's cousin), 3
George Washington University, The, viii, ix
Gerber, Joe, 40, 47, 144, 159, 177, 180, 183, 185-86
Gibson, D. Parke, 113
Giles, Herman, 18
Glenside, PA, 177
go-karts, 47, 59, 148
Godfather, The (film), 67
Gold & Glory Sweepstakes (1924-36), 69
Goodyear Tire & Rubber Company, 50-51, 53, 89, 123, 141, 148-150
Gordon, Jeff, 121
Grand National 53, 172
Grand National Series (NASCAR), 41, 53, 73-74

Grand National Race (1969), 40
Grand Prix cars, 102, 106, 161
Gray, Charles, 15
Greased Lightning (film), 48
Great Britain, 81
Great Depression, the, 1
Greatti, Eddie, 59
Green, Ernest, 21, 130, 162
Griswold, John, 30, 32
Guag, Lee, 141
Gurney, Dan, viii, 106, 113,
    125-127, 159
Guttenberg, Karl, 19

H

H/gas class (drag racing), 29
Haas, Carl, viii, 50, 81-82, 100,
    103, 107, 110, 113, 124,
    126-127, 133
Haines, Wilson, 29-30
Hamid, George, 131,137
Hamlet, Gen. James, 164
Hammond, Vernon, 174
Hampton , VA, 167
Hank's Speed Shop-Berwyn, PA, 8
Harbor Fuel Oil, 50
Harlem, NYC, 31, 37-38, 43
Harley-Davidson motorcycles, 98
Harrisburg, NC, 184
Hart, Brian, 61
Harvard Club of New York City,
    vii, ix
Hassan, Gogo, 161-62
Havertown , PA, 36
Hazelton, Henry, 21
Heller, Art, 71-72
Hell's Angels, 98
Henderson, David, 177-78
Henderson, Hank, 177
Henderson, Kenny, 178
Henderson Industries, 177
Henry, Ed, 59, 60
Heppenstall, Ray, 69, 80-82

Hewland transmissions, 93, 107
Higginbotham, Judge Leon, 151
Hill, Mr. and Mrs. (author's
    parents' employers) 1, 2
Hill, Tony, 30, 32
Hines, Ron, 48, 56, 61-63, 65-69,
    80-82, 88-89, 99, 134-135,
    137-140, 144-145, 149-154,
    156, 158, 161, 173
Hobbs, David, 108
Hog Island, 18
Holiday Inn hotels, 50
Holocaust, the, 89
Hollywood, 8, 48, 63, 79
Hollywood Sam, 68
Holmes, Buddy, (author's cousin)
    11-15
Holmes, Howdy, 83, 95
Holmes, Jesse and Marion
    (author's uncle and aunt), 11, 12
HONK magazine, 4
Hop Up magazine, 4
Hospitality House Motor Inn,
    Arlington, VA, 111
Hot Rod magazine, 2, 3, 4
hot rods and hot rodding, 4-13
Hotel Harrington, Washington,
    D.C., 27
Howard, Ernest and Freddie, 90,
    92, 94, 96-97
Howard Johnson's restaurants, 18
Howard University, 162
Howmet turbine race car, 69
Humphrey, Jeanne, ix
Hungary, 26
Hunt, Joe, 105
Husted, Wolfgang, 101, 102
Hyatt hotel, Chicago, 57

I

IBM, 161
"If " (Rudyard Kipling poem), 95
ignition systems, 33, 101-102

Indiana, 65
Indianapolis, IN, 110
Indianapolis 500, 1, 22, 47, 49, 79, 86, 111, 159
Indianapolis Raceway Park, 102
Indianapolis Motor Speedway, 113
Indy Racing League (IRL), 104
Inman, Sgt. Bernie, 24
Innis, Rice, 3
Internal Revenue Service (IRS), 113
International Association of Machinists and Aero-Space Workers, 130
International Inn, 27
International Motor Sport Association (IMSA), 78-79, 97-98
interracial marriage, 60-61, 72-73, 144, 173

J
J. Walter Thompson Agency, 73
Jack, Rajo, 18
Jackson, Rev. Jesse, 58, 63
Jackson, Jim, 162
Jackson, Maynard (Atlanta mayor), 87-89
Jackson, Paul, 49, 54
Jackson, William, 33
Jackson Five, the, 58
Jacksonville, NC, 186
Jamaica, 95
Jamaican athletes, 119
James, Nancy, 140
Jaws of Life, 140
Jefferson, Dr. Rowland, 55, 61
Jenkins, Bill "Grumpy", 41, 44
Jenkins, Leroy, 164-167
Jenkins distributor, 46
Jersey City, NJ, 23
JFK Automotive Center (Philadelphia School District), 36-37
Joe Hunt Magnetos, 105

Johncock, Gordon, 111
Johnson, Carol, 123, 128, 134, 141-43
Johnson, Jack, 118
Johnson, Herman, 95, 135
Johnson, Larry, 115
Johnson Publishing Company, 57
Jones, Bill, 7-8, 14
Jones, Booker T. Washington, 178
Jones, Dick, 134-135
Jones, Herb, 172, 174, 177, 179, 182-85
Jones, Parnelli, 126-127
Jones, Percy, 56, 58

K
K&G Speed Shop, Havertown, PA, 36, 41
Kappa Alpha Psi fraternity, 66
Katona, Gloria, 145-146, 148, 153
Katona, Les, 145-48, 153, 158-59
Kennedy, John F., 178
Kent Oil, 142
King, Don, 117, 119-120
King, Grant, 103, 105-07, 109-11, 145, 160, 181
King, Jackie, 36
King, Martin Luther Jr., Rev 13, 33, 35, 115, 165
King Arthur's Round Table, 147
Kipling, Rudyard, 95
Kirkland, Kerry, 162
Kirshner, Joel, 36
Kool cigarettes, 71
Korean War, 23
Ku Klux Klan, 22, 183
Kuhl, Paul, 151, 155

L
Labor Day weekend, 22, 82-83
Lagos, Nigeria, 161-62
Laguna Seca race, Monterey, CA, 76-77, 90-98, 109-110

Lane, Ace, 150
Lane, Ace Jr., 150
Langhorne Speedway, PA, 22
Langley, Elmo, 41
Lanier, Steve, ix
Las Vegas, NV., 93, 111-12,
    115-16, 128
Lawrence Engineering, 145
Lawrence Township, NJ, 117
Lawrence Township Democratic
    Club, 59
Lawrence Township Police
    Department, 59
Lawrenceville, NJ, 59, 65, 128
Lazier, Bob, 83, 95,
Lee, Mae, 140, 141, 142
Lee, Wendell, 141
Leighton, Mel, 18, 46-47
Lexington, OH, 78
Levi's, 109
"L'il Abner" (comic strip), 60
Lilliard, Leo, 58
Lime Rock, CT, 40, 76, 82-83,
    99-101,158
Lipman, Sen. Wynona, 162
Little Huk, 32
Little Rock High School, Little
    Rock, AR, 21
Little Rock Nine, the, 21
Lloyd's of London, 110
Lomax, Dr. Walter P. Jr., 162
London, U.K., ix, 62, 110, 161
Long Beach , CA, 89, 105, 108
Long Beach Grand Prix, 89, 105,
    108
Long Island, NY, 61, 73
Los Angeles, CA, 47, 49, 55, 98
Losch, William, 162
Louis, Joe, 2
Louisville, KY, 71, 112
Lovelace, Linda, 107, 113
Lyles, Lenny, 72
Lyles, Rapid Ronnie, 45

M

M&M Sunoco (Washington
    Crossing, PA), 162
MacInnes, Bruce, 158-59, 167, 168
McAfee, Marvin, 55
McGuire Air Force Base, NJ 39
Madison Avenue, 72
Mafia, the, 8, 93
Mahler, John, 50, 53
Mainline, Philadelphia, PA, 1, 49,
    168
Mainline Lumber and Millwork
    Company, 6
Mallory Park, U.K., 62
Malvern, PA, 7
Mandel, Leon, 92
Mangone, Frank, 149-150
Manhattan Project, 162
Manley, Leonard, 56
Markland, Don, 126
Martin, John, 103
Martini, Jerry, 39
Mason-Dixon Speedway, MD, 10
Massachusetts 179, 180
Massachusetts 54th Infantry
    Colored Regiment, 180
Matthews, Joe Jr., 162
Matthews, Joe Sr., 162
Matthews, Tommy, 162
Mays, Charley, 113, 115-16, 119
Mechanics Digest, 4
Mehl, Leo, 50-51, 129, 141, 148
Melville, Richard, 90, 95
Mercer County Airport, NJ, 163
Mercer County Courthouse, NJ,
    153
Merritt, Bobby, 150, 153, 185
Mid-Ohio race, 77, 105
Mid-Ohio race course, 78
Milby, Jesse, 24
Milford, VA, 15
Miletich, Vel, 71, 126

Miller, Bruce (author's brother), 33, 35-39, 82, 116, 141

Miller, Dexter (author's brother), 4, 6-8, 35-39, 41-46

Miller, Earl, 19

Miller, Eddie, 95

Miller, Evelyn (wife of Bruce), 82, 116

Miller, Julius and Ethel (author's parents), 1-2, 4, 6, 7, 43-44, 75

Miller, Leonard T. "Lenny" (author's son), viii, 29, 33, 37, 75, 78, 102, 106, 116-117, 121, 141, 143, 149, 151, 153-154, 156-158, 162-169, 174-175, 183-86

Miller, Rose (author's wife), 10, 20, 27, 30, 33, 59, 75, 78, 89, 100-101, 102, 116-17, 121, 124, 141-143, 149, 154, 162-163, 167

Miller, Stephanie (author's daughter), 30, 37, 75, 80, 102, 116- 117, 141, 162, 167

Miller Brewing Company, 130

Miller Brothers drag racing effort, 41

Miller Brothers Team, the, 35-42, 116

Miller Brothers, Volpe and Baynard, 44

Miller Days, 124-27

Miller Racing, Inc. 49

Miller Racing Group, 186

Milwaukee , WI, 133-34, 139

Milwaukee Fairgrounds, 134

Milton, Byron, 149

Mission Rebels, the (San Francisco gang), 31

Mississippi, 109

"Mr. Diplomat" (drag racer), 38, 40-41, 116

Mitchum, Robert, 22

Mitnaugh, Paul, 163

Modified racing, 171-175, 177-178, 181-182, 183

Monaco, 106

Monadnock Speedway, Winchester, NH, 181

Monterey, CA, 90, 99, 119

Montreal, 46

Moore, Todd, 185

Morehouse College, 157, 162-63, 167

Moroso Motorsports Park (Palm Beach Gardens, Fla.), 167

Morrisville , PA, 172

Motorsports
African Americans and, vii-viii
and mechanical skills, vii

Mount Holly, NJ, 64

Mt. Pocono , PA, 180

Mousy, 46

Myers, Harvey, 115

N

Nader, Ralph, 31

NASCAR, viii, 14, 21-23, 41, 47- 49, 53, 56, 63, 98, 120, 129, 148, 155, 172-73, 175, 177-178, 183, 185-186

Nashville, TN, 73, 178

National Association for the Advancement of Colored People (NAACP), 32, 104

National Basketball Association (NBA), 23, 67

National Football League (NFL), 72, 120

National Hot Rod Association (NHRA), 30, 35, 40, 44, 46

National Speed Sport News, 144

Negro Airmen International, 163

Neuhoff, Bill, 95

NHRA M/S, automatic trophy class 30, 32-33

New Hampshire International Speedway, 184

New Jack City (film), 45

New Jersey, 57-58, 68, 128, 133,
    137, 151, 154-55, 159, 160, 163,
    167, 174, 177
New Jersey Department of
    Corrections, 23-24
New Jersey legislature, 162
New Jersey State Assembly, 120
New Jersey State Championship
    (4th Annual V/S Class), 42
New Jersey State Championship
    (dirt track racing, 1980), 156
New Jersey State Fair, 138
New Jersey State Federation of
    Colored Women's Clubs, 131
New Jersey State Police, 23
New Jersey Turnpike, 24, 124
New York City, vii, 23, 30-31, 37,
    58, 64, 66, 68, 72-75, 79,
    116-117
New York Department of
    Transportation, 124
New York Hilton hotel, 113, 117
New York State Fairgrounds,
    Syracuse, NY, 154
New York University, 30, 35
New Zealand, 108
Newark , NJ, 23, 39
Newman, Paul, 83, 100-101
Nigeria, 161
Nixon, President Richard, 165
no-name cornerback, 118
Norfleet, Bobby, 86
Norristown , PA, 4, 11, 18, 43
North, Oliver, 166
North American Grand Prix
    Association, 124-25, 127
North Carolina, 183-85
North Carolina State Police, 80
Northeast Division 1 (NHRA), 46
Nyack , NY, 143

O
Offenhauser, 53
Officers Candidate Test (U.S.
    Army), 21
Ohio, 50
Oliver, Sumner "Red," 65, 69, 111
Ontario , CA, 77, 133-35
Ontario Motor Speedway, 134
open-wheel racing, 46-47, 87
Operation PUSH, 56-58, 74
Oppenheimer, J. Robert, 162
Oreos, 42, 43
Owego, NY, 173-74
Owens, Brig, 49, 54
Owens, Jesse, vii

P
Palm Beach, FL, 168, 169
Palm Beach Gardens, FL, 167
Paoli , PA, 1
Park, Steve, 25
Patton, Gen. George S., 121
Peace Corps, 27
Peachtree Dekalb Airport, Atlanta,
    163
Pebble Beach, 73
Peek, Coyle, 56, 58, 61-64, 156
Penn Station , NYC, 74
Pennington (NJ), 39, 153, 157
Pennsylvania, 1, 13, 15, 18, 25,
    29-30, 32, 44, 74, 76, 86, 104,
    179, 185
Pennsylvania State Championship
    Race, 9
Pennsylvania State Police, 8
Pennsylvania Turnpike, 18
Pennzoil, 68
Penske, Roger, 77, 102, 113
Penske team, 102
Pep Boys, 4, 104
Permatex Sportsman race, 1974, 73
Petty, Lee, 22
Petty, Richard, 41

Philadelphia, PA, 9-10, 17-18, 20, 25, 35-36, 49, 66, 68, 104, 113, 124, 128
Philadelphia Eagles, 166
Philippines, the, 26
Phillips, Freddie, 80, 96
Phillips Academy, Andover, MA, 66
Phoenix International Raceway, 144
Pine, Norman, 29
Pinkard, Harry "Pinky", 65
Pittman, Robert A., 75, 92
Pizzi, Tony, 41, 44
Planters Peanuts, 140
Platt, Elliott, 105
Playboy magazine, 81
Players magazine, 81-82
Pocono International Speedway, Mt. Pocono, PA, 59, 180
Pook, Chris, 105, 107
Port Royal, VA, 12
Porter, Oscar, 89
Powell, Gen. Colin, 162
Princeton, NJ, 115
Procrasa, Abe, 75
Proctor, Sylvia, 65, 117
Pryor, Richard, 48
Pueblo incident, 38
Purnsley, Arnold, 163-164
Purple Room, the, 159

Q

Quality Inn Philadelphia Airport hotel, 124
Queen Mary, the, 89, 106

R

R & W Enterprises, 129, 185
radios, 108
Radnor School District , Radnor, PA, 1
Rahway Prison , Rahway, NJ, 28, 37

Rainbow/PUSH Sports Conference 1999, viii
Ralt chassis, 135
Randson, Todd, 157
Reading Fairgrounds (PA), 154
Real Great Society, the, (New York City gang), 31
Rebel Hill (Upper Merion Township, PA), 2
Redman, Brian, 108
Redmond, Elias "Doodle Bug", 4
Reds, Los Angeles race shop owner, 98
Regal Racing, 78
Regan, Donald, 126
Republican Party, 165
Revolutionary War, 180
Ribbs, Bunny, 109, 135
Ribbs, Willie T,. 105, 130, 135-36
Richter, Les, 99
Ricks, Margaret, 65
Ridley, Lillian, ix
Riley, Herb, 162
Riverside, CA, 96, 99, 110-111
Riverside Park Speedway, Agawam, MA 177, 183
Road Atlanta, 77-78, 87
Robert Bosch ignition systems, 101-102
Roberts, Fire Ball, 22
Robeson, Paul, 119-120
Robeson, Paul Jr., 119-120
Robinson, Albert "Bo", 145-47
Robinson, Albie, 145-47
Robinson, Frank, 121
Robinson, Jackie, vii, 95, 121, 151
Robinson, Jane, 147
Robinson, Kim, 147
Robinson, Randall, 20
Roby, IN, 69
Rockingham (NC), 183
Rocky IV (film), 39
Rodman, Dennis, 152

Rogue, Mr. and Mrs. Howard, 117
Roman Brio team, 102
Ross, Diana, 71
Rotary Club, 82
Roush team, 102
Royale Formula Super Vee, 74, 76
Rutherford, Johnny, 140

S

S.H.A.R.P. Racing Limited, 61, 62
Savoy, Yvonne, 65
Saxton, Ernie, 144
Schuppan, Vern, 108
Scott, Archie, 2
Scott, Benny, 47, 49, 56, 58-61,
    65-66, 76-84, 86-99, 103-111,
    113, 115-117, 124-125, 128
Scott, Bill "Bullet", 47, 97
Scott, Mel ,56, 58
Scott, Schill, 55, 60-61, 72, 90,
    93-94, 97-98
Scott, Wendell, viii, 28, 41, 47-48,
    85-86, 100, 144, 155-156, 159,
    172, 186
Seabridge, Chief, 59
Sears & Roebuck (Sears), 41
Sebring, FL, 86
Second Baptist Church, Wayne,
    PA, 17
Seidel, Richard, 24
Semus, Peter, 61, 62
Sessions, Warner, 165-66
Shand, Bill, 144
Shangri-La Speedway, Owego,
    NY, 173-75, 180
Shiloh Baptist Church, Trenton,
    NJ, 143
Shirley, Larry, 174
Shropshire, Tom, 130
Sigma Pi Phi Fraternity, 162
Silverstone (U.K.), 62
Simon, John, 171, 173
Simms, Greg 48-49

Simpson, Bill 105, 111
Simpson driver suits, 105, 111
Singer, Bill, 69, 138, 144, 150-151
Sink, Gen. (U.S. Army), 23
Sissell Automotive, CA, 36, 40
Skip Barber Racing School,
    158-159, 167-168
slip streaming (drafting), 59
Smith, Elliott, 31
Smith, Ernest and Fay, 117
Smith, Richard, 24
Smith, Sgt. (U.S. Army), 21
Smith's tachometer cable, 102
Social Dynamics, Inc., 90
Somerset (NJ), 128
Sox, Ronnie, 45
Sparrow, Buddy, 3, 5
Speed Weeks (1974), 73
speedometer, 14
Spencer, Jimmy "Mr. Excitement",
    173-74
Sports Car Club of America
    (SCCA,) 47, 53-54, 59, 61, 90,
    123, 129
Sprull, Bob, 77, 81
Stallone, Sylvester, 39
Steve (young man from New Jersey
    shore area), 160
St. Francis Hospital, Trenton, NJ,
    140-143
stick-and-ball sports and athletes,
    vii, 2, 117
stock cars and stock car racing,
    9-10, 22-23, 40-41, 47-48, 87,
    173-174, 185-186
STP Corporation, 85
Street Stocks, 180, 183-184
Stumpo, Anne, 63, 82
Summit Point, WV, 75, 129
Sunoco Race of Champions Series,
    40, 144, 177, 180
suspension, 32-33, 147
Sweden, 29

sweet potato pies, 109-110
Syracuse, NY, 154- 155

T

Tannenbaum, Jack, 31,35, 156
Tasnady, Al, 155
technical inspection, 96-97
Ted Bates Advertising Agency,
71-72, 79, 87
television, 55
Temple University, 17
Tennessee, 73
Tennessee State Hobby Division,
74
Teterboro Airport, NJ, 177
Texas, 133, 136, 148
Texas International Speedway,
College Station, TX, 136-37
Third World Film Productions, 48
Thomas, Clarence, 151, 165-66
Thomas, Rev. Daisey "Fret"
(author's cousin), 17-18
Thomas, Randy, 31
Thompson, CT, 182
Thompson, Billy, 167-69
Thompson, Mr. and Mrs. (Tommy
Thompson's parents), 142-144
Thompson, Tommy, 123,128,
130-131, 133-144, 147, 149,
156, 158-59, 163
Thompson International
Speedway, 182
Thunder Road (film), 22
Thursday Night Thunder, 139
Torg, Dr. Joseph MD, Philadelphia
Eagles team surgeon, 166
Townsend, Rick, 186
Townsend Racing Products, 186
transmissions, 13-14, 33, 107, 158
Tree, 67
Trenton, NJ, 56, 69, 111-12, 117,
133-34, 137, 145-46, 158, 166,
169

Trenton Speedway, NJ, 41, 69,
130-131, 137-139, 144, 163
Trenton Times, 130-131, 144
Trenton YMCA, 136, 138
Trenton-Robinsville Airport, NJ,
163
Tui racers, 76
Tucker, Alice, 18
Tucker, Mrs. (Alice Tucker's
mother), 18
Turner, Curtis, 22
Tuskegee Airmen, 19, 163-64, 166
Tyler, Kenny, 29
Tyson, Dr. Bertha, 19

U

Uncle Toms, 42
Union, 172
Union Station, Washington, DC,
166
United Airlines, 31, 125
United Auto Workers, 21
United Minority Enterprise
Association, 171
United Nations, 35
United Parcel Service, 164
United Progress, Inc., 146-147
United States Air Force, 26
United States Army, 20-22, 89, 162
United States Auto Club (USAC),
41, 47, 86, 136, 139, 144
United States Capitol building,
166
United States Cavalry, 142
United States Department of
Housing and Urban Develop-
ment, 161
United States Department of
Labor, 30, 161
United States Peace Corps, 27
University of Pennsylvania, 27, 66
Unser, Al, 71, 89, 108, 124
Unser, Bobby, 61, 89, 106, 167

Unser, Louie 53
Unser, Mother (mother of Al and
    Bobby), 89, 106
UOP Shadow team, 102
Upper Merion High School ,4
U.S. 30 Drag Strip, Gary, IN, 149

V

V/S class (drag racing) 36-39,
    41-42
Valley Forge , PA, 18
Valley Forge Military Academy, 1
Valvoline, 56, 108, 123, 149
Vanguard Racing, Inc., 49, 53 , 55,
    102
Vargo Dragway, Cross Keys, PA,
    30, 32, 40-41
Vega, Lt. (U.S. Army), 21
Vereen, Fred Jr., 162
Vermont, 76
Viceroy cigarettes, 85, 88-89,
    90, 91, 92, 94, 96, 98, 102, 106,
    108, 111-113
Vietnam, 142
Villanova University, 5
Virginia, 11
Virginia Beach, VA, 167
Virginia State College, 35
(Robert Bosch) Volkswagen Gold,
    Cup Series 74, 76, 79, 82, 105,
    139
Volpe, Ollie, 41, 44, 49
Volusia Speedway Park,
    Barbersville, FL, 175
Volvo P-1800 with Dana
    posi-traction, 24-25, 30
Volvo PV-544, 29, 167
Volvo Wizard, the, 167
Voss, Ken, 48

W

Wagner, Albert C., 24
Wagner, Ralph, 179, 181, 183

Washington, DC, viii, 43, 166
Washington, George, 2
Washington Crossing (PA), 162
Washington Post, the, 27
Washington Redskins, 49
Wasserman, Marty, 23
Watkins, Ted, 31
Watkins Glen, NY, 62, 79, 101,
    131, 133
Watson, Doc, 136
Watts, Los Angeles, 30-31
Wayne, PA, 1, 3, 6-7
Wayne, John, 10
Weitzes, Eppie, 108
Wells, Eugene, 66, 68
West Chester, PA, 9-10, 75
West Chester High School, 20
West Chester State Teachers
    College, 6, 18, 19, 23
West Conshohocken, PA, 38
West Palm Beach (Fla.), 167
Westfield River (Mass.), 178
Wheeler, Humpy, 120, 148
White, Harry, 17
Whitey, 39
Whitney, Ron, 128-130, 135,
    149-150, 154, 173, 181
Whitney, Ron Jr., 149
Wilkins, Walter, 75
Wilks, John, 119, 162, 165
Williams, Hosea, 88, 111
Willingboro, NJ, 99
Wilson Haines Volvo, Mt. Holly,
    NJ, 30
Wiltshire, George, 56, 58, 63
Winchester, VA, 181
Wings Field, Norristown, PA, 19
Winston Racing Series National
    Invitational (NASCAR), 175
Witon, Armentale, 85
Woods, Chris 175, 178-185
Wood, Mr. (Gen. Robert E., Sears
    chairman), 35-36

Woods, Mrs. (mother of Chris),
    182-183
Woodson, Rev. S. Howard, 69, 143
Wooster, Shirley, 23
Worcester, MA, 180
World War II, 2, 18, 23, 43, 164
Wright, Kenny, 35, 36, 38, 41-42,
    116, 136-137, 139, 140, 145, 156
Wright, Libby, 116

Y

Yarborough, Cale 80
Yeager, Chuck, 10
Young, Rev. Andrew, 90
Young, Billy, 32
Young, James P., 69, 94, 96, 129,
    143, 148

Z

Z, Mr. (CIA), 25-26
Zacharias family, 174-175, 180
Zeitler, John, 82, 92-94, 97

Leonard W. Miller, a veteran of both amateur and professional motor racing has owned and managed teams in NASCAR, USAC, SCCA, IMSA, and the NHRA. In 1972, he entered a team in the Indianapolis 500 and in 1975 participated in the inaugural Long Beach Grand Prix as one of the top 60 teams in the world. Miller was inducted into the Black Athletes Hall of Fame for his achievements in motor racing and is an expert historian regarding African American involvement in the sport.

Silent Thunder chronicles Miller's love of automobiles and his participation in motor racing from 1939 –2001. He has started more African American drivers in motor racing than any other single car owner since World War II. Miller is still an active car owner today.